Socialist and Nonsocialist Industrialization Patterns

PRAEGER SPECIAL STUDIES IN
INTERNATIONAL ECONOMICS AND DEVELOPMENT

Socialist and Nonsocialist Industrialization Patterns

A COMPARATIVE APPRAISAL

Paul Gregory

PRAEGER PUBLISHERS
New York · Washington · London

The purpose of Praeger Special Studies is to make specialized research in U.S. and international economics and politics available to the academic, business, and government communities. For further information, write to the Special Projects Division, Praeger Publishers, Inc., 111 Fourth Avenue, New York, N.Y. 10003.

PRAEGER PUBLISHERS
111 Fourth Avenue, New York, N.Y. 10003, U.S.A.
5, Cromwell Place, London S.W.7, England

Published in the United States of America in 1970
by Praeger Publishers, Inc.

Library of Congress Catalog Card Number: 72-123723

Printed in the United States of America

PREFACE

During the past decade, Western economists have become increasingly interested in patterns of industrial growth. The outgrowth of this interest has been an extensive body of empirical research devoted to the determination of these patterns and to their sources and consequences. Through this study, I hope to fill a gap in this literature by presenting an alternative industrialization pattern--"the socialist industrialization pattern"--which has been largely ignored by Western economists working in this area. The importance of this alternative pattern need not be emphasized, for over one billion people live in the 12 centrally planned socialist countries which follow it. In addition, the socialist model has attracted the attention of economic planners of the developing economies, who are faced with the practical problem of choosing between alternative development patterns.

The approach of this study is primarily empirical, which does not make for easy reading. For those readers who wish to avoid the actual derivation of the socialist industrialization pattern, I would suggest that they read Chapter 1, which deals with the methodology, and Chapter 9, which summarizes the principal findings of this study and explores the implications of the socialist model. The statistics used should not be an obstacle to the general reader, since multiple regression and variance analysis are the principal techniques employed.

ACKNOWLEDGMENTS

I would like to acknowledge my indebtedness to Professors Abram Bergson and Hollis Chenery for their assistance. An additional note of gratitude should be expressed to Professor Frederic Pryor for his comments on an earlier draft. Numerous other individuals participated in this study through their advice and comments, and I would like to take this opportunity to thank them all collectively. I emphasize that the faults and errors which remain are to be attributed solely to the author. I would also like to thank the staff of the Harvard University Russian Research Center for their extensive assistance and support, as well as the Harvard University Department of Economics for its generous provision of computer time. The Ost-Europa Institut of the Free University of Berlin and the Deutsches Institut für Wirtschaftsforschung provided invaluable assistance during the data-gathering stage.

CONTENTS

LIST OF TABLES

TABLES IN THE APPENDIXES

APPENDIX B

Table   Page

APPENDIX C

APPENDIX D

LIST OF FIGURES

INTRODUCTION

Consensus is a rare commodity, especially concerning
Soviet and Eastern European industrialization; nevertheless,
there is substantial agreement among economists of both
Western and socialist nations that the socialist pattern of
industrial development, as it has evolved in the USSR and in
Eastern Europe, differs significantly from the pattern set by
the industrialized Western economies. The terminology is
different; the Western economist refers to the "Soviet industrialization model," whereas his socialist counterpart speaks
of "socialist industrialization." Both have in mind a form of
rapid and forced industrialization that is directed by a central
plan and is characterized by the rapid decline of the nonsocialist sector, high rates of capital accumulation, and the
marked predominance of the producer goods sector over the
consumer goods sector.

In market economies, a complex set of factors has in-
teracted to cause the rise and decline of industrial sectors
in the course of modern economic growth: Industry demand
curves shift at varying rates over time owing to the differences
in income elasticities, the pattern of which tends to be fairly
invariant across national boundaries.[1] As a result, the structure of final demand can be expected to change in a predictable
way in an economy subject to market forces as national per
capita income grows.

During the course of industrialization, the prices of products of rapidly expanding sectors tend to decline more rapidly
(or rise less rapidly) than the prices of products of slowly
expanding sectors. Consumers, maximizing utility, and producers, minimizing costs, substitute the now relatively cheaper
products for those which have become relatively more expen-
sive, thereby reinforcing the income effect's impact on the
structure of final demand.

Uniform patterns of industrial development can also be
expected from the supply side: The general similarity of
sectoral production functions plus diffusion of technology ensures that the differential impact of increases in the level of
development on sectoral cost curves is relatively uniform
among economies in the long run, insofar as substantial technological gaps represent disequilibrium situations. In addition,

the gains from economies of scale tend to be concentrated in certain sectors, while the remaining sectors do not benefit materially from the growing size of the market. Systematic changes in the relative cost structure result in differential rates of import substitution among economic sectors; therefore, over time a changing proportion of total demand is satisfied through domestic production.

Dynamic supply and demand factors, which vary with the level of economic development and scale of the economy, underlie the distinct pattern of structural transformations which have materialized in the course of economic growth. The public sector represents an unknown in this process because, owing to the magnitude of its expenditures, it is in a position to alter radically the structure of final demand. One need only cite the structural distortions created by changes in the pattern of government expenditures during wartime in order to appreciate the potential impact of the public sector. However, the uniform patterns of change which have been observed over time within the industrial sector serve as indirect evidence either that the size and structure of the public sector's demand for goods and services are relatively uniform among countries or, to the contrary, that the impact of such differences has not been strong enough to outweigh the uniform trends emerging from the private sector.

The system of economic control developed by socialist command economies counteracts the dynamic market forces which cause distinct industrial development patterns in market economies. First of all, a system of comprehensive central planning, reinforced by a managerial incentive mechanism which primarily rewards plan fulfillment, replaces quantity and price determination through supply and demand. Instead, centrally fixed targets determine which sectors are to expand rapidly or are to be accorded low priority. Administrative rationing of producer goods provides a double warranty that enterprises operate in accordance with general plan directives. The socialist double-price system frees the relative price structure from the relative cost structure and provides a mechanism whereby demand increases can be met with increases in indirect taxation in the consumer goods sphere with supply remaining constant. In addition, administrative rationing of investment goods replaces private marginal efficiency of investment calculations, substituting planners' time preferences for private time preferences in order to direct the desired flow of investment throughout the economy. A foreign trade monopoly, following an autarkic trade policy, regulates administratively the rate of import substitution. Insofar as cost minimization is neglected in the managerial incentive equation relative to plan fulfillment, the substitution effect is relegated to a minor role.[2]

Working within an institutional framework which precludes the spontaneous generation of sectoral expansion paths, socialist central planners are free to choose the industrial development pattern prescribed by planners' preferences. This leads us to consider how such preferences are formed, i.e., to the selection of criteria used by planners in setting sector goals.

The planning prescription which emerges from elaborations on the Marxian two-sector model of the economy is simple: The larger the portion of its total resources which an economy devotes to (reinvests in) the production of investment (heavy) goods, the more rapid the rate of growth of total product. Any economy which imputes a heavy weight to growth rates and a low rate of discount to future consumption must heed this "economic law of expanded reproduction" in making its sector planning decisions. A bias toward heavy industrial goods is therefore necessarily imparted to the formation of socialist planners' preferences. This bias has been a crucial factor in determining the direction of socialist development patterns, and it still remains firmly imbedded in the socialist ideology.

The official economic textbook of the Communist Party gives the following advice concerning sectoral priorities during the course of socialist industrialization:

> The industrial branches which produce the means of production--machinery, equipment, metal, coal, gas, construction materials--that is, heavy industry, play the most crucial role. For this reason, socialist industrialization promotes first of all the development of heavy industry, the cornerstone of which is the machinery sector. A developed machinery industry is required to reequip all the branches of the economy with modern technology--machinery, tools, and equipment. It is the most important source of technological progress. Industrialization is to be implemented on the basis of the law of preeminent development of the production of means of production.
>
> This characteristic sequence of development of industrial branches is extremely important for socialist industrialization.[3]

An added benefit derived from the promotion of heavy industry is the correlation between the share of total resources which an economy devotes to heavy industry and the capacity of that economy to manufacture military hardware. In this regard, production of heavy industrial products would be doubly attractive to socialist planners because the ensuing high growth rates of total product would make possible high future levels of consumption but would yield a high degree of current military power.

Although it is possible to import both capital equipment and military hardware, paying with foreign exchange earned from exports of light industrial and agricultural products, socialist central planners would naturally tend to discount this alternative. The risk of relying on unfriendly foreign markets for military equipment is obvious. From the point of view of socialist central planners, reliance on uncertain foreign markets for material supplies is equally objectionable. Given the marked interrelation in a modern economy, insufficient supplies of a single bottleneck commodity, especially one supplied by foreign producers, could wreck an entire material balance plan. For this reason, it is to be expected that socialist central planners would opt for autarky in order to remain independent of capitalist markets, i.e., for a policy of building up a self-sufficient domestic productive capacity. [4]

If socialist planners' preferences correspond to the a priori expectations noted above, one can predict with some degree of certainty a sectoral target plan heavily skewed (relative to "normal" levels in nonsocialist economies) in the direction of heavy and defense-oriented industries and away from consumer-oriented light industries.

The mere drafting of an economic plan, however well it expresses planners' preferences, does not guarantee its automatic fulfillment. First, insofar as perfect centralization of decision-making authority is impossible to achieve, a dichotomy between the central decision and the actual enterprise decision is likely, especially if the enterprise incentive system does not perfectly coordinate local and central objectives. For this reason, the role of the enterprise decision in determining the eventual structure of production within a centrally planned economy should not be ignored.

A second possible cause of a divergence between plan and performance is the fact that real production and consumption constraints can make central targets infeasible. A closed economy, shifting more and more towards the production of heavy industrial goods, would at some point reach a binding constraint because the labor effort required in production is being rewarded with a smaller amount of current consumption in return for a larger amount of future consumption (in the form of capital goods). Insofar as future consumption will probably be discounted quite heavily by individuals, the proper mix of factor services will not be forthcoming, unless a new form of social consciousness is created (thereby altering subjective time preferences).

Other constraints restrict the freedom of choice of socialist planners. In a closed economy with no final demand and fixed factors, and having fixed coefficient production functions, the long-run rate of growth will eventually be limited by the rate of growth of the slowest expanding sector (assuming the economy is indecomposable). The indiscriminate expansion of certain sectors at the expense of others could therefore prove costly for long-term growth. Other potential production constraints are the scarcity of managerial talent, optimal scale requirements, and resource limitations.

In sum, the above observations raise the possibility of a socialist pattern of industrial development distinct from the capitalist pattern. First, socialist institutional arrangements prevent the spontaneous generation of industrial development patterns through market forces; second, ideological, growth, and defense considerations require a socialist development pattern skewed in the direction of heavy industrial products.

The objective of this study is to investigate the socialist pattern of industrialization (1) to determine whether a distinct socialist pattern exists; (2) to describe its characteristics; and (3) to consider the sources and consequences of such differences. Implicit in this approach is the assumption that the singularity of the socialist industrial pattern vis-à-vis the nonsocialist (western) pattern can be determined by formal statistical testing of null hypotheses.

It could be argued that an investigation of this sort is unnecessary because the avowed objective of socialist planners is and has been to produce an industrial development pattern distinct from the nonsocialist pattern. However, one must not forget that major divergences from the historical Western pattern represent moves into uncharted territory which could activate any of the constraints mentioned above, creating a dichotomy between stated socialist objectives and performance. An interesting by-product of such an analysis would be increased understanding of the constraint system limiting industrial development patterns.

In this study, the three questions posited are

1. Does the choice of the economic system significantly affect the industrial structure of economies or are the structural differences observed in the real world to be explained by chance factors and universal economic and environmental factors which are independent of the economic system?

2. What are the sources of socialist industrialization, i.e., to what extent did the structural changes in socialist countries result from demand changes and from import substitution or export expansion? Did structural change occur because of basic changes in the pattern of domestic demand resulting from the transformation from consumer to planner orientation, or did it occur because of radical alterations in traditional trade patterns?

3. What are the consequences of socialist industrialization as far as growth, military power, and consumer welfare are concerned? Can the socialist pattern of industrialization be used by the developing economies?

Thus, the pattern of development of the industrial sector in socialist economies vis-à-vis nonsocialist economies over time and in cross-section is the topic of this study. Although the primary emphasis is on the internal structure of the manufacturing sector, attention is devoted to trends in broader aggregate sectors, manufacturing and industry (manufacturing plus construction), insofar as it is difficult to analyze the structural patterns of a given aggregate without cognizance of the relationship of that aggregate to other aggregates.

The manufacturing sector is defined according to the International Standard Industrial Classification (ISIC) as industry (excluding construction) minus mining and gas and electricity. A two-digit classification is employed to divide the manufacturing sector into twenty subsectors (ISIC 20-39). In turn, various combinations of these subsectors are examined. Ideally, these combinations should represent homogeneous product groups, such as machinery, producers goods, consumer goods, etc. Of course, the ideal is unattainable; instead, rough groupings are employed (such as metal products and chemicals) which include quite diverse product groups used for diverse ends. Subsector shares of total manufacturing value added and labor force serve as indicators of structural patterns within the manufacturing sector; the ratios of industry and manufacturing value added to gross national product (GNP) serve as indicators for the aggregate sectors.

The periods studied are the late 19th and the 20th centuries for a sample of industrialized capitalist countries for which data are available, the 1912 to post-World War II period for the USSR, the post-World War II period for two cross-sections of socialist (Eastern Europe and USSR) and nonsocialist economies, and finally a nonsocialist cross-section from the late 1930's.

Chapter 1 introduces the methodology employed in this study, states the hypotheses to be tested, and discusses the use of analysis of covariance and multiple regression in analyzing socialist economic structures. In Chapter 2, special attention is accorded to the sources and derivations of socialist data (with an account of the actual calculations of USSR and Eastern European value added provided in Appendix A). Next, Chapter 3 examines the structural development of the USSR industrial sector from 1912 to 1962, using a series of selected bench-mark years from different periods of Russian and Soviet economic history. Chapter 4 compares the USSR development pattern with the long-run evolution of the manufacturing and industry sectors in the United States, Canada, Germany, and the United Kingdom. In Chapter 5, we analyze the industrial structures of six Eastern European countries (Hungary, Poland, East Germany, Czechoslovakia, Romania, and Bulgaria) prior to and the following World War II. This chapter also includes application of homogeneity tests to the prewar and postwar Eastern European structures, the postwar Eastern European structures and the USSR plan-period structures, and the postwar Eastern European structures and a postwar cross-section of nonsocialist structures. In Chapter 6, the USSR and postwar Eastern European industrial structures are compared with the theoretical normal Western structures defined by a postwar Western cross-section. Here special emphasis is accorded the USSR industrial structure vis-à-vis the normal pattern during various periods of Russian and Soviet economic history.

A direct comparative appraisal of two postwar cross-sections, one socialist and the other nonsocialist, is provided in Chapter 7, with special attention to differences in the regression sector elasticities and intercepts. Chapter 8 then decomposes the sources of industrialization in the USSR and Eastern Europe; studies sectoral industrialization patterns in terms of domestic demand expansion, export demand expansion, and import substitution; and contrasts the sources of industrialization in the USSR and in Eastern Europe with the Western experience.

The final chapter summarizes the study's principal findings and describes the patterns and characteristics of socialist industrialization. The broader implications of socialist industrialization, its impact on the end use of total product and economic policy, and the system of constraints into which the socialist pattern was integrated are discussed. Also the relevance of the socialist industrialization model to the developing world is covered, and topics for further research are suggested.

NOTES

1. Hendrik Houthakker, "An International Comparison of Household Expenditure Patterns."

2. The general comments made above are based mainly upon material in Abram Bergson, The Economics of Soviet Planning, Chs. 3, 5, 7, 8, 13.

3. Politische Ökonomie, pp. 372.

4. Alexander Erlich, The Soviet Industrialization Debate, pp. 146-53; Ia. A. Kronrod, Obŝestvennyi Produkt i ego Struktura pri Sotsializme, Ch. 3; Franklyn Holzman, "Foreign Trade," pp. 301-02.

Socialist and Nonsocialist Industrialization Patterns

CHAPTER 1   A GENERAL METHOD FOR ANALYZING SOCIALIST INDUSTRIAL STRUCTURES

Mathematical statistics provides an impressive set of tools for testing the significance of the impact of economic systems on industrial structures and for isolating socialist structural characteristics. The analytical framework used here involves a mixture of descriptive statistics, regression analysis, and covariance analysis. Insofar as the methodology itself forms an integral part of this study, we devote this chapter to a discussion of methods and procedures. It should be noted that the discussion does not go beyond the intuitive level.

COVARIANCE AND REGRESSION ANALYSIS AND SOCIALIST INDUSTRIAL STRUCTURES

A hypothesis is required concerning the impact of the economic system on the industrial structure.

Hypothesis: The economic system as such has no statistically significant effect on the industrial structure. All differences between systems can be explained by random error and by system-independent factors.

A method must be devised to test this hypothesis. In notational form, it can be tested by postulating the following covariance model:

$$y_{ijk} = m_k + a_{ik} + \sum_{m-1}^{t} d_m v_{ijm} + e_{ijk} \qquad (1)$$

$$i = 1, 2$$
$$j = 1, 2, \cdots, p$$
$$k = 1, 2, \cdots, n$$
$$m = 1, 2, \cdots, t$$

The i subscripts refer to economic systems, 1 representing an observation from the socialist world and 2 representing an observation from the nonsocialist world. The j subscripts refer to the observation number within the i-th group. The k subscripts refer to the n economic sectors. The m subscripts are discussed below.

The model (1) states that y_{ijk} (the sector k output of observation j from group i) diverges from an additive constant (m_k) for three reasons:

1. Because of random error (e_{ijk}),

2. Because factors other than the economic system influence y_{ijk}, i. e., the v_{ijm} values, which represent factors influencing the economic structure, where the d_m coefficients define the relationship between y_{ijk} and (v_{ijm}).

3. Because the economic system itself (a_{ik}) significantly affects y_{ijk}, the values of the socialist group to differ from the values of the nonsocialist group.
The null hypothesis of a zero system-effect for sector k is accepted or rejected on the basis of whether $a_{1k} = a_{2k} = 0$ (for acceptance) or $a_{1k} \leq a_{2k} \leq 0$ (for rejection). *

For present purposes, a procedure should be devised to test the significance of the system-effect not only on a particular sector, but also on all sectors simultaneously, which requires a <u>multisectoral general covariance model</u>--the model used for actual significance tests in this study. Nevertheless, it is more appropriate to discuss the analytical framework in terms of a simple one-sector covariance model.

Under ideal test conditions, the v_m would be held constant and would thus be eliminated from the model (1), which would reduce to the simpler model

$$y_{ijk} = m_k + a_{ik} + e_{ijk} \quad (v_m \text{ constant}). \tag{2}$$

The v_m could also be eliminated if they had no significant impact on the y_k, e. g., if the coefficients d_m were all zero. Under either of these two situations, the model is reduced to the analysis of two separate effects: the random error effect (e_{ijk}) and the system effect (a_{ik}). Within this simplified framework, analysis of variance could be employed to test the significance of structural variation between economic systems.

---

*It is assumed throughout that $\Sigma \ a_{ik} = 0$ and that the error term (e_{ijk}) is distributed normally with a zero mean and constant variance.

In the realm of economics, it is generally difficult to reduce such models from complex interaction models to simple analysis of variance problems because (1) ideal test conditions cannot be constructed and (2) owing to the phenomenon of general interdependence, the entire set of coefficients is rarely zero.

Analysis of covariance does, however, allow simulation of ideal test conditions. In general terms, this is done by adjusting the y_k for the effect of the v_m variables. Once the y_k values are corrected by eliminating the influence of all factors other than the system-effect, the model reduces to a simpler analysis of variance involving only the random error effect and the system-effect:

$$\hat{y}_{ijk} = m_k + a_{ik} + e_{ijk}, \tag{3}$$

where $\hat{y}_{ijk}$ represents y_{ijk} corrected for the influence of other factors besides the system-effect.*

Within the analysis of covariance, the causal variables (the v_m) are termed covariate adjustors. They are generally classified into two categories: environmental covariates and explanatory covariates. An understanding of the distinction between explanatory and environmental covariates is crucial to the extent that the proper interpretation of final results rests upon this distinction.

Environmental covariates are variables which are significantly correlated with the dependent variable (in this case y_k) yet are independent of the system-effect. Explanatory covariates, on the other hand, are correlated with both the dependent variable and the system-effect.

The impact of adjusting y_k for environmental covariates is to reduce the error variance, whereas the net result of adjusting it for explanatory variables is to eliminate that part of the system-effect which is attributable to the effect of the system on the explanatory variables.

The foregoing is best illustrated by means of concrete examples. For instance, natural resource endowments are independent of the economic system, yet evidence suggests that they affect the industrial structure. In order to test the significance of the system-effect, the influence of natural

---

*The adjustments are made by regressing the v_m values on the y_k values, thus deriving least-squares estimators of d_m, and then employing the derived coefficients in the adjustment process.

resource endowments on the industrial structure must be removed; otherwise homogeneity tests on the unadjusted y_k
values might attribute group differences caused by differences
in natural resource endowments among groups to the system-
effect, thereby yielding a spurious conclusion.

The interpretation of the impact of adjusting y_k for explanatory variables is more complex. An autarkic trade policy
is a concomitant of centrally planned socialism, and the degree
of autarky has a potential impact on the structure of industry.
Assume the following situation: After adjusting for all covariates with the exception of autarky, the system-effect is significant. After adjusting y_k for the degree of autarky, the system-
effect becomes insignificant. What is the proper interpretation?
It is that socialist economies tend to have industrial structures
which differ significantly from nonsocialist structures, not
because they are socialist per se but because socialist economies tend to be autarkic. This means that if nonsocialist
economies were to become as autarkic as socialist economies,
structural differences would disappear.

The socialist system results in a high degree of autarky,
which in turn creates an industrial structure significantly
different from the nonsocialist structure. Therefore, when
one eliminates the autarky effect, one is, in a sense, eliminating the impact of socialism as well. For this reason, it is
important to segregate environmental covariates from explanatory covariates, which is not an easy task because most
covariates are of a mixed nature.

REGRESSION PROCEDURES

Despite its flexibility in dealing with the homogeneity of
total structures, covariance analysis primarily indicates
whether socialist industrial structures differ significantly
from nonsocialist structures, i.e., it tests the significance
of the system-effect. Evidence of the existence of a distinct
socialist industrial pattern is of importance; however, it
fails to define the characteristic features of the socialist
pattern, which is best done with regression coefficients.

Regression analysis can be employed in a variety of ways
to describe the differences between socialist and nonsocialist
industrial patterns. In fact, three complementary approaches
are employed in this study:

1.   The first approach is to estimate the socialist and the nonsocialist parameters--the d_m of (1) above--directly by regressing the socialist sample and the nonsocialist sample separately. The two parameter sets are then compared.*

2.   The second regression approach is to compare actual socialist structures with normal Western industrial structures. This procedure requires the extrapolation of the socialist values by using the estimated Western parameters. In this way, one compares actual socialist industrial structures with "normal" nonsocialist industrial structures. A distinct pattern of socialist residuals would then be indicative of a development pattern peculiar to the socialist group and distinct from the nonsocialist group. In employing this procedure one is essentially asking what would have happened had the socialist

---

*To examine socialist and nonsocialist coefficient sets, two samples must be available: a socialist and a nonsocialist sample. The two samples are then fitted by multiple regression yielding two parameter sets: the socialist parameter set, denoted by $d^{k'}$ (an n x 1 vector, where k denotes the economic sector and n represents the number of independent variables in the regression equation), and the nonsocialist parameter set, denoted by $d^{k'}$ (another n x 1 vector). The desired test for homogeneity of industrial development experiences on a sector-by-sector basis would be whether $d^k = d^{k'} \leq 0$. The simplest possible case would be the one in which the socialist sample yields a set of insignificant coefficients, $d^k = 0$, and the nonsocialist sample yields a set of non-zero coefficients $d^{k'} \leq 0$. Under such circumstances, one can conclude that the socialist industrial development model differs significantly from the nonsocialist model, and that a different theoretical model postulating a different set of explanatory variables must be formulated to explain the variation within the socialist sample.

A less obvious case would be the one in which both samples yield significant coefficients. If the coefficient signs differ, one can again assume a distinct socialist pattern. However, if the coefficient signs agree and the coefficients differ only in magnitude, the Chow test of equality between coefficients in two relations must be employed to test whether the coefficient differences are actually significant, e.g., whether the samples are drawn from two different universes or whether the differences are the result of random error. For a description of the Chow test, consult J. Johnson, Econometric Methods, pp. 136-37.

economies followed the industrial pattern of the nonsocialist
group. This approach assumes that a nonrandom pattern of
residuals is indicative of a distinct socialist industrial development pattern. It contains no built-in test procedure to explore
the possibility that divergences of the actual socialist structures from the normal structures are the result of random
factors; however, taken in conjunction with covariance tests,
this possibility is eliminated. Contrasting actual structures
with normal structures is most useful in the sense that it
allows detailed comparisons of individual socialist structures
with a conglomerate structure at almost any level of aggregation.*

    3. The third regression approach is to include the
economic system directly in the regression equation in the
form of a dummy variable. Dummy variable analysis of this
sort is identical with the simple covariance analysis described
above, and it is used to provide sector-by-sector breakdowns
of the system-effect in order to gauge the magnitude of the
system-effect by sector.**

-----

*A comparison of actual socialist manufacturing struc-
tures with normal Western patterns requires the nonsocialist
coefficient set $(d^{k'})$ and the socialist independent variable
matrix X^s (where X^s is an m x n matrix, with m denoting the
number of socialist observations and n the number of independent variables). Residuals of the actual socialist output
pattern y^k (y^k is an m x 1 vector of actual value-added shares
of sector k) from the $\hat{y}^k$ predicted by normal Western development patterns are computed as follows: $\hat{y}^k = X^s d^{k'}$; $u^k = y^k -
\hat{y}^k$, where u^k is an m x 1 vector of residuals of actual socialist
structures from normal Western structures. The u^k vector
can be interpreted as the vector of differences between the
actual socialist structures of sector k and the structures
which would have resulted had the socialist countries followed
the normal nonsocialist development pattern. A nonrandom
distribution of the u^k vector would indicate that the socialist
countries as a group diverged systematically from the normal
nonsocialist pattern.

    **Economic systems are by nature nonquantifiable; never-
theless, the economic system itself can be entered into the
regression equation as a dummy variable in the following
manner: $y^k = Xd^{k*} + W\theta^k$, where y^k is an r x 1 vector of
value-added shares of sector k of the combined socialist and
nonsocialist samples, X is an r x n matrix of independent
variables of the combined socialist and nonsocialist samples,

MULTISECTORAL DEVELOPMENT MODEL

It is crucial to specify the model upon which the subsequent covariance and regression analyses are based for two reasons.[1] First, a properly specified model ensured the meaningfulness of comparisons of socialist and nonsocialist structures. If the model is improperly specified, then differences between socialist and nonsocialist structures could very likely reflect specification error rather than actual differences in the two developmental patterns.

Second, the model facilitates the decomposition of the residuals into groups of causal factors. Therefore, one is able to examine the socialist development pattern not only in terms of the total model but also in terms of the separate impact of individual causal factors.

Model Specification

The model used in this study describes an economy of p sectors. The output of each sector (y_k) equals final domestic demand for k (D_k) plus intermediate demand for k (W_k) plus net foreign demand for k $(E_k - M_k)$. In notational form this reads:

$$y_k = D_k + W_k + E_k - M_k \qquad k = 1, \cdots, p \qquad (4)$$

To develop a model suitable for regression, each component of (4) must be analyzed separately. Final domestic demand for k (D_k) is determined by per capita income (I), which itself is determined by total resource endowments H, K, and R (where H denotes human resources, K denotes capital

---

d^{k*} is an n x 1 vector of combined regression coefficients of sector k, Θ^k is a scalar dummy variable, and W = 1 if the observation is drawn from the nonsocialist sample and W = Θ if drawn from the socialist sample. The inclusion of the dummy variable Θ^k rests upon the assumption that the impact of the economic system on the structure of sector k can be viewed as a parallel upward or downward shift of regression planes; therefore, one can test the significance of the impact of the system upon the economic structure by determining the significance of Θ^k, but the sign of Θ^k is indicative of the direction of the system impact.

resources, and R denotes natural resources). We assume
that the state of technology is embodied in H and K:

$$D_k = D_k(H, K, R) \qquad\qquad k = 1, \cdots, p \qquad (5)$$

Intermediate demand for k (W_k) is determined by the
vector of final outputs of the p sectors and by the matrix of
input-output coefficients (a_{ki}), which themselves are determined by the state of technology and factor prices. In the
static case, constant coefficients are assumed:

$$W_k = \sum_{i=1}^{p} a_{ki} y_i \qquad\qquad k = 1, \cdots, p \qquad (6)$$

Export demand for k (E_k) is determined by relative prices,
which are determined by total resource endowments (H, K, R):

$$E_k = E_k(H, K, R) \qquad\qquad k = 1, \cdots, p \qquad (7)$$

Import demand for k(M_k) is determined by relative prices,
which are determined by total resource endowments and scale
factors (N), such as the size of the domestic market:

$$M_k = y_k(H, K, R, N) \qquad\qquad k = 1, \cdots, p \qquad (8)$$

Equations (4)-(8) yield the following model to be estimated:

$$y_k = y_k(H, K, R, N) \qquad\qquad k = 1, \cdots, p \qquad (9)$$

In varying degree for different national units and for the
same economic unit over time, some economies are more
open to the world market than others; therefore, actual output
structures diverge from those which would have obtained had
the economy fully utilized its trade potential. Thus, two economies with identical total resource endowments and scale
features can have different output vectors because one is isolated from the world market. The degree of openness of the
economy (trade orientation), denoted by V, should therefore
be included in the complete model:

$$y_k = y_k(H, K, R, N, V) \qquad\qquad k = 1, \cdots, p \qquad (10)$$

Definition of Variables

Insofar as measures of human capital resources (H) and
physical capital resources (K) are not available, per capita

income (I), measured in constant 1960 US dollars, is employed in this study as a surrogate for H and K; therefore I and R together measure total resource endowments.

Natural resource endowments (R) are measured indirectly through their relationship with the structure of trade. *

---

*The relative shares of primary exports and manufactured exports of total exports are correlated with the development process itself (see Maizels, Industrial Growth and World Trade, pp. 57-65). Under the assumption that nations trade according to comparative advantage, the ratio of primary exports to manufactured exports would be an indirect indication of the level of natural resource endowments if one assumes the following relationship between this relationship and natural resource endowments:

$$\log E_{pm} = \log a - b \log I + c \log N + d \log R,$$

where E_{pm} denotes the ratio of primary to manufactured exports, I denotes per capita income, N denotes population and R denotes natural resource endowments. R is estimated in the following manner:

$$\log R = \log E_{pm} - \log \hat{a} + \hat{b} \log I - \hat{c} \log N = \hat{R},$$

where $\hat{a}$, $\hat{b}$ and $\hat{c}$ are regression coefficients derived from regressing I and N on E_{pm}. A large positive value would denote rich natural resource endowments. A large negative value denotes poor natural resource endowments.

It could be argued that the socialist countries do not observe comparative advantage in their trade relations with other countries and that therefore the socialist R values do not reflect natural resource endowments. If one assumes a rough degree of rationality on the part of the socialist state trade monopolies, then comparative advantage should be observed in a rough manner. In any case, the socialist values derived in this manner seem fairly realistic. For example, in terms of natural resource endowments, Czechoslovakia is closest to Japan, East Germany to the UK, the USSR to the US, Bulgaria to Ecuador, Romania to India, Hungary to Mexico, and Poland to Canada. In Chapter 7, the presocialism natural resource endowments are estimated and used for the postwar R values in addition to the original natural resource estimates. This second set of estimates is also imperfect owing to the large degree of measurement error in estimating presocialism per capita income in Eastern Europe.

Population size is chosen to represent N, the scale factor, because population is the best measure of the size of the domestic market. We also measure trade orientation (V) indirectly.*

In summary, the model actually estimated in this study is: ·

$$y_{tk} = y_{tk}(I_t, N_t, R_t, V_t) \qquad \begin{aligned} k &= 1, \cdots, n \\ t &= 1, \cdots, p \end{aligned} \qquad (11)$$

In time series, y_{tk} denotes the value-added share of sector k at time t, I_t denotes per capita income at time t, N_t denotes population at time t, R_t denotes natural resource endowments which are invariant with respect to time and therefore do not enter into time series and V_t denotes trade orientation at time t. The t subscripts can also refer to different national economic units (cross-sections) at the same point in time. In this case, R_t is no longer constant.

We use two types of dependent variables (the y^k): sector value added ÷ GNP and sector value added ÷ manufacturing value added (for the manufacturing subsectors only). Several considerations went into this choice of the dependent variables. The implicit dependent variable proposed by the multisectoral development model (IM) was ambiguously called the "output" of sector k. An unambiguous measure of this variable which can be used over space and time is not available, so one must choose between several imperfect alternatives. One common alternative is to express sectoral output (on a normalized per capita basis) in terms of a common monetary unit at a single

---

*A possible measure of trade orientation V is the trade ratio (TR), i.e., the ratio of exports plus imports to total output; however, the trade ratio varies with size and level of development, according to Simon Kuznets, <u>Modern Economic Growth</u>, pp. 300-03. For this reason TR reflects not only trade orientation but also the level of development and size of a given national economic unit. For purposes of this study, V is estimated in the following manner:

$$\text{Log } V = \log(TR) - \log(\hat{TR}) = \hat{V},$$

where log ($\hat{TR}$) is the estimated value of TR from the double-log regression of I and N on TR. A large positive value of log V denotes a trade-oriented economy, whereas a large negative log V denotes an autarky-oriented economy.

point in time. A second alternative is to express sectoral output as a portion of total output (or of industrial output), in which case domestic monetary units can be used.

Owing to the large amount of measurement error involved in computing purchasing power parities for socialist countries, we chose the second alternative. The aggregative sectors, such as manufacturing and industry, are necessarily expressed as shares of total output; however, one can express the various manufacturing subsectors either as shares of total output or as shares of total manufacturing output. The latter can be related to the former by means of the following simple algebraic operation:

$$y_k^a = F(v_1, v_2, \cdots, v_t) \qquad (12)$$

or
$$m[\, y_k^a = F(v_1, v_2, \cdots, v_t)\,] \qquad (13)$$

$$y_k = G(v_1, v_2, \cdots, v_t, m), \qquad (14)$$

where y_k^a is the output of sector k divided by GNP, m is the ratio of manufacturing value added to GNP, the v's are the independent variables and y_k is the value added by sector k divided by manufacturing value added.

Equation (14) indicates that to explain the internal structure of the manufacturing sector by using y_k instead of y_k^a, one must include not only the original independent variable set but also the relative level of industrialization (the manufacturing sector's share of GNP, or m). By using (14) instead of (12), one can decompose the structural development of the manufacturing sector into two factors. The first factor represents that portion which is explained by the original independent variable set, under the assumption of a normal development pattern for the aggregate manufacturing sector relative to GNP, i.e., that the actual m does not diverge significantly from the m predicted by the level of development. The second factor m, on the other hand, measures the impact on the internal structure of manufacturing of deviations of m from the normal m pattern, e.g., the impact of the relative level of industrialization.[2]

Failure to include m as an explanatory variable in addition to the original independent variable set involves the tenuous assumption that all countries having equal income, population and resource levels will generate identical aggregative structures and, therefore, identical intermediate demand structures. Using m as an independent variable obviates this assumption, and for this reason it is expected that the inclusion of m will provide a better specification and therefore a better statistical fit, which is extremely important when comparing structures on the basis of extrapolations.

The operational rule followed in this study for the choice of the dependent variable (y_k or $y_k a$) is to use the manufacturing subsector's share of manufacturing value added (y_k) whenever it is practical to include the ratio of manufacturing value added to GNP (m) as an independent variable. In other cases, such as time series where it is difficult to enter more than one independent variable, both manufacturing shares and total product shares (y_k and $y_k a$) are used to study the structure of manufacturing.[3]

NOTES

1. The model outlined in this section is the Chenery model, with certain minor modifications. See Hollis Chenery, "Patterns of Industrial Growth," pp. 624-54.

2. This use of the relative level of industrialization is suggested by United Nations, A Study of Industrial Growth.

3. The material presented above was derived from a variety of sources, notably Maurice Kendall, A Course in Multivariate Analysis, pp. 105-43; Henry Scheffe, The Analysis of Variance, Ch. 6; E. J. Williams, Regression Analysis, Ch. 7; Arthur Goldberger, Econometric Theory, pp. 227-31.

CHAPTER 2   DATA SOURCES AND DERIVATIONS

A truly detailed and exhaustive account of all data sources used in this study would occupy a separate volume; therefore we had to establish some guidelines to determine what should be detailed. Inasmuch as the majority of data for Western countries is drawn directly from United Nations publications and from official national statistical handbooks which are readily available to the general reader, only very general details will be given concerning the Western data. On the other hand, the assumptions and procedures involved in deriving socialist industrial structures and constant-price income data must be clearly stated; therefore more attention will be devoted to the derivation of the socialist data in the course of this chapter.

STRUCTURE OF INDUSTRY DATA

The principal dependent variable used here is the subsector share of total manufacturing value added. An alternative dependent variable is the manufacturing subsector share of total product. The GNP shares of the manufacturing and industry sectors are also employed as dependent variables. In addition, subsector shares of total manufacturing labor force are also compiled.

The definition of value added used in this study is the United Nations definition, which designates value added as the total value of gross output (valued at factor cost) less the cost of all purchased goods used during the period (i.e., raw materials, supplies, fuels, electricity and goods sold in the same condition as purchased) and the cost of all services of an industrial nature provided by others (i.e., fabricating, assembling, repair and maintenance). [1]

Value added is generally estimated by deducting material costs from gross output valued at factor cost. In the case of

15

socialist economies, it is more expedient to estimate value
added from the factor input side, since material costs are
generally not known and the value of gross production at factor
cost is difficult to estimate because of the complicated
structure of indirect taxation. Even if one were able to adjust for indirect taxation, the factory prices of products still
do not include a rental charge on capital (only a depreciation
charge, which is likely to be understated). Insofar as capital
rental charges do enter into Western value added, they must
also be included in socialist value added for the sake of comparability.

We generally estimate socialist manufacturing value added
in this study as follows: (1) industrial branch wage bills are
computed; (2) industrial branch capital stock is estimated and
capital charges are computed by imputing a rate of return on
capital; (3) actual industrial branch depreciation charges are
noted. Industrial branch value added is then computed as the
sum of industrial branch wage bills, imputed capital services
and actual depreciation charges.

Estimating socialist manufacturing value added in this
manner raises several difficult questions: What rate of return on capital should one employ among socialist economies?
Should the same rate of return be used for East Germany, a
relatively advanced industrial nation, as for Bulgaria, a
relatively backward industrial nation? Only if we could compute marginal rates of return on capital, could we impute
differential rates of return. We decided to impute a uniform
rate of return on capital for all socialist countries.*

We chose the relatively low rate of 8 percent for the im-
putation of capital services because it seemed preferable to
err on the low side: much of our emphasis will be placed on
the ratio of value added in light industries to value added in
heavy industries. The higher the rate of return chosen, the
more important the more highly capitalized heavy industrial
branches become relative to the less highly capitalized light
industrial branches. This strengthens any case based upon
an abnormally high ratio of heavy to light industrial branches
under socialism.

_____

*If, as is commonly thought, the marginal productivity of
capital is higher at a low level of development, then capital
services in less developed socialist economies would be underestimated relative to capital services in more developed
socialist countries. This means that the value-added shares of
heavily capitalized branches are underestimated for less developed socialist countries.

Russian and Soviet value added in the prewar period is estimated by subtracting material costs from the value of gross production (net of indirect taxes). Prices of 1912, 1925, 1927, 1928 and 1929 are used. The NEP (New Economic Policy) prices include material and labor costs, amortization, rent and direct taxes. Nutter notes that the pre-1930's Soviet price weights are "reasonable approximations to the cost of production . . . because the market still played a substantial role in the Soviet economy."[2]

Another important question concerns the use of a uniform rate of return for all industrial branches within an economy. Under conditions of perfect competition, a free enterprise system should generate equal marginal rates of return on capital in all industrial branches in the long run, although these conditions are seldom met. Owing to administrative rationing of investment goods, it is generally argued that socialist economies tend to allocate the most modern and productive equipment to top-priority sectors (generally heavy industrial sectors), whereas light industrial sectors must make do with less modern and productive equipment. The use of uniform rates of return among sectors means, therefore, that light industrial branches are overstated relative to heavy industrial branches; nevertheless, for reasons similar to those stated above, we decided to impute the same 8 percent rate of return for all industrial sectors.

The problem of varying census coverage must be discussed within the context of both socialist and nonsocialist data, since uniform coverage is necessary if one desires to compare the socialist and nonsocialist data. In general, we used industrial census data to estimate value-added shares. A significant number of these censuses, especially for earlier years, do not cover small industrial units. To the extent that one is interested in structures and not absolute values, non-uniformity of coverage would be of no concern if all sectors were affected uniformly by omissions. However, in many cases the omission of only a small proportion of total manufacturing value added can significantly alter the structure of final manufacturing output. For this reason, we used only data which cover all industrial establishments. In numerous cases, we made adjustments for incomplete coverage on the basis of more complete wage bill and labor force information, either under the assumption of equal branch value added per person employed in census and noncensus industries or according to the distribution of wage bills between census and noncensus industries.

In the case of Soviet and Eastern European economies in
the postwar period, census data generally cover only state
industry and cooperative industry (the socialist sector) or
state industry alone. Therefore we estimated private handicraft and cooperative production on the basis of labor force
and wage bill data. Direct estimates of noncensus industrial
production are employed to compute prewar USSR manufacturing value added. Only in the case of the 1955 East German
estimates does the coverage adjustment have a more than
marginal impact.

The system of industrial classification used in Eastern
Europe and in the USSR, by no means uniform within the
socialist bloc, differs quite substantially from the ISIC standard
used in this study.[3] These differences are spelled out in considerable detail on a country-by-country basis in the United
Nations publication The Growth of World Industry, 1953-1965,
National Tables. A complete discussion of adjustments to
eliminate differences in industrial classification is beyond the
scope of this study; nevertheless, the two most important and
frequent adjustments can be mentioned:

1. According to socialist statistical practices, fine
mechanics and optics are classified as metal products (ISIC
35-38), whereas the ISIC system places them under miscellaneous manufactures (ISIC 39). In some cases--East Germany,
for example--fine mechanics and optics account for about 6
percent of total manufacturing value added; the adjustment is
therefore more than marginal.

2. Mining of ferrous and nonferrous ores is included in
basic metals, mining of construction materials is included in
nonmetallic minerals, and mining of raw chemicals is included in chemicals according to socialist classifications; the
ISIC places such activities outside the manufacturing sphere.

In addition to these two major types of adjustments,
numerous adjustments were made on a country-by-country
basis in order to ensure comparability between the two samples.

Most of the time series data utilized in this study of manufacturing value-added structures are in current prices. In
fact, it is an open question whether current price data are not
preferable in our context insofar as the changing price structure
is itself a concomitant of the development process and current
price structures are representative of contemporary prefer-
ence and cost conditions. An important question arises in the
case of cross-sections of industrial structures: To what extent do the cross-section price structures reproduce the historical pattern of price changes, which occurs during modern

economic growth?[4] An even thornier question is raised by
the differences in socialist and capitalist relative cost (price)
structures, especially in the area of consumer goods and
producer goods. The magnitude of this question is so immense
that it is beyond consideration.

There is one major exception to the use of current price
data in time series: the 1933 and 1937 USSR industrial structures are in constant 1927/28 prices. In terms of the industrialization process, they are therefore valued in early-year
prices; thus, although sector share changes between 1928
and 1933 and 1937 are indicative of real changes in physical
quantities, the shares of newer industries are overstated
relative to what they would have been had they been valued
in current-year prices.*

INCOME, POPULATION, NATURAL RESOURCES
AND TRADE ORIENTATION:
THE INDEPENDENT VARIABLES

The independent variables perform two interrelated
functions throughout this study: (1) they serve as covariate
adjustors; (2) they act as independent variables in regression
analysis.

Per Capita Income

We use per capita income in 1960 US dollars as a crucial
independent variable throughout this study. The United Nations estimates of per capita income in current US dollars
(using calculated parity rates) for Western countries are used,
coverted into 1960 dollars using the US GNP deflator.[5] United
States, German, Canadian and English per capita incomes
over time were estimated by extrapolating 1960 per capita
income (in US dollars) using the Maddison total output and
population indexes for these countries.[6]

---

*The differences between current price manufacturing
structures and constant price manufacturing structures in
1933 were not great, but they were substantial by 1937. See
Abram Bergson, "Prices of Basic Industrial Products in the
USSR, 1928-1950."

USSR per capita income in constant 1960 dollars during
the 1912-1962 period was estimated in the following manner:
Cohn estimates 1960 USSR GNP at 235.5 billion US dollars,
which equals $1,109 on a per capita basis. Employing a
variety of GNP and population indexes, we extrapolate this
figure back to 1928. [7]

To estimate per capita income during the NEP period
and in 1912, we adopted extremely rough procedures. Nutter
estimates that 1913 Russian GNP equaled 97 percent of 1928
Soviet GNP. [8] This figure, corrected for population change,
is used to estimate Russian 1912 per capita GNP in dollar
values. Per capita income in 1925 and 1927 was crudely estimated by the current author.*

The Ernst estimates of Eastern European per capita incomes in dollar values are used in this study, first converted
in 1960 dollars using the U.S. GNP deflator and then extrapolated to the proper year using the indexes provided by Ernst.[9]

The deficiencies of comparing income levels over long
periods of time and long distances are well-known, and diffi-
culties are compounded by the use of a single currency. The
per capita income measures over time and space, while not
unique, do depend on the base year (country) prices used.
The use of US prices probably results in the overestimation
of per capita GNP (in US prices) relative to per capita GNP
in the domestic prices of the country in question. In addition,
one may question the utility of using the crude USSR pre-1928
estimates. One should keep in mind, however, that in

---

*The 1925 and 1927 GNP estimates were derived in the
following manner: Bergson's 1937 factor income-originating
weights from Abram Bergson and Oleg Hoeffding, Soviet
National Income and Product, 1928-1948, p. 33, are used to
aggregate the following sectoral indexes: The service sector
index is an index of employment in the service sector. The
transportation index is an unweighted index of ton-kilometers
and passenger-kilometers. The agriculture index is an index
of employment in agriculture. The data are from Statsprav
1928, pp. 82, 526, 618. The industry index is from Nutter,
The Growth of Industrial Production in the Soviet Union, p.
517 for 1927; an hours-worked index for 1925 is from
Statsprav 1928, p. 324. The resulting GNP index is:

1928	100	1925	76.6
1927	97.4	1913	97.1

regression analysis orders of magnitude are quite important, and even these crude estimates should reflect proper orders of magnitude. Also, the results are relatively insensitive and are not significantly altered by a wide margin of error in the estimation of per capita income.

Population

We use the United Nations' Demographic Yearbook (selected years) estimates of population of socialist and non-socialist countries.

Ratio of Primary Exports to Manufacturing Exports

Primary exports are defined according to the ITIC system as food (0), unmanufactured tobacco leaf (121), inedible (2), synthetic fabrics (266), crude oil or partly refined oil (331), natural gas (341), oils and fats (4) and wild animals (941). The United Nations' Yearbook of International Trade Statistics (selected years) provides the data for calculating the ratio of primary exports to manufactured exports for the majority of the countries in both samples. In most cases, we adjusted the USSR and Eastern European trade data to achieve conformity with the Internat'l Trade Ind Class (ITIC) system of classification. For prewar years, the League of Nations' Statistical Yearbook (selected years) and International Trade and Balance of Payments Yearbook (selected years) provide the necessary data.

The changing structures of American, Canadian, German, and English trade over time were computed from information in Maizels and Hoffman. Holzman's data on the USSR structure of trade over time and information contained in Statsprav 1927 serve as the basis for computing the changing structure of USSR trade over time. [10]

Ratio of Exports Plus Imports to Total Output

Data on the trade ratio (exports plus imports divided by gross domestic product, merchandise only) are readily available from a combination of the United Nations' Statistical Yearbook (selected years), for gross domestic production, and its Yearbook of International Trade Statistics, for exports plus imports. The trade ratios over time for the

Western time series countries are found in Kuznets' study of
long-term trends. USSR trade ratios over time are from the
Holzman article mentioned above for bench-mark years from
1913 to 1959. For years not covered by the Holzman figures,
extrapolations were made on the basis of constant-price
volume indexes and constant-price GNP indexes. [11]

Postwar Eastern European trade ratios were computed
from the Ernst ratio of imports to GNP (both in dollar values)
and the ratio of exports to imports. [12] In most cases the latter
ratio was roughly unity; therefore the trade ratios are approximately double the Ernst ratios.

NOTES

1. United Nations, The Growth of World Industry, 1953-
1965, National Tables, p. vii.

2. M. Smith, ed., Statističeskii Spravočnik SSSR, 1928,
pp. 364-65, hereafter cited as Statsprav 1928 (or 1927); G. W.
Nutter, The Growth of Industrial Production in the Soviet
Union, p. 123.

3. United Nations, Classification of Commodities by
Industrial Origin, "Statistical Papers," Series M, No. 43.

4. For a discussion of this problem and some prelimi-
nary evidence, see Simon Kuznets, Modern Economic Growth,
pp. 374-84.

5. United Nations, Yearbook of National Accounts
Statistics, 1964; United Nations, National Income Statistics
1938-1948.

6. Angus Maddison, Economic Growth in the West,
Appendixes A and B.

7. The Cohn GNP estimate is from Stanley Cohn, "The
Gross National Product in the Soviet Union," p. 76. The GNP
indexes are from Joint Economic Committee of Congress, New
Directions in the Soviet Economy, Part II-A, p. 104; Abram
Bergson and Simon Kuznets, eds., Economic Trends in the
Soviet Union, p. 36; and from Abram Bergson, The Real
National Income of Soviet Russia Since 1928, p. 225, henceforth

referred to as Real SNIP. The population indexes are from
Joint Economic Committee of Congress, New Directions in
the Soviet Economy, Part III, p. 608; and from Frank Lorimer, The Population of the Soviet Union, p. 30. The 1928-58
GNP figures are based upon indexes valued at 1937 factor cost.
The 1960 and 1962 figures are linked to 1958 using an index
employing 1955 factor costs weights.

      8.   For the Nutter 1913 estimates, see G. W. Nutter,
"The Soviet Economy: Retrospect and Prospect, " p. 3.

      9.   Maurice Ernst, "Postwar Economic Growth in
Eastern Europe, " New Directions in the Soviet Economy,
Part IV, pp. 877, 890. Domestic price GNP estimates are
first converted into West German prices by means of calculated exchange rates and quantity indexes; these estimates
are then converted into US prices using the computed dollar-
mark parity conversion rate.

      10.   Alfred Maizels, Industrial Growth and World Trade,
Tables A. 1 and A. 3; Walter Hoffman, Das Wachstum der
Deutschen Wirtschaft seit der Mitte des neunzehnten
Jahrhunderts, pp. 153, 154; Franklyn Holzman, "Foreign
Trade, " p. 292; Statsprav 1927, pp. 366-67.

      11.   Simon Kuznets, "Quantitative Aspects of the Econo-
mic Growth of Nations: X Level and Structure of Foreign
Trade: Long-term Trends"; Holzman, op. cit., pp. 289-90.

      12.   Ernst, op. cit., p. 900.

<table>
<tr><td>CHAPTER</td><td>3</td><td>THE STRUCTURE OF THE
USSR MANUFACTURING
SECTOR, 1912-62</td></tr>
</table>

The changing structure of the USSR manufacturing sector over time is the topic of this chapter. Bench-mark structures from distinct periods of Russian and Soviet economic history (the prerevolutionary period, the NEP period, the First and Second Five-Year Plan periods, and the postwar period are analyzed). The USSR structural trends will be compared with Western time series trends in Chapter 4.

We include a prerevolutionary bench-mark in order to specify the structural base from which the Soviets began their industrial development. We chose 1912 because of the census of factory production of that year and because it represents a year of fairly normal economic activity.

Imperial Russia, especially in the 1880's and during the period between the 1905 revolution and World War I, experienced rapid industrial growth.[1] We shall therefore consider the impact of this rapid industrialization on the industrial structure that the Soviets were to inherit. Russia in 1912 was essentially a free enterprise economy despite the "panoply of measures ranging from high protective tariff via subsidies, profit guarantees, tax reductions, and tax exemptions accorded to industrial enterprises, to manifold laxities in enforcing bothersome laws and ordinances and police and military help in case of labor conflicts, and culminating in huge government orders at extremely high prices."[2] According to Gerschenkron, the Ministry of Finance's lopsided interest in heavy industrial branches resulted in "the relative top-heaviness of the Russian industrial structure as well as its relative concentration upon producers' goods . . . the Russian government's discrimination against 'light industries' and against small enterprises in any branch of industry was applied with even greater consistency and ruthlessness."

The industrial structure during NEP is represented by a series of bench-mark years: 1924/25 (1925), 1926/27 (1927),

1927/28 (1928), and 1928/29 (1929). During the NEP period,
a substantial amount of private economic activity was
sanctioned, although the so-called "commanding heights" remained under state control. This marked a reversal from
the socialization excesses of the War Communism period,
when attempts were made to outlaw all market relations and
to socialize all industrial activity down to small economic
units. The NEP period saw extensive leasing of previously
socialized small-scale enterprises by the state to private
entrepreneurs, the almost total return of retail trade to private hands, the remaining of agriculture in individual hands,
and the lack of a comprehensive central plan to regulate
economic activity. The NEP economy was not a centrally
planned socialist economy; it was a peculiar hybrid of command and market.

The bench-mark years 1933 and 1937 fall within the First
and Second Five-Year Plan periods, respectively, during
which time the vast transformation of the Soviet economic
structure took place. In contrast with the NEP period, the
private sector ceased to play a significant role both in industry,
as a result of the total socialization of industrial activity, and
in agriculture, as a consequence of almost complete collectivization during this period. Commencing with the first two
Five-Year Plans, economic activity was directed by a central
plan which handed down specific production targets to the
enterprise. A state monopoly of foreign trade exerted strict
control over the foreign sector, which was viewed as a tool
of plan implementation. It was during this period that the
institutions peculiar to centrally planned socialist economies
emerged in full force, and if a distinct socialist development
pattern is to be isolated, it should be observed first during
this period.

The years 1955, 1960 and 1962 represent postwar bench
marks of the USSR manufacturing structure. The institutions
and working arrangements of this period are continuations of
those developed during the 1930's, despite the discussions of
economic reform beginning in the late 1950's.

In summary, bench-mark industrial structures have been
selected from four distinct periods of Russian economic development: the pre-Revolution period, the NEP period, the
1930's and the postwar period. The variety of institutional,
ideological and political factors characterizing each period
provides the necessary variation required to analyze the
impact of these factors on the industrial structure.

USSR INDUSTRIAL STRUCTURE, 1912-62

As can be seen in Table 1, Sections D-H, the manufacturing sector maintained a fairly constant total product share of
around 18 percent between 1912 and 1928. A major discontinuity occurred between 1928 and 1937, during which time
manufacturing increased its total product share to 29 percent.
After 1937, manufacturing's total product share fluctuated
from a high of 31 percent in 1955 to a low of 27 percent in 1960.
The construction sector experienced a general decline in
its total product share throughout the entire 1912-37 period.
If one ignores the decline in its output share between 1912 and
1925, which could reflect the incomplete recovery from the
war and the Revolution, construction's share of GNP declined
from a 7 percent average in the NEP period to 5 percent in
1937; the manufacturing share increased from 19 percent to
29 percent of GNP during the same period. On the other hand,
while manufacturing's GNP share was declining from 31 percent to 27 percent between 1955 and 1960, construction increased its GNP share from 6 percent to 11 percent. During
the two periods, there must have been a partial trade-off
between manufacturing and construction.
The trends in industry's (manufacturing plus construction)
share of total product represent a blend of the product trends
of its two component sectors. By 1928, the industry sector
had almost regained its pre-Revolution GNP share of 25 percent, after falling to a low of 21 percent in 1925. Between
1928 and 1937, the industrial sector outpaced the growth of
GNP, increasing its GNP share from 24 percent in 1928 to
35 percent in 1937. Also from 1937 to 1955 and from 1955 to
1960, industrial production grew at a faster rate than total
output, attaining a level of 38 percent of GNP in the early
1960's.

The Structure of USSR Manufacturing:
Value-Added Shares

The structural changes which took place within the manufacturing sector during the 1912-62 period (see Table 1) can
be summarized as follows:
1.   In terms of the broadest aggregates, heavy and light
manufacturing, the transition from the pre-Revolution output
mix of 1912 to the NEP output mix of 1925 was much less

dramatic than the transition from the late NEP output mix of
1928 to the mid-Five-Year Plan mix of 1933. Between 1912
and 1925, the heavy manufactures' share of manufacturing
value added rose from only 28 percent to 29 percent and light
manufactures' share declined from 71 percent to 70 percent;
between 1928 and 1933 alone, heavy manufactures' share rose
from 31 percent to 51 percent and light manufactures' share
declined from 68 percent to 47 percent, with even more rapid
shifts occurring between 1933 and 1937.

    2. The changes in relative output shares which occurred
between 1937 and 1955 are moderate in comparison with the
rapid shifts of the earlier period. Between 1937 and 1955,
heavy manufactures' share increased from 63 percent to 64
percent and light manufactures' share decreased from 36 percent to 35 percent of total manufacturing value added.*

    3. The particular sector most responsible for the rapid
increase of the heavy manufactures' share between 1928 and
1937 was metal products (engineering), whose share of total
manufacturing value added more than doubled between 1928
and 1933, rising from 14 percent to 30 percent, and attained
a 37 percent share by 1937. Again, as in the case of total
heavy manufactures, the increases in metal products' share
prior to 1928 and after 1937 were mild relative to the 1928-37
period. Between 1912 and 1928, metal products' share increased from 10 to 14 percent of manufacturing value added,
and from 37 percent to 39 percent between 1937 and 1962.

    4. Less dramatic value-added share increases were
recorded by the other heavy manufacturing sectors between
1928 and 1937: Basic metals (metallurgy) increased its value
added share from 5 percent to 8 percent, and chemicals (including rubber products and coal and oil products) increased
its share from 9 percent to 14 percent of manufacturing value
added. It is interesting to note the relative constancy of the
nonmetallic minerals' (mostly construction materials) share
during the 1928-37 period. Heavy intermediate manufacturing
(metallurgy, chemicals, nonmetallic minerals) increased its
share of total manufacturing value added from 17 percent to
26 percent between 1928 and 1937.

    5. Several interesting features should be noted concern-
ing relative shares within heavy intermediate manufactures
during other periods. First, one should note the importance

---

*Had the 1937 structure been valued in 1937 prices, the
increase in heavy manufactures' share and the decline in light
manufactures' share would have been more substantial.

TABLE 1

The Value-Added Structure of Manufacturing,
Russia and USSR, 1912-62

		1912	1925	1927	1928	1929	1933	1937	1955	1960	1962
A.	Per Capita Income (1960 US$)	353	277	334	336	347	417	493	865	1109	1198
B.	Subsector Percentage of Total Manufacturing Value Added										
1.	Food Products (ISIC 20-22)	29.7	29.1	22.0	23.0	21.5	16.8	12.0	9.2	8.5	9.7
2.	Textiles (ISIC 23)	19.8	21.1	25.2	24.9	24.4	14.8	12.2	8.2	7.3	6.7
3.	Clothing, Footwear (ISIC 24)	4.9	7.1	9.1	8.8	8.8	5.2	4.3	7.1	6.9	6.5
4.	Wood Prods. (ISIC 25, 26)	14.4	4.3	4.9	4.9	4.8	5.6	3.8	6.8	5.5	5.3
5.	Paper Prods. (ISIC 27)	.7	2.1	1.5	1.4	1.6	1.6	1.5	.9	.8	1.0
6.	Printing (ISIC 28)	.8	3.0	2.1	2.0	2.0	1.8	1.2	1.7	1.5	1.4
7.	Leather Prods. (ISIC 29)	1.2	2.9	3.1	2.8	2.5	1.5	1.4	.7	.8	.7
8.	Chemicals, Rubber, Coal, Oil Prods. (ISIC 30-32)	7.2	10.0	8.0	8.6	8.8	12.1	14.2	6.6	7.6	7.4
9.	Non-metallic Minerals (ISIC 33)	2.9	3.6	3.9	3.8	4.0	3.1	4.0	5.5	8.5	8.4
10.	Basic Metals (ISIC 34)	7.4	3.9	5.2	4.9	4.9	5.8	7.6	13.5	12.9	12.5
11.	Metal Prods. (eng.) (ISIC 35-38)	10.3	11.9	14.0	14.0	15.5	30.4	36.9	38.7	38.2	39.3
12.	Misc. Manufactures (ISIC 39)	.9	1.1	.9	1.0	1.4	1.4	.9	1.0	1.5	1.0
	Total	100.0	100.0	100.0	100.0	100.0	100.0	100.0	100.0	100.0	100.0

	1912	1925	1927	1928	1929	1933	1937	1955	1960	1962
C. Major Aggregates of the Manufacturing Sector as Percentages of Total Manufacturing Value Added										
1. Heavy Manufacturing (ISIC 30-38)	27.7	29.4	31.1	31.3	33.1	51.3	62.7	64.3	67.2	67.6
2. Light Manufacturing (ISIC 20-29)	71.4	69.6	68.0	67.6	65.6	47.3	36.4	34.7	31.3	31.4
3. Heavy Intermediate (ISIC 30-34)	17.4	17.5	17.1	17.4	17.6	21.0	25.8	25.6	29.0	28.3
4. Textiles, Clothing, Leather Prods. (ISIC 23, 24, 29)	25.8	31.1	37.4	36.5	35.7	21.5	17.9	15.0	16.0	13.9
5. Other Light Manufactures (ISIC 25-28)	16.0	9.4	8.5	8.3	8.4	9.0	6.5	9.4	7.8	7.7
D. Manufacturing Value Added ÷ GNP	18.1	16.8	17.4	17.5	20.5	23.1	29.3	30.7	26.9	28.0
E. Construction Value Added ÷ GNP	7.1	4.3	6.5	6.8	7.0	6.0	5.2	6.2	11.3	10.4
F. Industry Value Added ÷ GNP	25.2	21.1	23.9	24.3	27.5	29.1	34.5	36.9	38.2	38.4
G. Mining, Gas, Electricity Value Added ÷ GNP	3.2	2.5	2.6	2.6	3.0	3.7	4.8	4.6	4.7	4.6
H. F + G	28.4	23.6	24.5	26.9	30.5	32.8	39.3	41.5	42.9	43.0

(Continued)

TABLE 1--Continued

Sources: Section A, consult text, Chapter 2; Sections B and C, Appendix A; Sections D-H, as follows:

1912: S. N. Prokopovič, Opyt isčislenia narodnogo dokhoda 50 gubernii evropeiskoi Rossii v 1900-1913 g.g., p. 24, estimates that 21.3 percent of national income originated in manufacturing, mining, gas and electricity and 7.2 percent originated in construction in 1913. The same ratios are assumed for 1912. Goldsmith, "The Economic Growth of Russia, 1860-1913," Table B-2, estimates that about 17 percent of total industrial value added (including gas and electricity) originated in mining (with gas and electricity less than 1 percent of the total) in 1908. The same ratios are assumed for 1912, which yields a manufacturing share of 18.1 percent and a mining, gas and electricity share of 3.2 percent of GNP.

1925: The 1925 shares of GNP are estimated by extrapolating the 1928 shares, using the industry and GNP indexes in Chapter 2 and a construction index (based upon hours worked in construction from Statsprav 1928, p. 527), yielding the following GNP shares: Total industry equals 19.3 percent of GNP and construction equals 4.3 percent of GNP. Of the 19.3 percent total industry share, 18.1 percent represents the manufacturing share and 2.5 percent represents mining, gas and electricity share, according to net product data in Statsprav 1927, pp. 216-19, 254-55.

1927: The 1927 GNP shares are estimated in the same manner as the 1925 shares by extrapolating the 1928 shares. Total industry accounts for 20.0 percent and construction for 2.5 percent of GNP. According to Nutter, The Growth of Industrial Production in the Soviet Union, pp. 509-17, manufacturing, in turn, equals 17.4 percent and mining, gas and electricity equals 2.5 percent of GNP.

1928: Bergson, Real SNIP, p. 153, estimates USSR 1928 GNP at 29.56 billion rubles (1928 factor cost). Raymond Powell, "Industrial Production," p. 185, estimates 1928 total industry value added and construction value added at 5.95 and 2.00 billion rubles, respectively. According to Nutter, The Growth of Industrial Production in the Soviet Union, pp. 509-17, manufacturing accounts for about 83 percent and mining, gas and electricity account for the remainder of the 5.96 billion rubles.

1929: On the assumption that GNP grew exponentially between 1932 and 1937, USSR 1929 GNP equals 33.11 billion rubles (Bergson, Real SNIP, p. 155). Using Powell, "Industrial Production," p. 187, and Powell, A Material-Input Index of Soviet Construction, Revised and Extended, p. 3, it is estimated that in 1929 total industry value added equaled 7.79 billion rubles and construction value added equaled 2.32 billion rubles. According to Nutter, The Growth of Industrial Production in the Soviet Union, pp. 509-17, manufacturing accounts for 87 percent and mining, gas and electricity account for 13 percent of the 7.79 billion.

30

1933: Assuming exponential growth between 1928 and 1937, 1933 GNP (1928 prices) equals 51.91 billion rubles. According to the two Powell indexes, value added in total industry equals 13.92 and value added in construction equals 3.10 billion rubles (1928 prices). According to Powell's Soviet Construction, pp. 42-47, 62-63, mining, gas and electricity account for 22 percent of industrial capital stock and 14 percent of industrial labor force in 1934. Both figures refer to large-scale industry only. Large-scale industry, on the other hand, accounts for 89 percent of industrial labor force in 1933, and it is crudely assumed that it also accounts for 89 percent of industrial output. Weighting capital and labor with .25 and .75 weights and multiplying by .89, it is estimated that mining, gas and electricity account for roughly 14 percent of the 13.92 billion rubles.

1937: Bergson, Real SNIP, p. 145, estimates USSR 1937 factor cost GNP at 193.4 billion rubles. Powell, "Industrial Production," p. 185, estimates 1937 industry and construction value added at 65.9 and 10.0 billion rubles. The 65.9 billion figure includes a portion of fishing and lumbering, which should be excluded. According to Nutter, Growth of Industrial Production, pp. 509-17, lumbering and fishing accounted for 8 percent of industry value added in 1929, i.e., less than 2 percent of GNP. Owing to lack of information, no adjustment is made; at the most, adjustment would cause a one percentage point decline in the various ratios. According to Nutter, Growth of Industrial Production, pp. 348-49, mining, gas and electricity grew at about the same rate as total industrial output between 1933 and 1937; therefore the 65.9 billion rubles are broken down in the same fashion as for 1933.

1955: Stanley Cohn, "The Gross National Product in the Soviet Union," p. 73, estimates that in 1955 total industry plus construction accounted for 41.4 percent of GNP valued at factor cost. According to Morris Bornstein, Soviet National Accounts for 1955, p. 84, construction accounts for 15 percent of this total; therefore construction equals 6.2 percent of GNP and total industry equals 35.3 percent of GNP. According to Joint Economic Committee, Current Economic Indicators for the USSR (June, 1965), p. 50, mining, gas and electricity account for 13 percent of this 35.3 percent.

1960, 1962: In 1959, industry equaled 31.0 percent and construction equaled 10.9 percent of GNP. These shares are extrapolated to 1960 and 1962 using indexes in Joint Economic Committee, Current Economic Indicators for the USSR (June, 1965), p. 20, and in James Noren, "Soviet Trends in Outputs, Inputs and Productivity," p. 280. On the basis of the Noren value-added weights and Current Economic Indicators employment data (pp. 74-79), it is estimated that the mining, gas and electricity share in 1960 was 15 percent of total industrial value added.

31

of basic metals in the 1912 manufacturing structure, at which
time it accounted for 7 percent of manufacturing value added,
a share which was not regained until 1937. Second, one should
note the postwar decline of chemicals vis-à-vis other heavy
intermediate manufactures. In 1937, chemicals' value-added
share was 14 percent; in 1955 it was 7 percent. On the other
hand, basic metals' share increased from 8 percent to 14
percent during the same period, and nonmetallic minerals'
share increased from 4 percent in 1937 to between 8 percent
and 9 percent in the 1960's.

    6.   Disaggregating the factors behind the rapid decline
in the light manufactures' share of total manufacturing value
added between 1928 and 1937, the following trends should be
mentioned: Between 1928 and 1937, the four major consumer
goods sectors (food products, textiles, clothing and leather
products) all declined in terms of value-added shares by more
than 50 percent. Food products declined from 23 percent to
12 percent, textiles from 25 percent to 12 percent, clothing
from 9 percent to 4 percent, and leather products from 3 percent to 1 percent of manufacturing value added. On the other
hand, no distinct trend can be isolated for the other light
manufactures group between 1928 and 1937; it maintained a
share close to 8 percent during the entire period.

    7.   Throughout the entire 1912-60 period, food products'
share of manufacturing value added declined, from a high of
30 percent in 1912 to a low of 9 percent in 1960. The most
rapid decline occurred between 1929 and 1937, at which time
food products' share dropped from 22 percent to 12 percent
of manufacturing value added.

The Structure of USSR Manufacturing:
Labor Force Shares

    Industrial branch labor force is measured in full-time
equivalents and not by the actual physical number employed.
This distinction is quite important in the case of the USSR
labor force data because a large proportion of employment
in small-scale enterprises was on a part-time basis during
the pre-Revolutionary period and NEP period. Failure to
adjust for part-time employment would therefore overem-
phasize light manufacturing employment relative to heavy
manufacturing employment during the early periods of Soviet
development in comparison with employment shares during
later periods, when part-time employment was less important.

Less information is available on USSR labor force distributions than on value added distributions. For example, the
important 1937 bench mark is missing from the labor force
data because of lack of data on small-scale enterprises.

Several trends in labor force shares should be noted:

1.   In terms of the broadest manufacturing aggregates,
it is evident that the same trends hold for manufacturing labor
force shares as for value-added shares. The most abrupt
structural shifts occurred during the first two Five-Year
Plans; the changes preceding and following this period were
more gradual and moderate. Between 1928 and 1933, heavy
manufactures' share of total manufacturing labor force increased from 28 percent to 43 percent, and light manufactures'
share declined from 71 percent to 56 percent. On the other
hand, the transition from the 1913 structure to the 1925 NEP
structure witnessed an increase in heavy manufactures' share
from 26 percent to 27 percent.

Owing to lack of information for 1937, it is difficult to
evaluate the extent of the structural transformations which
took place between the Second Five-Year Plan period (the
late 1930's) and the postwar period. Between 1933 and 1956,
heavy manufactures' share of manufacturing labor force increased from 43 percent to 57 percent, and light manufactures'
share declined from 56 percent to 42 percent. If final product
trends reflect labor force trends, then the major portion of
these share changes had already been attained by 1937.

2.   The sector most responsible for the rapid increase
in heavy manufactures' labor force share between 1928 and
1933 was the metal products sector, whose share of total
manufacturing labor force increased from 14 percent to 20
percent during this period. The three heavy intermediate
manufacturing sectors (basic metals, chemicals, and nonmetallic minerals) increased their combined labor force share
from 14 percent to 23 percent, the most marked increase
occurring in the chemicals sector, whose labor force share
increased from 3 percent to 8 percent. On the other hand,
nonmetallic minerals and basic metals both increased their
labor force shares: nonmetallic minerals from 6 percent to
8 percent and basic metals from 5 percent to 7 percent.

3.   As in the case of the aggregate heavy manufactures
sector, the structural changes prior to 1928 were insignificant,
with no distinct trends emerging in the various heavy intermediate sectors and metal products. For example, chemicals
maintained a constant 3 percent labor force share between
1913 and 1928, nonmetallic minerals increased its labor force

TABLE 2

The Labor Force Structure of Manufacturing,
Russia and USSR, 1913-60

		1913	1925	1928	1933	1956	1960
A.	Labor Force Percentage of Total Manufacturing Labor Force						
1.	Food Products (ISIC 20-22)	21	16	17	13	12	11
2.	Textiles (ISIC 23)	39[a]	20	24	18	10	10
3.	Clothing, Footwear (ISIC 24)	[a]	17	16	12	7	10
4.	Wood Prods. (ISIC 25, 26)	12	13	8	9	9	7
5.	Paper Prods. (ISIC 27)	1	1	1	1	1	1
6.	Printing (ISIC 28)	2	2	3	2	2	1
7.	Leather Prods. (ISIC 29)	[a]	3	2	1	1	1
8.	Chemicals, Rubber, Coal, Oil Prods. (ISIC 30-32)	3	3	3	8	4	5
9.	Non-metallic Minerals (ISIC 33)	5	5	6	8	6	8
10.	Basic Metals (ISIC 34)	6	4	5	7	9	9
11.	Metal Prods. (ISIC 35-38)	12	15	14	20	37	37
12.	Misc. Manufactures (ISIC 39)	[b]	2	1	2	1	1
	Total	100	100	100	100	100	100
B.	Labor Forces of Major Aggregates of Manufacturing as Percentages of Total Manufacturing Labor Force						
1.	Heavy Manufactures (ISIC 30-38)	26	27	28	43	57	59
2.	Light Manufactures (ISIC 20-29)	75	72	71	56	42	41
3.	Heavy Intermediate Manufactures (ISIC 30-34)	14	12	14	23	20	22
4.	Textiles, Clothing, Leather Prods. (ISIC 23, 24, 29)	39	40	42	31	18	18
5.	Other Light Manufactures (ISIC 25-28)	15	16	12	12	12	9

[a]Textiles, clothing, and leather combined.

[b]Miscellaneous manufactures not estimated, probably between 1 percent and 2 percent of manufacturing labor force in 1913.

Sources: Appendix A; G. W. Nutter, The Growth of Industrial Production in the Soviet Union, Table C-1.

share from 5 percent to 6 percent during the same period, and basic metals' labor force share declined from 6 percent in 1913 to 5 percent in 1928.

4.   The lack of information concerning the 1937 labor force structure makes it difficult to judge the extent of structural transformations within the heavy manufacturing sector which occurred between the prewar and postwar periods. Between 1933 and 1956, metal products' share of manufacturing labor force increased from 20 percent to 37 percent, but one can only speculate as to how much of this increase had been attained by 1937. It is interesting to note, however, the decline in heavy intermediate manufactures' share between 1933 and 1956 from 23 percent to 20 percent, owing mainly to the substantial drop in chemicals' share from 8 percent of manufacturing labor force in 1933 to 4 percent in 1956.

5.   Several notable trends explain the rapid decline in light manufactures' share of manufacturing labor force between 1928 and 1933. Whereas the labor force shares of the aggregate light manufacturing sector declined by 15 percentage points between 1928 and 1933, the combined textiles, clothing and leather sector alone declined by 11 percentage points. Adding to this the four percentage point decline in food products' labor force share, one can account for the total decline. This means that the brunt of the relative labor force share losses between 1928 and 1933 was borne by the textiles, clothing and leather sector. On the other hand, other light manufactures (wood products, paper and printing) maintained a constant labor force share between 1928 and 1933.

6.   The major labor force share losses after 1933 were still borne by textiles, clothing and leather, whose collective share of manufacturing labor force dropped from 31 percent to 18 percent between 1933 and 1956, accounting for over 90 percent of the decline in the aggregate light manufacturing sector during this period.

Relative Value Added Per Worker Sector Trends

Tables 1 and 2 provide insights into the relative trends in output per worker among economic sectors in the USSR, for the ratio of value-added share of sector i divided by its labor force share to the value-added share of sector j divided by its labor force share equals the ratio of value added per worker in sector i to value added per worker in sector j. We calculate relative sector value added per worker in Table 3.

TABLE 3

Value Added Per Worker Ratios,
Russian and USSR Manufacturing Sectors,
Selected Years

	1912(3)	1925	1928	1933	1960
Value Added per Worker					
1. Heavy Manufactures to Light Manufactures	1.14	1.10	1.16	1.42	1.50
2. Metal Prods. to Textiles, Clothing, Leather	1.24	1.03	1.14	2.12	1.16
3. Heavy Manufactures to Food Prods.	.76	.59	.82	.91	1.25
4. Metal Prods. to Heavy Intermediate Manufactures	.69	.53	.82	1.70	.78

Source: Tables 1, 2.

The relative value added per worker ratios of Table 3 are by necessity poor measures of changes in sectoral labor productivity differentials over time, owing to the distorting influence of relative price changes. The 1928 and 1933 figures are, however, in constant 1927/28 prices; therefore they reflect sectoral labor productivity trends. We note the following trends concerning the 1928 and 1933 figures:

1.   The important feature of Table 3 is the discontinuous jump in value added per worker (relative productivity) differentials between 1928 and 1933 in favor of the heavy manufacturing sectors. In 1928, value added per worker in heavy manufactures was roughly 15 percent greater than value added per worker in light manufactures. By 1933, output per worker in heavy manufactures was over 40 percent greater than output per worker in light manufactures.

2. The discontinuity is even greater in the case of the major subsectors of heavy and light manufacturing. In 1928, value added per worker in the metal products sector was about 15 percent greater than in the combined textiles, clothing and leather sector; by 1933 value added per worker in the metal products sector was more than double that of the textiles, clothing and leather sector.

3. A smaller discontinuity can be observed by comparing value added per worker differentials in the food products sector and the aggregate heavy manufacturing sector. In 1928, the average worker in heavy manufacturing was about eight-tenths as productive as in food products; in 1933 the average worker in heavy manufacturing was nine-tenths as productive.

4. Within the heavy manufactures sector, the major value added per worker increases between 1928 and 1933 were concentrated in the metal products sector, which experienced extremely rapid product growth between 1928 and 1933 relative to growth in employment. On the other hand, heavy inter-mediate manufacturing grew less rapidly than metal products measured in terms of product, and more rapidly measured in terms of labor force. This is reflected in the reversal of the metal products-heavy intermediate manufactures output per worker ratios between 1928 and 1933.

Although a specific investigation of the differential rates of capital accumulation among sectors has not been under-taken, a significant portion of these discontinuous changes in value added per worker differentials is to be explained by the concentration of investment in those sectors which experienced the most rapid productivity gains. A significant portion of the remainder can be attributed to the importation of tech-nology for high-priority sectors and to the setting of high rela-tive wages in priority sectors to attract the best-quality labor into those sectors.

As a result of this industrialization policy, the productiv-ity of resources channeled into priority sectors increased more rapidly than the productivity of resources in low priority sectors. Production costs per unit of output therefore rose more rapidly in low-priority than in high-priority sectors be-tween 1928 and 1937, thereby altering the relative price structure in favor of investment and defense items. This means that the postwar industrial value-added structures (in current prices) reflect the new post-industrialization price structure and underestimate the heavy manufacturing value-added shares relative to what they would have been in constant preindustrialization prices. One can see from this that the

1960 sector value added per worker ratios do not reflect labor productivity trends between 1933 and 1960 because of the radical changes in the relative price structure during this period.[3]

SUMMARY AND CONCLUSIONS

The material presented in this chapter is best evaluated in light of the development experience of other nations, which is done in the ensuing chapters. However, an appreciation of the magnitude of the structural transformations which occurred in the USSR in the composition of total output, e.g., the rising shares of manufacturing and industry and the changing structure of the manufacturing sector itself, especially between 1928 and 1933, facilitates an understanding of the results which follow. That the USSR was able markedly to change its manufacturing output mix within a period of five years (1928-33) should not be allowed to pass without special notice, for it illustrates the singular capacity of centrally planned economies to restructure themselves rapidly in accordance with planned economic objectives. By channeling investment into priority industrial sectors, by controlling wage rates, recruitment campaigns and financial resources of firms and by regulating the importation of Western industrial technology, the Soviets created something akin to a dual industrial economy between 1928 and 1937, i.e., a modern heavy industry and a relatively backward light industry. Even within the heavy industry sector, Soviet development strategy called for the advance of only certain sectors, particularly engineering and metallurgy, which indicates the simplicity of sectoral planning objectives during this period.

NOTES

1. R. W. Goldsmith, "The Economic Growth of Russia, 1860-1913"; Alexander Gerschenkron, "The Rate of Industrial Growth in Russia Since 1885."

2. Alexander Gerschenkron, "The Early Phases of Industrialization in Russia: Afterthoughts and Counterthoughts," pp. 152-54.

3. See Abram Bergson, "Prices of Industrial Products in the USSR, 1928-1950"; Bergson, Real SNIP, p. 237; Philip Hansen, The Consumer in the Soviet Economy, pp. 87-89.

CHAPTER **4** THE DEVELOPMENT
OF THE MANUFACTURING
SECTOR IN THE USSR
AND FOUR WESTERN
NATIONS

In this chapter, we study the development pattern of the
USSR manufacturing sector vis-à-vis the historical experience
of four industrialized Western nations: US (1870-1963), Canada
(1891-1963), UK (1907-65) and Germany (1873-1936). The
USSR data were given in Table 1 and the Western data are
found in Appendix B.

We carry out this comparative appraisal of the USSR
industrial development pattern on several levels. First,
the aggregate trends in the ratios of manufacturing value added
and industrial value added to total product are examined by
computing least-squares trend lines with respect to per capita
income. Second, the USSR sample is subdivided into two
groups, a 1925-29 "preplan" group and a 1933-62 "plan" group
to determine whether one can detect a structural break in the
USSR development pattern between the two periods. Third,
the USSR plan and preplan manufacturing structures are tested individually against the composite Western sample for
structural homogeneity. Fourth, regression trend lines of
the individual manufacturing subsectors are computed and
compared for the USSR, US, Canada, UK and Germany, as
well as for the combined Western sample.

MANUFACTURING AND INDUSTRY

Insofar as the size of the industry and manufacturing sectors relative to GNP can significantly influence the internal
structure of the manufacturing sectors it is of considerable
interest to examine the USSR trends vis-à-vis our sample of
developed Western economies.

The regressions of per capita income and population on the manufacturing sector's share of total product (which we henceforth call MS) and on the industry (manufacturing plus construction) sector's share of total product (IS) are recorded in Table 4 and are graphed in Figures 1 and 2. In all cases, we used double log functional forms; therefore the elasticity coefficients measure the percentage change in the manufacturing (or industry) share of GNP for every percentage change in the independent variable.

Starting with the simple regressions (A equations) of per capita income (I) on the manufacturing share of total product (MS) and on the industry share of total product (IS), we note that in terms of income-share elasticities and intercepts, the USSR development experience does not distinguish itself radically from that of the four sampled Western industrial economies. The USSR manufacturing and industry income-share elasticities of .373 and .384, respectively, are larger than the US and Canadian elasticities (.344 and .269, and .156 and .177, respectively) but are smaller than the UK and German elasticities (.474 and .529, and .544 and .651, respectively). It is interesting to note the closeness of the USSR elasticities to the unweighted averages of the Western elasticities: the former is .373, whereas the average Western elasticity is .384. The USSR and the average Western sample industry elasticities are .384 and .407, respectively.[*]

Table 4 gives the population elasticities also (B equations), but the significant degree of multicollinearity between per capita income and population, both of which are subject to an upward time trend, makes them difficult to interpret.

---

[*]One can also compare the USSR elasticities with other income elasticity estimates. Chenery and Taylor, "Development Patterns," compute an industry elasticity of .344 from Western cross-section data. Peter Temin, "A Time-Series Test of Patterns of Industrial Growth," computes an industry income elasticity of .32 from time series data. Chenery, "Patterns of Industrial Growth" (p. 633), computes a cross-section elasticity of .44 for manufacturing, and Maizels, Industrial Growth and World Trade (p. 53), computes a manufacturing elasticity of .26 from OEEC time series data. It is interesting to note that the manufacturing and industry share elasticities (.387 and .397, respectively) derived from a postwar cross-section of socialist countries are almost identical with the USSR historical elasticities. See Chapter 7.

TABLE 4

Estimates of Production Patterns, Manufacturing and Industry, USSR and Selected Western Countries

Country	Regression Coefficients for Manufacturing				Regression Coefficients for Industry			
	Intercept	Log I	Log N	R²	Intercept	Log I	Log N	R²
USSR A	-3.81	.373	--	.76	-3.61	.384	--	.90
B	5.41	1.193	-2.798	.84	.07	.711	-1.117	.93
US A	-3.94	.344	--	.95	-3.23	.269	--	.92
B	-3.83	(.079)	.373	.97	-3.15	(.080)	.266	.93
Canada A	-2.84	.156	--	.45	-2.43	.177	--	.64
B	-9.37	(-.169)	.292	.61	-1.23	(-.076)	.229	.75
Germany A	-4.66	.544	--	.90	-5.22	.651	--	.90
B	-4.57	.385	.236	.93	-5.08	.386	.392	.94
UK A	-4.47	.474	--	.84	-4.71	.529	--	.87
B	-7.98	-.567	2.78	.96	-7.96	-.436	2.579	.95
Western Pool A	2.36	.152	--	.10	2.10	.139	--	.10

Notes: Regression A: ln MS (IS) = a + blnI.
Regression B: ln MS (IS) = a + blnI + clnN.
The coefficients in ( ) are insignificant at .95.

Sources: Author's computations based on data in Table 1 and Appendix B.

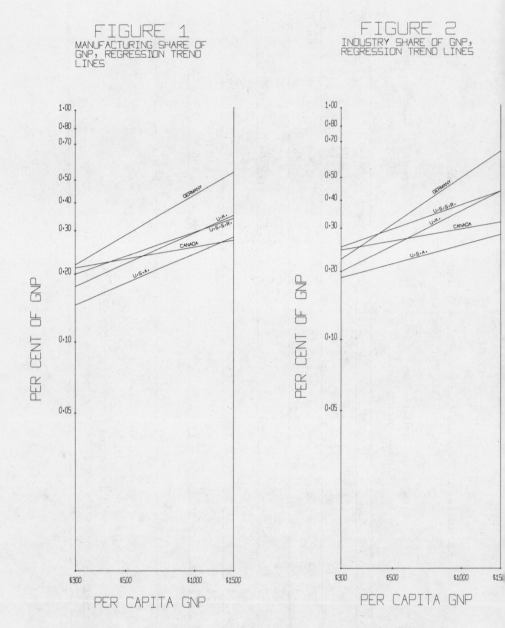

Source: Author's computations based on data in Table 4.

42

Figures 1 and 2 contain the regression trend lines of the USSR, US, Canadian, German and UK manufacturing and industry sectors plotted from Table 4 for a $300-$1500 range. Figure 1 shows that the German (1873-1936) manufacturing shares of total product surpass the USSR shares at all income levels within the $300-$1500 range plotted. The UK manufacturing shares exceed those of the USSR at income levels above $750. On the other hand, the USSR manufacturing sector maintains a larger share of GNP than the respective Canadian and US manufacturing shares at almost all income levels.

Figure 2 shows that the German ratios of industrial output to total product exceed the USSR ratios at income levels above $400. On the other hand, the USSR ratios are larger than the US, Canadian and UK ratios at all income levels within the $300-$1500 range.

On the basis of this evidence, one can conclude that the USSR manufacturing and industry sectors occupy an intermediate position relative to the development experience of the US, Canada, the UK and Germany. The failure of the USSR manufacturing sector to distinguish itself in terms of income elasticities and intercepts from the development experience of the four Western economies examined is perhaps indicative of the statistical averaging process involved in regression analysis, which averages the high elasticities of the 1930's with the lower NEP and postwar elasticities. It also says nothing about the speed of industrialization, which was extremely rapid in the USSR.[*]

Turning now from total industry and manufacturing trends to the internal structure of manufacturing, we focus our attention on the USSR manufacturing trends relative to the US, Canadian, German and UK trends.

COVARIANCE ANALYSIS: USSR PLAN AND
PREPLAN MANUFACTURING STRUCTURES

We shall test the following hypothesis in this section:

The change in the economic system in 1928 (from
NEP to centrally planned socialism) did not cause

---

[*]According to Simon Kuznets, "A Comparative Appraisal," p. 345, the structural shifts which took place in the USSR between 1928 and 1940 required some 50 to 60 years in other developed economies.

any significant change in the structure of USSR
manufacturing. Instead, all observable changes
can be accounted for by changes in system-independent variables and by random error.

To test this hypothesis, it is necessary to determine
whether the structural changes which occurred after 1928 can
be accounted for by eliminating the economic factors which
might have caused them, as was outlined in Chapter 1. Con-
structing a test of this sort is made more difficult by the
limited number of observations in both groups. If 1912 is included in the preplan group, the total number of observations
from both groups is 10, the number being divided equally between the two groups. The result is a limited number of degrees of freedom, which makes hypothesis testing tenuous;
nevertheless, the formal tests have been carried out. Even
if one wishes to attach less than full significance to the results of the formal homogeneity tests, valuable insights can
be gained from the adjusted group means which are by-products
of the formal tests.

The model of Chapter 1 suggests a set of covariates whose
influence upon the structure of manufacturing should be eliminated before testing for homogeneity: per capita income (I),
size (N), natural resource endowments (R), trade orientation
(V), and the ratio of manufacturing output to GNP (MS). Natural resource endowments are by definition constant over
time, and because time series do not involve vast differences
in the size of markets, as do cross-sections, no attempt is
made to adjust for population differences. Covariate adjustments have been made for I and MS. Trade orientation has
been omitted because the initial covariance tests show that it
has no impact on the adjusted group means. The results are
given in Table 5. The structural dichotomy of the two structures is evident from Table 5. The preplan manufacturing
shares of food products and light manufactures (column 1) are
well above the combined USSR averages (column 5), whereas
the preplan manufacturing shares of metal products and heavy
intermediate manufactures are well below the combined averages. The opposite deviations from the combined means hold
for the plan structures (column 3). A comparison of within-
group standard deviations (columns 2 and 4) with overall standard deviations (column 6) reveals a significant degree of
structural uniformity within the two groups. A simple analy-
sis-of-variance test of structural homogeneity at this point
would result in the rejection of the hypotheses.

TABLE 5

The Unadjusted Group Means (M), Standard Deviations (S.D.),
Adjusted Group Means (M'), USSR, 1925-29, 1933-62

	(1925-29)		(1933-62)		(1925-62)		(1925-29)		(1933-62)	
(1)	M (2)	S.D. (3)	M (4)	S.D. (5)	M (6)	S.D. (7)	1-3 (8)	M' (9)	M' (10)	8-9
Dependent Variables, Percentages of Manufacturing Value Added										
Light Manufactures, Excl.										
Food Prods.	39	2	20	3	28	11	+19	36	22	+14
Food Prods.	24	3	11	3	17	7	+13	18	16	+2
Metal Prods.	14	1	37	4	27	12	-23	20	32	-12
Heavy Intermediate Manufactures	17	2	26	3	22	5	-9	21	22	-2
Independent Variables										
Per Capita Income (I)	$323	$31	$836	$332	$608	$358				
Manufacturing Percentage of GNP (MS)	28	2	28	3	23	6				
F value								$F(4, 2)= 191.4^*$		
Average Absolute Deviation								16.0		7.5

*Significant at .05.

Source: Author's computations based on data in Table 1.

The impact of per capita income and MS differences on
the original group differences is indicated by the adjusted group
means (columns 8-10). * The average absolute deviation of
the unadjusted group means is 16 percentage points. I and
MS differences between the two groups explain a significant
portion of these initial group differences in that the average
absolute (adjusted) group mean deviation is 7.5 percentage
points. The food products deviation drops from +19 percent
(unadjusted) to +2 percent (adjusted). The metal products and
heavy intermediate manufactures deviations decline from -23
percent and -9 percent, respectively, to -12 percent and -2
percent, respectively. On the other hand, the light manufactures (excluding food products) deviations is reduced only
slightly, from +19 percent to +14 percent.

The adjusted group mean differences are still highly significant, however, because the F statistic, which tests the
significance of adjusted group mean differences, is significant
at .05. Thus, the USSR preplan and plan structures are heterogeneous.

USSR PREPLAN AND PLAN MANUFACTURING
COMPARED WITH A WESTERN COMPOSITE

The evidence presented in the preceding section points
to a break in the USSR structural pattern after 1928 which cannot be accounted for by changes in economic variables. Instead, we accept the counter hypothesis that this structural
discontinuity must be attributed to radical institutional changes,
i.e., to the introduction of a plan-directed socialist industrial
development pattern.

An alternative approach is to conduct two separate homogeneity tests, one comparing the preplan USSR manufacturing
structure and the composite Western structure of Appendix B,
the other comparing the USSR plan manufacturing structure
and the same composite Western structure. To do so requires
a new hypothesis:

---

*The computational formula for the adjusted group mean is

$$\text{adj}(y_{.k}) = y_{.k} - \sum_{m=1}^{t} d_m(v_{.m} - v_{..m}),$$

where the . represent group means and the .. represent
combined means.

The choice of the economic system significantly affects the structure of manufacturing; therefore, one
can account for the structural differences between
the composite Western manufacturing structure and
the preplan USSR structure by way of system-independent factors and random error, but one cannot account
for the structural differences between the composite
Western manufacturing structure and the USSR plan
structure in the same manner because of the system-
effect.

The comparison of the two USSR structures with a composite Western structure involves a larger number of observations than above; therefore, one is less inhibited by the limited
number of degrees of freedom.
    A relatively simple way to eliminate per capita income dif-
ferences is to compare a particular USSR manufacturing structure with those of the four industrial Western countries at
points of time when per capita incomes were roughly equal.
For example, USSR 1955 per capita income ($865) corresponds
roughly to US 1904, Canadian 1926, UK 1924 and German 1913
per capita incomes. The comparative structures are given in
Table 6.

TABLE 6

USSR, US, UK, Canadian and German
Manufacturing Structures, Equal Per Capita Incomes
(percentage of manufacturing value added)

	(1) USA 1904	(2) Canada 1926	(3) UK 1924	(4) Germany 1913	(5) Avg. (1-4)	(6) USSR 1955
Food Prods.	19	29	17	19	21	9
Textiles, Clothing, Leather	26	13	29	25	23	16
Printing, Paper	9	16	8	5	10	3
Heavy Intermediate Manufactures	20	18	19	26	21	26
Metal Prods.	20	18	21	19	20	39

Sources: Table 1; Appendix B.

Columns 5 and 6 of Table 6 reveal striking differences between the USSR manufacturing structure and the average Western structure (per capita income constant): The USSR food products share is less than half of the average Western share, and its paper and printing share is less than one-third of the average Western share. On the other hand, the USSR metal products share is almost double the average Western share. The USSR combined textiles, clothing and leather share is seven percentage points below the average Western share whereas its heavy intermediate manufactures share is five percentage points above the average Western share.

It would be quite interesting to make a similar comparison of a USSR preplan manufacturing structure and Western manufacturing structures, holding per capita income constant; however, the USSR preplan per capita income levels are below $350, and only the US 1870 per capita income compares roughly with this figure. The structural similarity of the USSR 1928 and the US 1870 manufacturing structures is quite striking: The average absolute deviation of the 1870 US structure (Appendix B) from the 1928 USSR structure is 2.4 percent, whereas the average absolute deviation of Table 6 is 10.0 percent.

Although such comparisons are quite useful, they are quite crude insofar as factors other than per capita income influence the industrial structure. Full covariate adjustments have been undertaken, and the results are recorded in Table 7.

Before turning to the interpretation of Table 7 we shall group the covariates into the two covariate categories--environmental and explanatory covariates--discussed in Chapter 1. Per capita income, population and natural resource endowments are placed in the environmental covariate category, i.e., we assume that they are independent of the economic system. The manufacturing share of GNP (MS) and trade orientation (R) are placed in the explanatory covariate category.[*]

---

[*]The rationale for including MS in the explanatory variable class is complex. Chenery and Taylor have shown that income, size, trade, and resource variables, when grouped properly, explain a major portion of the variation of MS in a cross-section of nonsocialist economies; the remainder of the variation should be accounted for by random error. In the case of the planned socialist economies, a large MS ratio is the result of a conscious decision of socialist planners that a socialist economy should have a large manufacturing sector relative to its income level, size and resource endowments. The rationale for considering trade orientation (V) as an explanatory

TABLE 7

Covariance Analysis, Composite Western Group,
USSR Pre-Plan Group, USSR Plan Group;
Adjusted Group Means; F Tests of Structural Homogeneity

Unadjusted Group Means

	(1) Western Composite	(2) USSR Plan	(3) Difference	(4) USSR Pre-Plan	(5) Difference
1. Light Manufactures	28%	20%	+8	39%	-11
2. Food Prods.	17%	11%	+6	24%	-7
3. Metal Prods.	25%	37%	-12	14%	+11
4. Heavy Intermediate Manufactures	21%	26%	-5	17%	+4

Group Means Adjusted for Income (I),
Size (N) and Natural Resource (R) Differences

	(6) Western Composite	(7) USSR Plan	(8) Difference	(9) Western Composite	(10) USSR Pre-Plan	(11) Difference
1. Light Manufactures	28%	15%	+13	29%	28%	+1
2. Food Prods.	18%	9%	+11	18%	19%	-1
3. Metal Prods.	24%	43%	-19	23%	28%	-5
4. Heavy Intermediate Manufactures	21%	27%	-6	21%	21%	0
F Tests of Homogeneity		$F_{(4, 37)}=8.86$[a]		$F_{(4, 36)}=2.69$ [b],[a]		

Group Means Adjusted for Income (I), Size (N),
Natural Resource (R) and Size of Manufacturing (MS) Differences

	(12) Western Composite	(13) USSR Plan	(14) Difference	(15) Western Composite	(16) USSR Pre-Plan	(17) Difference
1. Light Manufactures	28%	14%	+14	29%	28%	+1
2. Food Prods.	18%	10%	+8	18%	19%	-1
3. Metal Prods.	24%	41%	-17	23%	28%	-5
4. Heavy Intermediate Manufactures	21%	26%	-5	21%	21%	0
F Tests of Homogeneity		$F_{(4, 36)}=6.00$[a]		$F_{(4, 35)}=3.11$ [a]		

[a]Significant at .05.
[b]Insignificant at .06.
Sources: Author's computations based on data in Table 1 and Appendix B.

The unadjusted group means and differences are given in columns 1-5 of Table 7. The difference columns give the differences between the Western composite group means and the two sets of USSR group means. Before adjustment, the structural differences between the two USSR groups relative to the Western composite group are easy to discern. The preplan light manufactures' value-added share and food products' value-added share are 11 and seven percentage points, respectively, larger than the composite Western group means; the respective USSR plan average value-added shares are eight and six percentage points below the composite Western means. The opposite is true of metal products and heavy intermediate manufactures, whose group means are 12 and five percentage points above the composite Western group means, whereas the USSR preplan group averages are 11 and four percentage points below the composite Western group means, respectively.

We carried out the covariate adjustments in two stages. First, the impact of the environmental covariates on the structure of manufacturing is removed, i.e., both the composite Western and the two USSR group structures are corrected for differences in per capita income, size and natural resource endowments (I, N, R). The results are recorded in columns 6-11 of Table 7. Second, MS is added to the original list of covariate adjustors, and the respective structures are corrected for differences in income, size, natural resource endowments and MS (columns 12-17). The trade orientation (V) adjustment is not recorded because of its negligible impact on the group mean adjustments.

The most notable general feature of Table 7 is that the elimination of covariate influences narrows the Western composite and USSR preplan group mean differentials, whereas it causes a widening of group mean differentials in the comparison of the Western composite and the USSR plan variables. This indicates a normal reaction to changes in economic variables on the part of the USSR preplan group ("normal" defined

---

variable is simpler: The political isolation, supply uncertainty and pressure to fulfill given targets without relying on outside producers make socialist economies autarky-oriented. Of course, it is highly speculative to assert that per capita income is independent of the system, because socialist development policy is aimed at maximizing growth rates. However, a dummy variable regression of socialism on per capita income would probably, at the present time, not yield a significant coefficient.

in terms of the relationships prevalent in the Western sample, which dominates the combined groups) and an abnormal reaction on the part of the USSR plan group to changes in economic variables.*

A detailed examination of Table 7 reveals the following features: The adjustment of the composite Western and USSR preplan structures to eliminate the influence of the environmental covariates (I, N, R) causes the disappearance of a major portion of the structural differences between the two manufacturing structures (columns 9-11). In terms of group mean differences, environmental covariate adjustments (for I, N, R) account for over 90 percent of the unadjusted group mean differences in light manufactures, for 86 percent of the unadjusted group mean differences in food products, for 100 percent of the unadjusted group mean differences in heavy intermediate manufactures, and a complete reversal from 11 percentage points below to 5 percentage points above the Western composite group mean in metal products. The F statistic (2.69) is significant at .05 but insignificant at .06. An entirely different result (columns 6-8) is yielded in the comparison of USSR plan and Western composite structures. Instead of narrowing group mean differences, covariate adjustment widens such differentials; this indicates that had the USSR plan and the Western composite economies been at equal income, size and natural resource levels, structural differences would have been even greater. In addition, the highly significant F statistic (8.86, as compared with the 2.69 preplan F statistic) indicates that the group mean differences are more statistically significant. Therefore, on the basis of the environmental, adjustments, we must assume the structural heterogeneity of the USSR plan structure and the composite Western structure.

The addition of the explanatory MS covariate as a covariate adjustor does not materially affect the previous results. In the case of the preplan USSR and Western composite structures (columns 15-17), its inclusion does not result in a further

---

*An example illustrates how this abnormal USSR plan period reaction can take place: Prior to adjustment, the USSR plan group's mean metal products share is significantly larger than that of the composite Western group. At the same time, the USSR per capita income levels are generally below those of the composite Western group. The regression coefficients, however, indicate that adjustment for income differences must result in an increase in the average USSR metal products value-added share, thus widening the differential.

narrowing of group mean differences. The F statistic (3.11)
is significant at the 6 percent level. In the case of the USSR
plan structure, the inclusion of MS provides a marginal narrowing of group mean differences; the F statistic (6.00) is
still highly significant, affirming the structural heterogeneity
of the plan USSR structure and the composite Western structure.
The adjusted group means and differences are in columns 12-14.

REGRESSION ANALYSIS: LONG-RUN STRUCTURAL
TRENDS OF USSR AND WESTERN
MANUFACTURING SECTORS

In the preceding section we investigated the significance
of observed composite group differences. Significant structural
differences which remain after removal of the impact of these
crucial economic variables are then attributed to true system
differences. The direct homogeneity tests on the two USSR
plan and preplan samples, as well as the more indirect homogeneity tests of the two USSR samples against a third sample,
suggests that the combined USSR sample represents, in all
actuality, two samples.

Under ideal conditions, the two USSR samples should be
fitted separately for the purpose of analyzing long-run trends
in the manufacturing sector. Separate fitting of regression
trends is not feasible in the present case because of the limited
number of observations in each group. Instead, we must combine the preplan and plan USSR samples into one sample. We
then fit 11 subsectors of the USSR manufacturing sector by
regression analysis to determine the USSR trends in subsector
value-added shares relative to per capita income and to compare
these trends with the long-term, trends of selected Western
countries.

The regressions are recorded in Tables 8 and 9 and are
graphed in Figures 3-13. Both manufacturing subsector shares
of manufacturing value added (y_k) and of GNP (y_k^a) are used
as regressands. The regressors are per capita income for
both dependent variables; in addition, the manufacturing sector's
share of GNP (MS) enters as an independent variable when the
dependent variable is expressed as a share of manufacturing.
The coefficients of multiple determination (not shown) are
generally above 80 percent for sectors 1-6 of Table 8 which
is not unusual for time series.

Table 8 gives the income and MS sector share elasticities
from the double log regressions of I and MS on manufacturing

subsector shares of manufacturing value added.* Table 9 gives
the income share elasticities from the double log regressions
of per capita income on manufacturing subsector share of
GNP. Figures 3-13 plot the manufacturing subsector trend
lines both in terms of manufacturing and GNP shares.

Several features of Tables 8 and 9 should be noted:

1. As far as the most highly aggregated manufacturing
sectors are concerned (rows 1-6), the differences between
USSR sectoral development patterns and those of the sampled
Western countries are of degree, not of direction. Examining
the manufacturing share of elasticities of Table 8 (rows 1-6),
one should note that the signs of the USSR I and MS manufacturing share elasticities are the same as those of the other
countries sampled. Minor exceptions are the negative Canadian
and UK MS elasticities of heavy intermediate manufactures.
The GNP share income elasticities of Table 9 (rows 1-6) tell
the same story: The USSR, US, Canadian, UK, German and
Western Pool GNP income share elasticities have identical
signs.

2. On the other hand, at a lower level of aggregation
(rows 7-11), directional differences between USSR trends and
Western trends are evident, especially in terms of subsector
manufacturing shares. The USSR chemicals sector has a
negative income share elasticity, whereas the Western countries
all yield positive elasticities. The USSR paper and printing
sector also has a negative income share elasticity, which
must be contrasted with a solid array of positive Western
elasticities.

One can best appreciate the differences in sectoral development patterns among the countries sampled by examining
the graphed sectoral trend lines of Figures 3-13. Each figure
(except Figures 10-13) contains plots of two sets of trend lines:
For each of the five countries, the normal regression equations
of per capita income on subsector share of manufacturing value
added and on subsector share of GNP, respectively, are plotted
separately.** We stress the following features of Figures 3-13:

_____

*MS enters in residual form: First I is regressed on MS.
The predicted MS is then estimated from the derived parameters.
The independent variable which finally enters the regression
equation is $(MS-\hat{MS})$. A double log form was used. The MS
deviation variable is independent of I; therefore, the I elasticity
and intercept are unaffected.

**The regression parameters are given in Tables 8 and 9.
In order to reduce the manufacturing share regressions (Table
8) to two dimensions, we assume normal manufacturing patterns $(MS - \hat{MS} = 0)$.

TABLE 8

Time Series Regressions of Subsector Shares of Manufacturing Value Added, USSR, US, Canada, Germany, UK

		USSR (1925-62)			US (1870-1963)			Canada (1891-1963)		
		Inter-cept	lnI	lnMS	Inter-cept	lnI	lnMS	Inter-cept	lnI	lnMS
1.	Light Mfg. (ISIC 20-29)	3.05	-.61 (8.69)	-.71 (3.46)	1.51	-.32 (5.03)	-1.57 (2.43)	2.47	-.44 (12.61)	-.33 (1.80)
2.	Heavy Mfg. (ISIC 30-38)	-4.61	.61 (6.18)	1.06 (4.02)	-2.69	.28 (5.97)	1.39 (1.39)	-5.13	.61 (15.91)	.43 (2.35)
3.	Food Prods. (ISIC 20-22)	3.10	-.80 (10.31)	-.77 (1.03)	-.31	-.22 (3.56)	-1.55 (2.48)	-.76	-.13 (.81)	-1.00 (1.06)
4.	Heavy Inter-mediate Mfg. (ISIC 30-34)	-3.95	.39 (9.02)	.36 (2.17)	-2.62	.16 (4.57)	.93 (2.88)	-5.76	.59 (5.25)	-.21 (.30)
5.	Metal Prods. (ISIC 35-38)	-6.63	.83 (5.23)	1.71 (4.14)	-4.05	.38 (5.89)	1.74 (2.82)	-5.90	.62 (5.38)	1.13 (1.92)
6.	Light Mfg. (excl. food prods.) (ISIC 23, 24, 27-29)	2.73	-.65 (7.29)	-.75 (2.20)	.47	-.27 (3.88)	-1.14 (1.39)	1.76	-.44 (5.20)	.23 (.45)
7.	Textiles (ISIC 23)	3.97	-.95 (10.45)	-.44 (1.03)	.93	-.53 (4.37)	-.80 (.50)	6.04	-1.29 (3.67)	.83 (.39)
8.	Basic Metals (ISIC 34)	-7.93	.84 (12.77)	.26 (.81)	-1.86	-.09 (2.33)	1.19 (4.16)	-7.30	.69 (3.38)	-2.09 (2.08)
9.	Chemicals (ISIC 30-32)	-1.34	-.17 (1.13)	1.19 (1.97)	-6.06	.52 (8.26)	1.84 (3.42)	-8.42	.85 (5.56)	1.19 (1.42)
10.	Non-metallic Minerals (ISIC 33)	-6.76	.59 (5.42)	1.20 (4.60)	-2.61	-.09 (1.33)	-2.03 (4.17)	-5.09	.22 (.28)	1.78 (.38)
11.	Paper, Printing (ISIC 27, 28)	-.88	-.41 (6.14)	-.81 (.60)	-4.54	.29 (3.75)	-1.08 (1.10)	-8.57	.92 (3.01)	1.25 (.68)

The header row "Regression Coefficients for" spans the Intercept, lnI, lnMS columns.

	Germany (1873-1936)			UK (1907-65)			Western Pool (1870-1965)		
	Intercept	lnI	lnMS	Intercept	lnI	lnMS	Intercept	lnI	lnMS
	Regression Coefficients for								
1. Light Mfg. (ISIC 20-29)	4.82	-.83	-1.20	6.04	-.98	-.53	2.23	-.43	-.33
		(6.52)	(2.04)		(9.50)	(1.08)		(8.35)	(3.32)
2. Heavy Mfg. (ISIC 30-38)	-8.93	1.23	1.76	-6.33	.81	.19	-3.97	.46	.13
		(8.46)	(2.15)		(.96)	(.42)		(8.33)	(.71)
3. Food Prods. (ISIC 20-22)	4.20	-.89	-1.17	4.29	-.89	1.06	.75	-.37	-.15
		(6.41)	(1.72)		(5.62)	(1.48)		(5.54)	(1.02)
4. Heavy Intermediate Mfg. (ISIC 30-34)	-7.00	.84	.49	-4.62	.44	-.17	-3.30	.25	.26
		(10.79)	(2.04)		(6.71)	(.52)		(4.70)	(2.32)
5. Metal Prods. (ISIC 35-38)	-13.00	1.72	3.22	-8.74	1.08	.40	-6.01	.66	.25
		(5.89)	(2.75)		(8.80)	(.66)		(8.00)	(1.38)
6. Light Mfg. (excl. food prods.) (ISIC 23, 24, 27-29)	4.42	-.86	-1.42	6.31	-1.10	-.23	1.48	-.41	-.11
		(4.72)	(1.52)		(9.73)	(.39)		(7.89)	(.94)
7. Textiles (ISIC 23)	-1.97	-.10	-.06	8.28	-1.51	-.51	4.38	-.99	1.17
		(.51)	(.05)		(11.53)	(.79)		(6.70)	(4.41)
8. Basic Metals (ISIC 34)	-6.53	.61	-1.19	-2.94	.06	-.07	-3.43	.13	-.07
		(2.26)	(.76)		(.26)	(.06)		(1.72)	(.40)
9. Chemicals (ISIC 30-32)	-16.74	2.15	3.65	-9.25	.98	-.09	-7.61	.74	.21
		(6.22)	(2.53)		(23.31)	(.41)		(9.47)	(1.27)
10. Non-metallic Minerals (ISIC 33)	-1.97	-.10	.06	-4.06	.12	-.28	-1.59	-.23	.91
		(.51)	(.05)		(.46)	(.06)		(1.18)	(2.21)
11. Paper, Printing (ISIC 27, 28)	-9.82	1.05	4.02	-2.52	.00	-.13	-6.43	.57	-.54
		(2.64)	(2.31)		(.01)	(.17)		(4.95)	(2.28)

Note: Figures in parentheses are t values.

Sources: Author's computations based on data in Table 1 and Appendix B

TABLE 9

Time Series Regressions of Subsector Shares
of GNP, USSR, US, Canada, Germany, UK

	USSR (1925-62)		US (1870-1963)		Canada (1891-1963)	
			Regression Coefficients for			
	Intercept	lnI	Intercept	lnI	Intercept	lnI
1. Light Mfg. (ISIC 20-29)	-.76	-.233	-2.43	-.022	-.01	-.284
2. Heavy Mfg. (ISIC 30-38)	-8.42	.984	-6.63	.623	-7.61	.764
3. Food Prods. (ISIC 20-22)	-.71	-.421	-4.25	.122	-3.24	.022
4. Heavy Intermediate Mfg. (ISIC 30-34)	-7.76	.760	-6.54	.501	-8.24	.750
5. Metal Prods. (ISIC 35-38)	-10.44	1,202	-7.99	.728	-8.38	.778
6. Light Mfg. (excl. food prods.) (ISIC 23,24, 27-29)	-1.08	-.276	-3.47	.078	-.72	-.283
7. Textiles (ISIC 23)	.16	-.572	-3.01	-.185	3.56	-1.129
8. Basic Metals (ISIC 34)	-11.74	1.216	-5.80	.256	-9.78	.841
9. Chemicals (ISIC 30-32)	-5.15	.202	-10.00	.866	-10.90	1.006
10. Nonmetallic Minerals (ISIC 33)	-10.57	.963	-6.55	.257	-7.57	.371
11. Paper Printing (ISIC 27,28)	-4.69	-.038	-8.48	.638	-11.05	1.074

	Germany (1873-1936)		UK (1907-65)		Western Pool (1870-1965)	
1. Light Mfg. (ISIC 20-29)	.16	-.286	1.57	-.508	4.59	-.273
2. Heavy Mfg. (ISIC 30-38)	-13.59	1.771	-10.80	1.283	-1.61	.610
3. Food Prods. (ISIC 20-22)	-.46	-.344	-.18	-.418	3.11	-.215
4. Heavy Intermediate Mfg. (ISIC 30-34)	-11.66	1.386	-9.09	.912	-.94	.405
5. Metal Prods. (ISIC 35-38)	-17.66	2.267	-13.21	-.551	-3.65	.810
6. Light Mfg. (excl. food prods.) (ISIC 23, 24, 27-29)	-.24	-.316	-1.84	-.621	3.84	-.253
7. Textiles (ISIC 23)	-6.63	.441	3.80	-1.033	6.74	-.841
8. Basic Metals (ISIC 34)	-11.19	1.158	-7.41	.532	-1.07	.282
9. Chemicals (ISIC 30-32)	-21.40	2.690	-13.72	1.452	-5.25	.892
10. Non-metallic Minerals (ISIC 33)	-6.63	.441	-8.53	.592	.77	-.082
11. Paper, Printing (ISIC 27,28)	-14.48	1.592	-6.99	.476	-4.07	.718

Notes: t values not given because these coefficients are calculated indirectly from Table 4 and Table 8.

Sources: Tables 4 and 8.

1.   The USSR heavy manufactures' shares of total manufacturing value added and of GNP exceed those of the selected
Western countries at all income levels, with the exception of
Germany, whose heavy manufactures' shares of both manufacturing and GNP exceed those of the USSR at high income levels.*

2.   The USSR light manufactures' shares of manufacturing
and of GNP are smaller than those of the selected Western
countries at practically all income levels.

3.   According to the Hoffman ratio,** the distinctive feature of USSR industrialization is that the USSR attained sector
equality (the point where the net product of the consumer goods
sector) at a relatively low level of per capita income. By
setting the two normal regression equations of the heavy and
light manufacturing sectors equal to each other (Table 8), we
compute that level of per capita income at which the net products of the two sectors are equal. The USSR reached sector
equality at a per capita income of $534; Germany, UK, US
and Canada attained, sector equality at $796, $1,000, $1,100
and $1,400, respectively. All of the per capita income figures
are in 1960 US dollars.

4.   The USSR food products' shares of manufacturing
value added are less than the Western shares at practically
all income levels. As a percentage of GNP, the US food
products' share is slightly below the USSR share at low income
levels. The relative USSR light-manufactures (excluding food
products) trends are the same as the food products trends.

5.   The USSR heavy intermediate manufactures and metal
products shares of both manufacturing and GNP exceed the
Western shares at practically all income levels, with the exception of the German shares, which exceed the USSR shares
at high income levels.

---

*German per capita income in 1936 equaled about $950;
therefore the high income observations for Germany represent
extrapolations of prewar trends, which can lead to rather
absurd results at higher income levels, owing to the log-linear
nature of the extrapolations.

**W. G. Hoffman, The Growth of Industrial Economies,
claims that the ratio of value added in the consumer goods
sector to value added in the producer goods sector can be employed as a surrogate measure of the level of development.
During the initial stages of industrialization, the consumer
goods sector dominates; however, in the course of industrialization, the producer goods sector grows at a faster pace. A
critical point in the development process occurs when the net
products of the two sectors are equal.

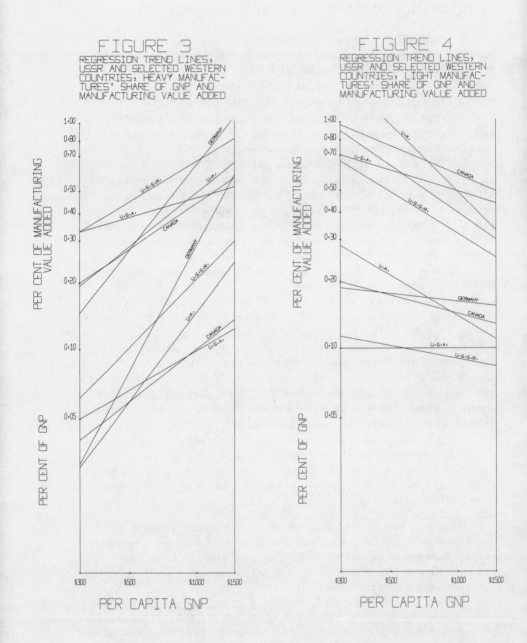

FIGURE 3

REGRESSION TREND LINES,
USSR AND SELECTED WESTERN
COUNTRIES, HEAVY MANUFAC-
TURES' SHARE OF GNP AND
MANUFACTURING VALUE ADDED

FIGURE 4

REGRESSION TREND LINES,
USSR AND SELECTED WESTERN
COUNTRIES, LIGHT MANUFAC-
TURES' SHARE OF GNP AND
MANUFACTURING VALUE ADDED

Sources: Author's computations based on data in Table 1
and Appendix B.

58

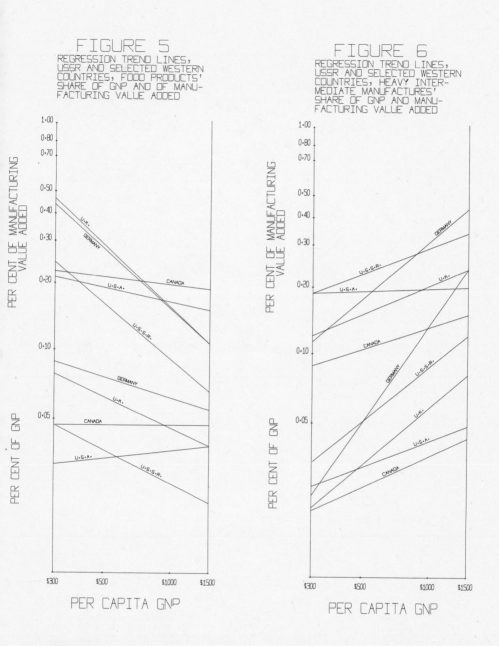

FIGURE 5
REGRESSION TREND LINES,
USSR AND SELECTED WESTERN
COUNTRIES; FOOD PRODUCTS'
SHARE OF GNP AND OF MANU-
FACTURING VALUE ADDED

FIGURE 6
REGRESSION TREND LINES,
USSR AND SELECTED WESTERN
COUNTRIES; HEAVY INTER-
MEDIATE MANUFACTURES'
SHARE OF GNP AND MANU-
FACTURING VALUE ADDED

PER CENT OF MANUFACTURING
VALUE ADDED

PER CENT OF GNP

PER CAPITA GNP

Sources: Author's computations based on data in Table 1
and Appendix B.

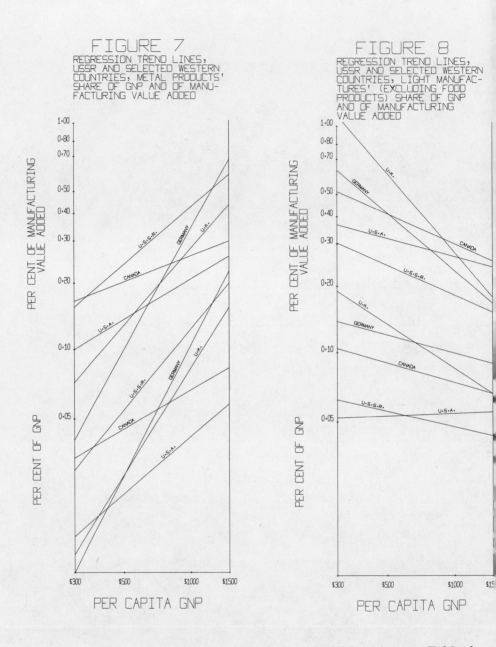

FIGURE 7
REGRESSION TREND LINES,
USSR AND SELECTED WESTERN
COUNTRIES, METAL PRODUCTS'
SHARE OF GNP AND OF MANU-
FACTURING VALUE ADDED

FIGURE 8
REGRESSION TREND LINES,
USSR AND SELECTED WESTERN
COUNTRIES, LIGHT MANUFAC-
TURES' (EXCLUDING FOOD
PRODUCTS) SHARE OF GNP
AND OF MANUFACTURING
VALUE ADDED

Sources: Author's computations based on data in Table 1
and Appendix B.

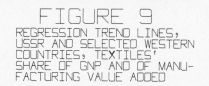

FIGURE 9
REGRESSION TREND LINES,
USSR AND SELECTED WESTERN
COUNTRIES, TEXTILES'
SHARE OF GNP AND OF MANU-
FACTURING VALUE ADDED

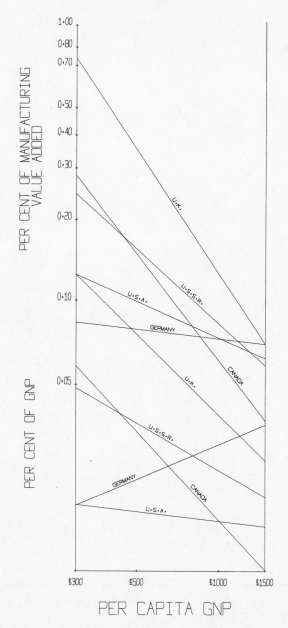

PER CAPITA GNP

Sources: Author's computations based on data in Table 1
and Appendix B.

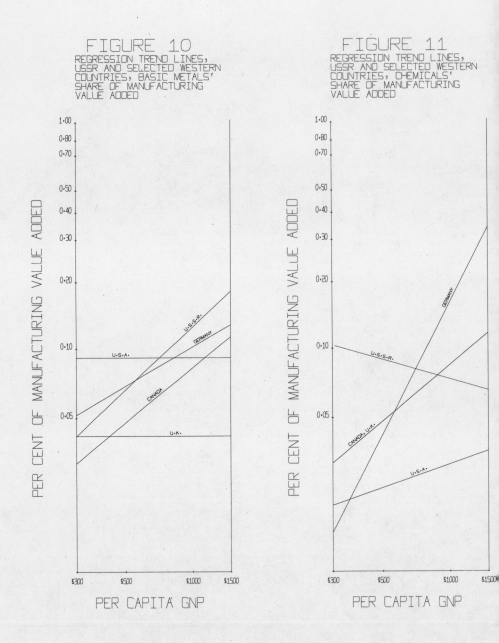

FIGURE 10
REGRESSION TREND LINES,
USSR AND SELECTED WESTERN
COUNTRIES, BASIC METALS'
SHARE OF MANUFACTURING
VALUE ADDED

FIGURE 11
REGRESSION TREND LINES,
USSR AND SELECTED WESTERN
COUNTRIES, CHEMICALS'
SHARE OF MANUFACTURING
VALUE ADDED

Sources: Author's computations based on data in Table 1
and Appendix B.

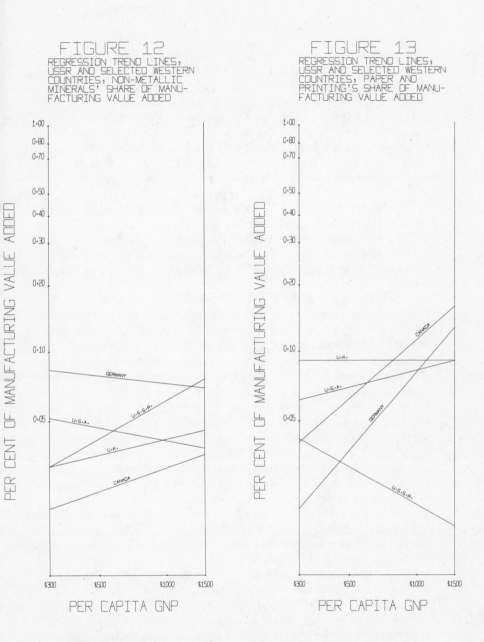

FIGURE 12
REGRESSION TREND LINES,
USSR AND SELECTED WESTERN
COUNTRIES, NON-METALLIC
MINERALS' SHARE OF MANU-
FACTURING VALUE ADDED

FIGURE 13
REGRESSION TREND LINES,
USSR AND SELECTED WESTERN
COUNTRIES, PAPER AND
PRINTING'S SHARE OF MANU-
FACTURING VALUE ADDED

PER CENT OF MANUFACTURING VALUE ADDED

PER CAPITA GNP

Sources: Author's computations based on data in Table 1
and Appendix B.

63

6. The trends in USSR textiles, basic metals, chemicals, nonmetallic minerals and paper and printing manufacturing value added shares relative to the Western trends are graphed in Figures 9-13. GNP shares (except textiles) are not graphed because these sectors represent very small percentages of GNP. It is interesting to note the rapid rate of increase in the USSR basic metals share relative to the other countries (Figure 10), the declining USSR chemicals share and the rising chemicals share in the other countries (Figure 11), the rapid rate of increase of the USSR nonmetallic minerals share relative to the other countries (Figure 12), and the declining USSR paper and printing share, contrasted with increasing shares in the other countries (Figure 13).

In summary, we note that compared with the long-run trends of the US, the UK, Canada and Germany, the USSR manufacturing development pattern distinguishes itself in several ways:

1. The relatively low light manufactures shares and the relatively high heavy manufactures shares at all income levels are characteristic of Soviet industrialization, but the early predominance of the producer goods sectors over consumer goods sectors at relatively low income levels is especially significant. The singularity of the USSR historical development pattern is challenged only by prewar Germany, generally at higher income levels. Insofar as comparisons of German and USSR structures at higher income levels represent hypothetical projections of the German prewar trends, the German challenge must be somewhat discounted.

2. The extremely rapid decline in food products value-added shares to very low absolute levels even at moderate income levels is unmatched by the other countries.

3. Of the five countries, only the USSR shows declining paper and printing and chemicals shares. On the other hand, the rates of increase of the USSR basic metals and nonmetallic minerals shares are unmatched.

The above comments apply to industrial structures relative to per capita income not relative to time. In terms of time, the historical development of the USSR manufacturing sector distinguishes itself even more markedly from the experiences of the industrialized Western nations. Figure 14 shows the historical development of the USSR metal products sector, which spearheaded the advance of the USSR heavy manufacturing sector, and it is interesting to compare the magnitude and rapidity of its expansion in the USSR with its expansion in the industrialized Western countries. As Figure 14 indicates,

FIGURE 14

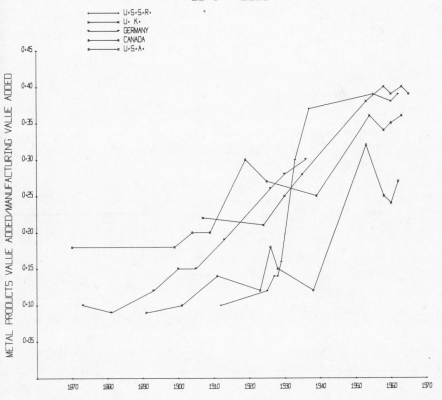

METAL PRODUCTS VALUE ADDED / MANUFACTURING VALUE ADDED,
USSR AND SELECTED WESTERN COUNTRIES,
1870 - 1965

Sources: Author's computations based on data in Table 1
and Appendix B.

the speed and magnitude of the USSR metal products share
increase between 1928 and 1937 was unmatched by the four
other countries examined.

CHAPTER **5** THE MANUFACTURING
SECTOR OF EASTERN
EUROPE UNDER TWO
ECONOMIC SYSTEMS

Prior to World War II, the economies of Eastern Europe
were organized essentially on a private enterprise basis; full-
scale socialist economic planning was first introduced into
Eastern Europe in the late 1940's and early 1950's, and by the
mid-1950's, the Eastern European economic system generally
paralleled that of the Soviet Union. The existence of a group
of countries whose economies have been subject to two radically different economic systems at different points of time
should provide valuable insights into the question of the impact
of changes in the economic system on the industrial structure.
Therefore, we propose to examine in this Chapter the structural transformations which took place in the countries of
Eastern Europe after the introduction of centrally planned
socialism and the relation of these structures to USSR and
nonsocialist structures.

As one might expect, prewar Eastern European industrial
data leave much to be desired.[1] Even if one were able to eliminate all measurement error, several conceptual problems
would still remain because the territorial changes which occurred at the end of World War II make long-term comparisons
of prewar and postwar structures quite difficult. For example,
the redefinition of Polish boundaries to include former German
territories, coupled with the loss of former Polish territories
to the Soviet Union, makes any comparison of prewar and postwar Polish industrial structures irrelevant. Another complex
problem is raised by the postwar emergence of East Germany
as a separate economic entity, since it had been an integral
part of the all-German economy, and its prewar structure
would reflect this fact. In addition, the vast population flows
resulting directly and indirectly from the war (the loss of the
German populations of Bohemia and east of the Oder-Neisse)
could have had a significant impact on the postwar economic
structure.

Another impediment to long-term structural comparisons is the fact that most of the available observations of prewar Eastern European industrial structures pertain to depression years, the distorting influence of which on the economic structure represents an unknown. The major exception is the 1929 Czechoslovak estimates, inasmuch as 1929 was a year of full utilization of resources and of high foreign trade volumes. [2]

One should keep the above reservations in mind in the course of this chapter. Data on the prewar and postwar industrial structures of six Eastern European countries are recorded in Tables 10 and 11, and the remainder of this chapter will be devoted to their examination and appraisal.

THE VALUE-ADDED STRUCTURE
OF POSTWAR MANUFACTURING

The average postwar Eastern European ratio of manufacturing value added to GNP is 34 percent and the industry ratio is 40 percent, as shown in Table 10. In the manufacturing sector, heavy manufactures accounts for 60 percent and light manufactures for 37 percent of manufacturing value added. The 60 percent heavy manufactures share is about evenly divided between metal products (29 percent) and heavy intermediate manufactures (30 percent); textiles, clothing and leather products account for 18 percent, food products for 12 percent and other light manufactures for 8 percent of the light manufactures share.

Given the diversity of income, population and resources within Eastern Europe, it is not surprising to note a degree of structural variance within the Eastern European sample, the pattern of which remains fairly consistent at various levels of aggregation. Within the manufacturing sector, the general variance pattern is above-average heavy manufactures shares for Czechoslovakia, GDR 1963 and Hungary 1963, below-average values for Bulgaria, Romania, GDR 1955 and Hungary 1957 and average values for Poland. The reverse pattern holds for light manufacturing sectors.

For example, the Czechoslovak, GDR 1963 and Hungarian 1963 heavy manufactures shares are eight, five and one percentage points above average; the Bulgarian, GDR 1955, Hungarian 1957 and Romanian heavy manufactures shares are seven, six, two and one percentage points below average and the Polish share is equal to the average share. The average light manufactures share is 37 percent. Hungary 1963

(35 percent), GDR 1963 (31 percent), Czechoslovakia (31 percent) and Hungary 1957 (35 percent) are below average; GDR 1955 (43 percent), Romania (40 percent) and Bulgaria (41 percent) are above average.

The above pattern is fairly consistent at lower levels of aggregation. The average metal products share is 29 percent. The GDR 1963 (34 percent), Czechoslovakia (34 percent) and Hungary 1963 (31 percent) are again above average; GDR 1955 (28 percent), Romania (28 percent) and Bulgaria (22 percent) are below average; and Poland and Hungary 1957 both equal the average share. The average textiles, clothing and leather share is 18 percent. Czechoslovakia, GDR 1963, Hungary 1963, Poland and (surprisingly) Bulgaria are below average, and the rest yield above-average shares. The small degree of variance in the heavy intermediate manufactures sector within the postwar Eastern European sample is noteworthy: all sample values are within four percentage points of the sample mean. The food products variance pattern runs somewhat counter to the general pattern: Poland (14 percent), Hungary 1963 (13 percent), GDR 1955 (13 percent) and Bulgaria (16 percent) are all above the 12 percent average, whereas Hungary 1957 (11 percent), GDR 1963 (9 percent), Romania (11 percent) and Czechoslovakia (9 percent) are all below average.

The average postwar Eastern European manufacturing value-added structures and variance patterns are best brought into perspective by means of comparative analysis. In the next sections, we compare the postwar structures with their prewar counterparts, with the USSR structures, and with a postwar cross-section of capitalist countries.

VALUE-ADDED STRUCTURES OF
PREWAR AND POSTWAR MANUFACTURING

Table 11 contains two bench-mark observations, one prewar and one postwar, of the value-added structures of the manufacturing sectors in five Eastern European countries: Hungary (1937 and 1963), East Germany (1936 and 1963), Czechoslovakia (1929 and 1965), Bulgaria (1936 and 1963) and Romania (1930 and 1958). Poland is not included in this prewar-postwar comparison because of the vast territorial changes that occurred at the end of the war.

TABLE 10

The Value-Added Structure of Manufacturing,
Eastern Europe, Selected Years
(Countries arranged descending order of per capita income)

		(1) Czecho-slovakia 1965	(2) GDR 1963	(3) Hun-gary 1963	(4) GDR 1955	(5) Hun-gary 1957	(6) Pol-and 1963	(7) Bul-garia 1963	(8) Rom-ania 1958	(9) Average
A.	Subsector Percentage of Total Manufacturing Value Added									
1.	Food Prods. (ISIC 20-22)	9	9	13	13	11	14	16	11	12
2.	Textiles (ISIC 23)	9	9	10	9	9	11	12	12	10
3.	Clothing, Footwear (ISIC 24)	5	4	5	8	10	5	4	7	6
4.	Wood Prods. (ISIC 25, 26)	4	4	4	7	5	5	6	7	5
5.	Paper Prods. (ISIC 27)	2	2	1	2	1	2	1	1	2
6.	Printing (ISIC 28)	1	2	1	2	1	1	1	1	1
7.	Leather Prods. (ISIC 29)	1	1	1	2	1	1	1	2	1
8.	Chemicals, Rubber, Coal, Oil Prods. (ISIC 30-32)	10	17	10	15	10	12	10	13	12
9.	Non-metallic Minerals (ISIC 33)	7	6	6	5	7	8	7	8	7
10.	Basic Metals (ISIC 34)	17	8	14	6	12	11	14	10	12
11.	Metal Prods. (ISIC 35-38)	34	34	31	28	29	29	22	28	29
12.	Misc. Mfg. (ISIC 39)	1	4	4	3	7	3	6	1	4
Total		100	100	100	100	100	100	100	100	100
B.	Major Manufacturing Aggregates as Percentages of Total Manufacturing Value Added									
1.	Heavy Mfg. (ISIC 30-38)	68	65	61	54	58	60	53	59	60
2.	Light Mfg. (ISIC 20-29)	31	31	35	43	35	37	41	40	37
3.	Heavy Intermediate Mfg. (ISIC 30-34)	34	31	30	26	29	31	31	31	30
4.	Textiles, Clothing, Leather (ISIC 23, 24, 29)	15	14	17	19	20	17	17	21	18

70

	(1)	(2)	(3)	(4)	(5)	(6)	(7)	(8)	(9)
5. Other Light Mfg. (ISIC 25-28)	7	8	6	11	7	8	8	10	8
C. Manufacturing ÷ GNP	31.7	52.2	28.2	45.4	24.0	33.3	31.2	20.0	33.5
D. Construction ÷ GNP	7.9	4.8	6.8	4.5	6.0	10.9	7.4	4.5	6.5
E. Industry ÷ GNP (C + D)	39.6	58.0	35.0	49.9	30.0	44.2	38.6	24.5	40.0
F. Mining, Gas, Electricity ÷ GNP	n.a.	n.a.	6.0	6.8	6.0	13.0	6.0	7.8	--
G. Total Industry ÷ GNP (E + F)	57.2	n.a.	41.0	56.7	36.0	57.2	44.6	32.3	--
H. Per Capita GNP, (1960 US $)	$1421	$1313	$938	$924	$838	$828	$638	$529	--

Sources: Parts A, B: Appendix A.
　　　　　Parts C-G:

Poland 1963: The Ernst estimate of the 1960 ratio of industry (including construction) value added to GNP is extrapolated to 1963 using the Ernst index (Maurice Ernst, "The Postwar Economic Growth in Eastern Europe," p. 833) to yield a 57 percent share. The Concise Statistical Yearbook of Poland, 1966, VIII, pp. 26, 52, gives the industry and construction shares of total labor force and capital stock; these shares are aggregated using .75 and .25 weights, respectively. In this manner, the industry and construction weights are estimated at .81 and .19, respectively. In order to break down the .81 figure, manufacturing and mining and gas-electricity value added are estimated from Appendix A. On the basis of these value-added estimates, mining and gas-electricity account for approximately 28 percent of total industrial value added.

Hungary 1957, 1963: Thad Alton, Hungarian National Income and Product in 1955, p. 76, provides estimates of the distribution of Hungarian national income in 1955 at factor cost. On the basis of data in L. Czirjak, "Indexes of Hungarian Industrial Production, 1938 and 1946-1965," p. 9, it is estimated that mining and gas-electricity account for approximately 20 percent of total industrial value added. In order to estimate the percentage distribution of Hungarian GNP in 1957 and 1963, the 1955 distribution is extrapolated using the Czirjak industrial production index; the Czirjak construction index; and the Ernst GNP index.

(Continued)

71

TABLE 10--Continued

East Germany 1955, 1963: The 1955 factor cost distribution of GNP is from Wolfgang Stolper, The Structure of the East German Economy, pp. 259, 418. The 1963 industry share is derived by extrapolating the 1955 share using the Ernst indexes of industrial production and GNP. On the basis of labor force and capital stock data from Statistisches Jahrbuch, 1964, pp. 26, 52, it is estimated that the respective 1963 industry and construction weights are .81 and .19, respectively.

Romania 1958: The official estimates of Romanian national income (net product) are used under the assumption that nonmaterial production equals 35 percent of total GNP, from J. M. Montias, Economic Development in Communist Romania, p. 271, and Pong Lee, "Structural Change in Rumanian Industry, 1938-1963," p. 221. Insofar as indirect taxation is more heavily concentrated in the industrial sector, the following correction of the official ratios is undertaken: The Stadnik estimates of the composition of Czech net product (1955), which do not impute a return to capital, are compared with the Alton 1955 estimates, which do impute a return to capital. See the Czech estimates below. The same structure of indirect taxation is then assumed for Romania.

Czechoslovakia 1965: The Stadnik 1965 factor cost estimates (Stadnik, Some Problems of Economic Growth in Czechoslovakia, Statistical Appendix) form the basis for computing the 1965 GNP distribution: The Stadnik 1965 ratios, which exclude a return to capital, are corrected by comparing the 1955 Stadnik ratios with the 1955 ratios from Thad Alton, Czechoslovak National Income and Product, 1947-1948 and 1955-1956, p. 60. Alton estimates the industry and construction shares at 38.2 percent and 7.9 percent; whereas Stadnik estimates them at 35.8 percent and 8.8 percent. The same relation is assumed to hold for 1965.

Bulgaria 1963: The Ernst estimate of the 1960 industry and construction shares is extrapolated to 1963 using the Ernst indexes of industrial output (including construction) and GNP (Maurice Ernst, "The Postwar Economic Growth in Eastern Europe," pp. 880-83). According to data in G. Lazarcik and A. Wynnyczuk, Bulgaria: Growth of Industrial Output, 1939 and 1948-1965, mining and gas-electricity accounted for approximately 16.5 percent of total industry value added in 1963 (assuming that ore mining accounts for 15 percent of basic metals including ore mining). The industry-construction breakdown is estimated by applying .75 and .25 weights to labor force and capital stock shares, from Statistićeski Spravočnik Bulgaria, 1965, pp. 9, 26.

Part H: See text, Chapter 2.

The prewar Eastern European average heavy manufactures share is 36 percent, and the average light manufactures share is 60 percent. Of the five countries, only the East German prewar heavy manufactures share exceeds 50 percent. Czechoslovakia (1929), Hungary (1937) and East Germany (1936) have above-average, whereas Bulgaria (1936) and Romania (1930) have below-average, heavy manufactures shares. Hungary, East Germany and Romania have below-average prewar light manufactures shares, and the other sampled countries have above-average shares. In other words, the prewar Eastern European structural variance pattern parallels the postwar pattern.

The postwar sector averages reveal a marked reversal in the heavy-light manufactures ratios: The average postwar heavy manufactures share is 61 percent (compared with the 36 percent prewar average), and the postwar light manufactures share is 31 percent (compared with the 60 percent prewar average).

Examining these trends at a lower level of aggregation, the following features are noted. The average metal products share doubled from 15 percent to 30 percent during the period studied, whereas the average heavy intermediate manufactures share increased from 20 percent to 31 percent, most of this increase being concentrated in basic metals, which increased from 4 percent to 12 percent of manufacturing value added.

Food products declined from a prewar average of 28 percent to a postwar average of 12 percent of manufacturing value added. At the same time, textiles clothing and leather declined from 23 percent to 17 percent. Paper and printing declined from a prewar share of 6 percent to a postwar share of 3 percent.

The average figures conceal marked intrasample differences. In general, the most prominent changes took place in Bulgaria and Romania, the two most economically backward countries of Eastern Europe. The value-added share of heavy manufacturing in Bulgaria increased between 1937 and 1963 from 22 percent to 53 percent, and the Romanian share increased from 30 percent to 59 percent between 1930 and 1958. The declines in the respective light manufactures shares were just as dramatic in these two countries. Similarly, the share of metal products more than quadrupled in Bulgaria (from 5 percent to 22 percent) and more than tripled in Romania (from 8 percent to 28 percent); on the other hand, the food products share fell to approximately one-third its prewar share in both countries.

TABLE 11

The Structure of Manufacturing Value Added, Eastern Europe, Prewar and Postwar Years
(subsectors as percentages of total manufacturing value added)

		(1) Food Prods.	(2) Textiles	(3) Clothing, Footwear	(4) Wood Prods.	(5) Paper	(6) Printing	(7) Leather	(8) Chemicals, Rubber, Coal, Oil Prods.
Hungary	1937	25	16	7	3	2	7	1	9
	1963	13	10	5	4	1	1	1	10
East	1936	15	14	5	4	4	3	1	12
Germany	1963	9	9	4	4	2	2	1	17
Czecho-	1929	16	22	17	8	4	2	2	6
slovakia	1965	9	9	5	4	2	1	1	10
Bulgaria	1936	46	23	3	3	1	2	2	9
	1963	16	12	4	6	1	1	1	10
Romania	1930	39	7	7	5	2	3	1	12
	1958	11	12	7	7	1	2	2	13
Prewar Average		28	16	8	5	3	3	2	10
Postwar Average		12	10	5	5	1	1	1	12

*Less than 0.50 percent.

Sources: Postwar values are from Table 10.

Prewar values: Hungary 1937: Net production data from Ungarns Industrie und Handel im Jahre 1937 form the basis for computing 1937 branch value added. The above data cover only factory production; they are corrected by multiplying the 1934 ratios of total branch gross production to factory branch gross production from Ungarns Industrie und Handel im Jahre 1935, pp. 38-39, by the factory production figures.

East Germany 1936: The net production figures for the German Reich are from Die Deutsche Industrie. The East German share of each branch is computed by applying the gross production shares from Bruno Gleitze, Ostdeutsche Wirtschaft, pp. 174-185.

74

(9) Non-metallic Minerals	(10) Basic Metals	(11) Metal Prods.	(12) Misc. Mfg.	(A) Heavy Mfg.	(B) Light Mfg.	(C) Heavy Intermediate Mfg.	(D) Light Mfg. (excl. food prods.)	(E) Textiles, Clothing Leather	(F) Paper, Printing
5	7	17	2	38	58	21	33	26	9
6	14	31	4	61	31	30	18	16	2
6	6	27	3	51	41	24	27	20	7
6	8	34	4	65	27	31	18	14	4
11	4	19	1	40	63	21	45	41	4
7	17	34	1	68	27	34	18	15	3
7	1	5	*	22	77	17	31	28	3
7	14	22	6	53	35	31	19	17	2
3	3	8	4	30	59	18	20	15	5
8	10	28	1	59	35	31	24	21	3
6	4	15	2	36	60	20	29	23	6
7	12	30	3	61	31	31	19	17	3

Czechoslovakia 1929: The branch net production figures are from Stadnik, Some Problems of Economic Growth in Czechoslovakia, Statistical Appendix. The breakdown between basic metals and metal products and between printing and miscellaneous manufactures was made on the basis of data from Mitteilungen des statistischem Amts der Tschechoslovakei, 1933, pp. 1478-83.

Bulgaria 1937: The data are taken directly from Statističeski Godišnik na Tsarstvo B'lgaria, 1937, pp. 390-411. Net production is defined as gross production minus the cost of own materials used, the cost of other materials used, fuels and electricity consumed and cost of work done elsewhere.

Romania 1930: 1934 branch value added per worker from Consiliul Superior Economic, Aspecte Ale Economiei Romanesti, 1939, p. 158, is multiplied by total branch employment in 1930 from Die Wirtschaftsstruktur Rumäniens in ihren Wesenmerkmalen und Entfaltungsmöglichkeiten, pp. 67-71.

The average Eastern European basic metals value-added
share tripled between the prewar and postwar period from 4
percent to 12 percent. In all countries, with the exception of
East Germany, basic metals rose from an insignificant share
of manufacturing value added to become a major manufacturing
sector. Between 1936 and 1963, the Bulgarian basic metals
sector increased its value added share from 1 percent to 14
percent; in Romania, the share increase was from 3 percent
to 10 percent between 1930 and 1958; and in Czechoslovakia
it was from 4 percent to 17 percent between 1929 and 1965.

THE HOMOGENEITY OF
PREWAR AND POSTWAR STRUCTURES

In order to determine the statistical significance of these
prewar-postwar group differences, we test the following hypothesis in Table 12:

The change of economic systems in Eastern Europe
did not bring about any significant change in the
structure of manufacturing. Instead, all observable
group differences are to be explained by changes in
factors which are independent of the economic system and by random error.

The proper testing of this hypothesis requires the elimination
of all significant covariate influences which could possibly
have caused the above observed differences. Natural resource
endowments and population were essentially constant in the
two periods, and we have little information on prewar MS in
Eastern Europe; therefore, the only available covariate adjustor is per capita income. * We emphasize the crudeness

---

*The prewar estimates of Eastern European GNP are
quite crude. We converted current price GNP estimates into
US dollars, using the then prevailing exchange rates, and then
converted these dollar figures into 1960 US dollars employing
the US GNP deflator. The current price, domestic currency
GNP estimates are drawn from the following sources: East
Germany 1936: Stolper, The Structure of the East German
Economy, p. 418; Czechoslovakia 1929: United Nations,
National Income Statistics 1938-1948, p. 230; Hungary 1936,
Bulgaria 1936, Romania 1930: Jahresbericht des Deutschen
Instituts für Konjunkturforschung, No. 18 (1938), Statistical
Appendix, p. 146.

TABLE 12

Unadjusted and Adjusted Group Means
and F Statistic, Prewar and Postwar Eastern
European Manufacturing Structures

	Prewar Unadjusted	Postwar Group Means	D	Prewar Adjusted	Postwar Group Means	D
1. Food Prods.	28%	12%	+16%	24%	15%	+9%
2. Light Mfg. (excl. food prods.)	29%	26%	+3%	27%	27%	0%
3. Metal Prods.	15%	29%	-14%	20%	26%	-6%
4. Heavy Intermediate Mfg.	20%	30%	-10%	22%	30%	-8%
Average Absolute Deviation			10.8%			5.8%
F Statistic				$F(4, 7) = 5.27$[*]		

*Significant at .05.
Sources: Author's computations based on data in Tables 10 and 16.

of the prewar Eastern European GNP estimates; nevertheless, they probably are roughly indicative of orders of magnitude.

Prior to adjusting for per capita income differences, the average absolute deviation of the postwar average sector shares from the prewar average sector shares is 11 percent. The adjustment reduces the average absolute deviation to 6 percent, i. e. , per capita income differences explain away approximately 50 percent of the prewar and postwar group differences. The food products deviation is reduced from +16 percent to +9 percent, the light manufactures (excluding food products) deviation is reduced to 0 percent, the metal products deviation is reduced from -14 percent to -6 percent and the heavy intermediate manufactures deviation is reduced from -10 percent to -8 percent. Thus, changes in per capita income levels explain over 50 percent of the postwar decline of food products and light manufactures (excluding food products) and over 50 percent of the postwar increase in metal products; the postwar increase in heavy intermediate manufactures remains, to a great extent, unexplained.

The F value provides a test statistic to evaluate the significance of the remaining group differences. The $F_{(4, 7)}$ value of 5. 27 is significant at . 95; therefore the hypothesis is rejected, i. e. , the significance of postwar and prewar group differences is accepted. In other words, the postwar and prewar Eastern European manufacturing structures are heterogeneous, and the heterogeneity is not explained by changes in economic variables (per capita income).

MANUFACTURING VALUE-ADDED STRUCTURES:
EASTERN EUROPE AND THE USSR

The F test demonstrated that the postwar structure of the manufacturing sector in Eastern Europe is significantly different from its prewar nonsocialist counterpart, which implies that the introduction of socialist central planning had a significant impact on the structure of Eastern European industry.

Insofar as Eastern Europe essentially adopted the Soviet economic system in the postwar period, it is valid to examine the homogeneity of postwar Eastern European and plan period Soviet industrial structures. With this question in mind, we compare the postwar Eastern European sample with the USSR plan sample (1933-62) in Table 13. By comparing the Eastern European sample with the entire 1933-62 USSR plan sample,

TABLE 13

Unadjusted and Adjusted Group Means
and F Statistics, Postwar Eastern European
Sample and USSR Plan Sample

	Unadjusted Group Means			Adjusted Group Means		
	Eastern Europe	USSR	Change	Eastern Europe	USSR	Change
A. 1. Food Prods.	12%	11%	+1%	11%	12%	-1%
2. Light Mfg. (excl. food prods.)	20%	20%	0%	20%	20%	0%
3. Metal Prods.	29%	37%	-8%	30%	36%	-6%
4. Heavy Intermediate Mfg.	30%	26%	+4%	32%	23%	+9%
Average Absolute Deviation			3.3%			4.0%
F Statistic		$F(4, 5) = 6.47$[a]				
B. 1. Food Prods.	12%	11%	+1%	12%	11%	+1%
2. Light Mfg. (excl. food prods.)	20%	20%	0%	20%	20%	0%
3. Heavy Mfg. (A3 + A4)	60%	63%	-3%	60%	63%	-3%
Average Absolute Deviation			1.0%			1.0%
F Statistic		$F(3, 7) = .91$[b]				

[a]Significant at .05.
[b]Insignificant at .05.
Sources: Author's computations based on data in Tables 1 and 10.

instead of with the postwar USSR sample, we gain not only
additional degrees of freedom but also are comparing "early"
and "late" USSR industrial structures with "early" and "late"
Eastern European cross-section structures.

Several features of Table 13 are worth noting. The average Eastern European and USSR manufacturing product mixes
are remarkable uniform within the light manufactures sector.
The unadjusted group means yield a 12 percent Eastern European food products share versus an 11 percent USSR share.
Both groups yield 20 percent light manufactures (excluding
food products) shares. These averages are only marginally
changed after covariate elimination of per capita income,
natural resource and MS differences. Although both groups
yield quite similar aggregate heavy manufactures shares
(Eastern Europe 60 percent, USSR 63 percent), the product
mix within the heavy manufactures sector varies significantly:
In comparison with the USSR, the Eastern European group devotes more of its heavy manufacturing output to heavy intermediate manufactures (30 percent) than to metal products
(29 percent). The same figures for the USSR are 26 percent
and 37 percent respectively.

This difference reflects itself in the homogeneity tests.
Judged on a four-sector basis (Table 13, Part A), the F statistic is significant at .05, yielding the conclusion that the
USSR and Eastern European structures are heterogeneous;
however, when metal products and heavy intermediate manufactures are combined into one sector (Part B), the $F_{(3,7)}$
statistic equals .91, which is highly insignificant, i.e., all
group differences disappear.

A related question is the extent to which the structural
shifts that occurred within the Eastern European manufacturing
sector between the prewar and postwar periods parallel those
which took place in the USSR between the preplan and the plan
periods. We examine this question in Table 14.

The average absolute deviation of the USSR preplan manufacturing structure from the prewar Eastern European manufacturing structure is 5.3 percent; the postwar Eastern European and USSR plan period average absolute deviation is 1.3
percent, which indicates a significant narrowing of group
differences. In other words, the homogeneity of Table 13 is
not the result of historical homogeneity of USSR and Eastern
European structures.

The narrowing of USSR and Eastern European structural
differences noted above implies a similar set of sectoral
growth elasticities in the USSR and Eastern Europe. Under

TABLE 14

Average Group Values, Sector Shares
of Manufacturing Value Added, USSR (1912-29, 1933-62)
and Eastern Europe (Prewar and Postwar)

	USSR (1912-29)	Eastern Europe (prewar)	D	USSR (1933-62)	Eastern Europe (postwar)	D
1. Heavy Mfg.	29%	36%	-7%	63%	60%	+3%
2. Light Mfg. (excl. food prods.)	38%	32%	+6%	20%	20%	0%
3. Food Prods.	25%	28%	-3%	11%	12%	-1%
Average Absolute Deviation			5.3%			1.3%

Sources: Tables 1, 13.

81

ideal conditions, one would compare USSR and Eastern European elasticities by regressing per capita income on manufacturing sector shares. The individual Eastern European per capita income estimates of the prewar period are subject, however, to a high degree of measurement error; therefore the USSR and average Eastern European regression lines are derived by using Wald's method of fitting regression lines from grouped observations in order to minimize the impact of measurement error.[3] The resulting regression lines are graphed in Figure 15.

Figure 15 underlines the similarity of USSR and average Eastern European long-term sectoral growth trends. In general, the slopes of the USSR regression trend lines have larger absolute values than the Eastern European regression lines; that is, the USSR sector-by-sector response to changes in income levels has been generally more elastic than the average Eastern European response. Only in the case of food products is the (negative) Eastern European slope (slightly) larger in absolute value than the USSR slope.

Comparisons of this sort should not be taken too seriously, because of the high degree of internal variance within the Eastern European sample; nevertheless, we note the striking similarity of average Eastern European and USSR long-run sectoral trends.

MANUFACTURING STRUCTURES: POSTWAR EASTERN EUROPE AND A POSTWAR WESTERN CROSS-SECTION

We have compared the structure of the manufacturing sector in postwar Eastern Europe with the prewar Eastern European structure and with the USSR plan structure. Another relevant comparison is to contrast the postwar Eastern European socialist structure with a contemporaneous cross-section of nonsocialist manufacturing structures, which is done in this section.

The unadjusted and adjusted (for I, N, R and MS) means of the postwar Eastern European cross-section and of the postwar nonsocialist cross-section are given in Table 15. The nonsocialist cross-section used in this and subsequent sections is composed of 41 observations from 29 countries. The observations are drawn from the 1953-65 period.[4]

Prior to adjustment for income, population, natural resource and MS differences, the average absolute deviation of

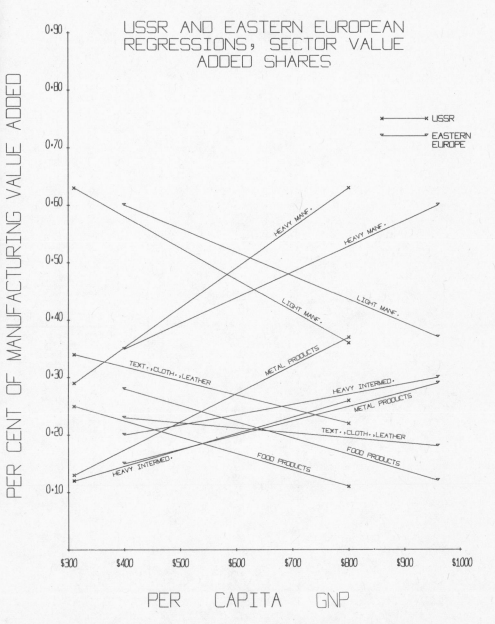

FIGURE 15

USSR AND EASTERN EUROPEAN
REGRESSIONS, SECTOR VALUE
ADDED SHARES

PER CENT OF MANUFACTURING VALUE ADDED

PER CAPITA GNP

Sources: Author's computations based on data in Tables
1 and 16.

TABLE 15

Unadjusted and Adjusted Group Means and F Statistic,
Postwar Eastern European and Postwar Nonsocialist
Cross-Sections, Manufacturing Sector

	Eastern Europe	Western Sample	D	Eastern Europe	Western Sample	D
1. Food Prods.	12%	20%	-8%	19%	22%	-3%
2. Light Mfg. (excl. food prods.)	20%	22%	-2%	19%	22%	-3%
3. Metal Prods.	29%	27%	+2%	28%	27%	+1%
4. Heavy Intermediate Mfg.	30%	23%	+7%	30%	23%	+7%
Average Absolute Deviation			4.8			3.5
F Statistic				$F(4, 40) = 3.73^*$		

*Significant at .05.

Sources: Author's computations based on data in Table 10 and Statistical Appendix (available from author).

84

the postwar Western from the postwar Eastern European group
means is 4.8 percent; the average absolute deviation of the
adjusted means is 3.5 percent.   Thus, the covariates account
for some 27 percent of the unadjusted group deviations.

The residual pattern of the unadjusted group means is
quite distinctive: The Western sample means of the two light
manufacturing sectors (food products and light manufactures,
excluding food products) exceed the Eastern European means
by 8 percent and 2 percent, respectively, and the Eastern
European sample means of the two heavy manufacturing sectors (metal products and heavy intermediate manufactures)
exceed the Western means by 2 percent and 7 percent, respectively.

Covariate adjustment eliminates approximately 63 percent of the original food products deviation (reducing it from 8
percent to 3 percent) and 50 percent of the original metal products deviation (reducing it from 2 percent to 1 percent); on
the other hand, it increases the original light manufactures
(excluding food products) deviation from 2 percent to 3 percent and leaves the original heavy intermediate 7 percent deviation unchanged.

The F statistic after adjustment is highly significant,
which indicates that the adjusted group differences are statistically significant; therefore one must conclude that the Eastern European and Western cross-section manufacturing structures differ significantly from one another.   The direction and
magnitude of the structural differences are shown by the pattern of deviations described above.

THE STRUCTURE OF MANUFACTURING LABOR FORCE:
PREWAR AND POSTWAR EASTERN EUROPE

The available data on the distribution of prewar and postwar Eastern European manufacturing labor force by industrial
branches are presented in Table 16; the remainder of this
section is devoted to an analysis of this information.*

---

*In reporting annual labor force data, the Eastern Euro-
pean statistical authorities do not use the concept of economically active population. Instead, several categories are excluded. As far as manufacturing labor force distributions are
concerned, the most important exclusion is apprentices. In
East Germany (1966), apprentices made up 5 percent of the

TABLE 16

The Structure of Manufacturing Labor Force,
Eastern Europe, Prewar and Postwar Years
(percent of total manufacturing labor force)

		(1) Food Prods.	(2) Textiles	(3) Clothing, Footwear	(4) Wood Prods.	(5) Paper	(6) Printing	(7) Leather	(8) Chemicals, Rubber Coal, Oil Prods.
Hungary	1937	13	20	10	6	2	6	2	5
	1963	20	11	7	4	1	1	2	6
East Germany	1936	12	16	6	5	2	4	1	7
	1963	9	11	6	6	2	2	2	11
Czecho-slovakia	1929	15	18	20	10	2	2	1	2
	1965	9	12	9	6	2	2	2	7
Bulgaria	1936	40	31	3	4	2*	--	1	7
	1963	18	14	6	8	1	1	--	6
Romania	1930	24	12	11	16	2	3	1	6
	1958	12	13	9	14	1	2	2	8
Poland	1963	13	14	8	6	2	1	1	8
Prewar Average		21	19	10	8	--	--	1	5
Postwar Average		14	13	8	7	2	2	2	8

(9) Nonmetallic Minerals	(10) Basic Metals	(11) Metal Prods.	(12) Misc. Mfg.	(A) Heavy Mfg.	(B) Light Mfg.	(C) Heavy Intermediate Mfg.	(D) Light Mfg. (excl. food prods.)	(E) Textiles, Clothing, Leather	(F) Paper, Printing
9	8	18	2	40	53	22	40	32	8
5	7	31	6	49	42	18	22	20	2
9	4	27	3	47	44	20	29	23	6
5	6	36	5	58	32	22	23	19	4
12	3	20	1	37	55	17	43	39	4
6	10	36	1	59	36	23	27	23	4
4	1	4	1	16	77	12	37	35	2
7	7	22	9	42	40	20	22	20	2
3	3	14	1	26	53	12	29	24	5
7	7	26	1	48	39	22	29	26	3
7	6	30	8	51	39	21	26	23	3
7	4	17	2	33	56	17	36	31	5
6	7	30	5	50	38	21	25	22	3

*Paper and printing.

Sources: See sources to Tables 10 and 11, pp. 71, 72, 74, 75.

The prewar Eastern European sample yields an average 33 percent heavy manufacturing labor force share. Hungary 1937 (40 percent), East Germany 1936 (47 percent) and Czechoslovakia 1929 (37 percent) have above-average shares, whereas Bulgaria 1936 (16 percent) and Romania 1930 (26 percent) have below-average shares. The reverse pattern holds for the variation around the 56 percent prewar Eastern European light manufactures mean, with the exception of Romania, which has a below-average 53 percent share.

The average prewar food products labor force share is 21 percent. Again Hungary (13 percent), East Germany (12 percent) and Czechoslovakia (15 percent) yield below-average shares, while Bulgaria and Romania yield above-average shares. The variation around the 31 percent textiles, clothing and leather average is worthy of note. Hungary (32 percent), Czechoslovakia (39 percent) and Bulgaria (35 percent) yield labor force shares which exceed the group average, while East Germany (23 percent) and Romania (24 percent) have below-average shares.

Within the heavy manufactures sector, the following features of Table 16 should be noted: The prewar metal products average labor force share is 17 percent, with Hungary (18 percent), East Germany (27 percent) and Czechoslovakia (20 percent) yielding above-average shares and Romania (14 percent) and Bulgaria (4 percent) yielding below-average shares. The same pattern holds for heavy intermediate manufactures. The group average is 17 percent, with Hungary (22 percent), East Germany (20 percent) and Czechoslovakia (17 percent) yielding average or above average shares and Romania (12 percent) and Bulgaria (12 percent) yielding below-average shares.

The structural transformations which occurred in the distributions of Eastern European manufacturing labor force between the prewar period and the 1960's closely parallel the transformations in the value-added structures noted above.

The average Eastern European heavy manufactures labor force share increased from an average of 33 percent in the

---

industrial labor force (Statistisches Jahrbuch der DDR, 1967, p. 189). The inclusion of apprentices in East Germany does not alter the percentage distribution among manufacturing sectors. Inclusion of apprentices would probably not alter the percentage distributions in the other Eastern European countries in Table 16. For detailed discussions of labor force concepts in Eastern Europe, consult Bureau of Census, International Population Statistics Reports, Series P-90, Nos. 13, 14.

prewar period to 50 percent in the postwar period. During the
same period, the average labor force share of the light manufacturing sector declined from 56 percent to 38 percent. Within the light manufactures sector, food products declined from
an average prewar share of 21 percent to an average postwar
share of 14 percent; the decline in the textile, clothing and
leather share from 31 percent to 22 percent was less dramatic.
Within the heavy manufactures sector, the metal products
share increased from the prewar average of 17 percent to the
postwar average of 30 percent; the increase in the heavy intermediate manufactures share from 17 percent to 21 percent
was more moderate. At a lower level of aggregation, one
should note the increase in the basic metals labor force share
from an average of 4 percent in the prewar period to a postwar average of 7 percent.

     The average trends conceal a great deal of diversity with-
in Eastern Europe. The most drastic overall labor force
shifts took place in Romania and Bulgaria. Between 1936 and
1963, the labor force share of Bulgarian heavy manufacturing
increased from 16 percent to 42 percent; the increase was
from 26 percent in 1930 to 48 percent in 1958 for Romania.

A COMPARISON OF EASTERN EUROPEAN
AND USSR LABOR FORCE DISTRIBUTIONS

     As shown in Table 17, the comparison of average USSR
preplan with average prewar Eastern European manufacturing
labor force distributions yields an average absolute deviation
of 5.2 percent, the largest deviations being concentrated in
the heavy manufactures, light manufactures and the combined
textiles, clothing and leather sectors. On the other hand, the
same comparison of postwar socialist Eastern European and
USSR plan distributions yields an average absolute deviation
less than one-quarter the original deviation (1.2 percent), the
largest sector deviation being the +3 percent USSR plan deviation in the heavy manufactures sector. The small metal products and heavy intermediate manufactures deviations are
surprising in view of the rather substantial value-added share
deviations. (See Table 14).

     In general, the structural similarity of the postwar East-
ern European and USSR (1937-62) manufacturing labor force
distributions, plus the rather substantial degree of variance
between the prewar Eastern European and USSR preplan

TABLE 17

Average Group Values, Sector Shares of Manufacturing
Labor Force, USSR (1912-29, 1933-62) and
Eastern Europe (Prewar and Postwar)

Average Group Labor Force Shares:

	USSR Pre-Plan	Eastern Europe Prewar	Change	USSR Plan	Eastern Europe Postwar	Change
1. Heavy Mfg.	27%	33%	-6%	53%	50%	+3%
2. Light Mfg.	62%	56%	+6%	38%	38%	0%
3. Food Prods.	18%	21%	-3%	12%	14%	-2%
4. Textiles, Clothing, Leather	40%	31%	+9%	22%	22%	0%
5. Metal Prods.	14%	17%	-3%	31%	30%	+1%
6. Heavy Intermediate Mfg.	13%	17%	-4%	22%	21%	+1%
Average Absolute Deviation			5.2%			1.2%

Sources: Tables 3, 16.

90

distributions, confirms the postwar convergence of USSR and
Eastern European manufacturing labor force structures.

The virtual elimination of USSR and Eastern European
structural differences indicates a similar pattern of sectoral
labor force share growth elasticities relative to GNP. To explore this further, we estimate the regression trend lines
from regressions of per capita income on sector shares of
manufacturing labor force. The sector regression trend lines
are given in Figure 16, which shows the striking similarity of
long-term USSR and Eastern European labor force share
trends. The USSR sector trend lines again tend to be more
elastic than the Eastern European trends, with the exception
of food products.

RELATIVE VALUE ADDED PER WORKER
IN EASTERN EUROPE

Table 18 is derived in the same manner as Table 3. As
was the case for the USSR, the derived Eastern European
ratios are not really comparable over time or among countries
because of variations in price structures over time and space.
Nevertheless, we assume that the changes in the Eastern
European price structures between the prewar and postwar
period roughly paralleled those which took place in the Soviet
Union during the 1930's, i.e., that the prices of investment
and defense items fell relative to consumer goods prices.

Using this assumption, we can note the basic similarity
between the Eastern European and Soviet patterns. Labor
productivity increased at a much more rapid pace in heavy
than in light manufacturing both in Eastern Europe and in the
Soviet Union. In Eastern Europe, this trend shows through
even in current prices, which understate the output of heavy
manufacturing.

In the course of this chapter, we compared the Eastern
European industrial structure in the postwar period with a
series of industrial structures. After analyzing the intrasample variance of the postwar Eastern European sample, it
was shown that the prewar and postwar Eastern European industrial structures are heterogeneous, i.e., that the observed
structural differences could not be explained by changes in
economic variables in the postwar period. On the other hand,
the postwar Eastern European and USSR plan period industrial
structures are remarkably uniform in terms of value-added

FIGURE 16

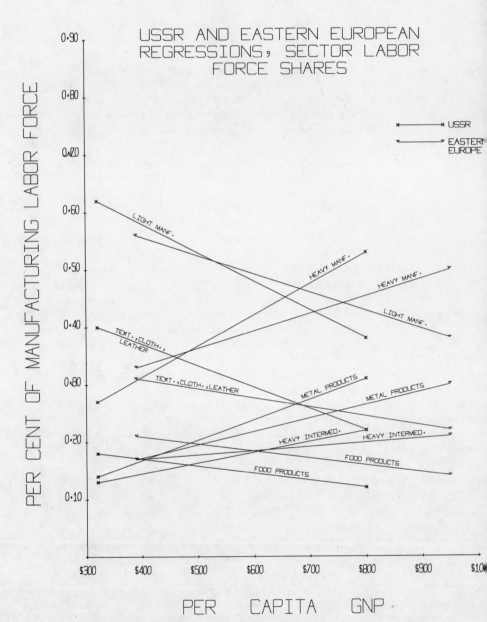

Sources: Author's computations based on data in Tables 2, 16.

TABLE 18

Sector Value Added Per Worker Ratios, Eastern Europe
and USSR, Prewar and Postwar Years

	(1) Heavy Mfg. to Light Mfg.	(2) Metal Prods. to Textiles, Clothing, Leather	(3) Metal Prods. to Heavy Intermediate Mfg.	(4) Heavy Mfg. to Food Prods.
Hungary 1936	.87	1.16	.98	.50
1963	1.69	1.25	.60	1.91
East Germany 1936	1.17	1.15	.83	.87
1963	1.33	1.27	.67	1.12
Czecho-slovakia 1929	.94	.91	.77	1.01
1965	1.53	1.45	.64	1.15
Bulgaria 1936	1.38	1.56	1.25	1.20
1963	1.43	1.18	.74	1.42
Romania 1930	1.04	.92	.38	.71
1958	1.36	1.33	.77	1.34
Poland 1963	1.44	1.31	.66	1.09
USSR 1928	1.16	1.14	.82	.82
1960	1.50	1.16	.78	1.25

Sources: Tables 3, 10, 11, 16.

shares, labor force distributions and sector value added per
worker ratios; a comparison of prewar Eastern Europe with
preplan USSR shows that this uniformity is not a carry-over
of earlier homogeneity. A final comparison of postwar socialist Eastern European industrial structures with a sample of
postwar nonsocialist structures reconfirms the heterogeneity
of the two groups.

In other words, the Eastern European bloc imitated quite
closely the industrialization pattern established in the Soviet
Union during the 1930's despite the vast differences between
the Soviet Union and Eastern Europe and despite the vast diversity within Eastern Europe itself. Especially noteworthy
is the one-sided expansion of metal products and metallurgy
regardless of the scale and level of development throughout
Eastern Europe. This was done to create a self-sufficient
economy independent not only of the capitalist world but also
independent of other socialist countries.

NOTES

1. The most reliable net production data are provided by
the German industrial census of 1936, which can be used to
reconstruct the 1936 value-added structure of industry in what
is now East Germany (GDR). The Stadnik estimates of the
1929 Czechoslovak industrial structure, derived from a series
of Czech industrial censuses, are also to be accorded a relatively high degree of reliability. On the other hand, industrial
census data of the other Eastern European countries are subject to a wider margin of error. In descending order of reliability, one should list the 1936 Hungarian estimates, the 1930
Romanian estimates and finally the 1937 Bulgarian estimates,
all of which are described in Table 11. The lack of coverage
of small-scale enterprises is the principal reason for the
disparity in the reliability of the various prewar structural estimates: The Hungarian factory industry net product estimates
are adjusted to include small-scale enterprises by multiplying
the factory industry net product figures by the ratios of total
branch gross production to factory branch gross production.
This procedure assumes equal net-to-gross product ratios in
factory and small-scale units. The Romanian 1930 estimates
are the product of branch per worker net product in factory
industry and total branch employment (factory and small-scale).
This procedure assumes equal net product per worker in both

factory and small-scale units.   The Bulgarian 1937 net product
estimates are not adjusted.   Statističeskii Godišnik 1937 (introduction) claims that all production units are covered, but this
is extremely doubtful.   Because detailed methodological ex-
planations are lacking, it is impossible to tell whether the
above net product estimates include indirect taxes.   The inclusion of excise taxes would probably result in the overstatement
of food products' value added but would probably have a small
impact in other sectors.   The derivation of the postwar Eastern European industrial structure estimates are discussed in
Appendix 2A and are summarized in Table 10.   Measurement
error is probably large in the case of the East German 1955
estimates because of the importance of the handicraft sector.
Our assumption of equal value added per worker should result
in an overestimation of handicraft value added and handicraft
production is concentrated in the light manufactures sectors.
The margin of error is also likely to be large in the Romanian
estimates, which omit a return to capital.   This omission results in the relative underestimation of the value added of
capital-intensive sectors.   There are no a priori grounds for
expecting biased estimates of the remaining Eastern European
structures.

2.   Milos Stadnik, Some Problems of Economic Growth in
Czechoslovakia, p. 28.

3.   J. Johnston, Econometric Methods, pp. 164-65.

4.   Multiple observations are given for the US, Canada,
Japan and the UK.   This increases the weight of highly developed economies in the sample.   United Nations, A Study of
Industrial Growth, p. 43, has shown year-to-year variation
to be insignificant during the 1953-1958 period.   The observations are taken from United Nations, Growth of World Industry,
1953-1965, National Tables.

CHAPTER **6** USSR AND EASTERN
EUROPEAN INDUSTRIAL
STRUCTURES
COMPARED WITH
WESTERN PATTERNS

This chapter compares actual socialist industrialization
patterns with the "normal" patterns which would have prevailed
if the capitalist pattern had been followed. First, the relevance
of cross-sectional evidence in comparing socialist and capitalist industrial development patterns is discussed in terms of
the difficulty of inferring historical patterns from cross-
sections. Second, actual USSR industrial structures at different points in time are compared with the so-called "normal"
capitalist industrial structures predicted by a nonsocialist postwar cross-section. Third, the USSR industrial structures are
compared with additional "normal" structures, computed from
a pre-World War II cross-section. Fourth, the postwar Eastern European cross-section is compared with the "normal"
Western pattern.

INFERENCES OF STRUCTURAL PATTERNS
FROM CROSS-SECTIONS

Chapter 4 examined the time series development patterns
of the USSR, US, German, Canadian and UK industry and manufacturing sectors in aggregate form and in structure. If the
Western time patterns could have been aggregated in a manner
which incorporated scale and resource differences, further
structural comparisons would not be necessary. Present
methods of dealing with time series data preclude the above.
First, it is theoretically difficult to incorporate natural resource factors into individual country time patterns because
of their relative constancy over time. Second, time series
parameters explain intracountry variation over time, not intercountry variation, e.g., why the 1962 USSR metal products

share exceeds the 1925 share by X percent, but not why the
1962 USSR metal products share is Y percent larger than the
1962 USA metal products share. *

Cross-section regressions provide a way out of this im-
passe, for they incorporate the entire complex of explanatory
factors into a single functional relationship to explain inter-
country variance; however, the utility of employing cross-
sections to compare socialist and nonsocialist industrial development patterns hinges upon the ability of the cross-section
to predict secular patterns of development.

Much attention has been devoted to this question. Although
there is general agreement that the ideal arrangement is a
complement of cross-section and time series data, the limited
availability of time series data which encompass a sufficiently
long period generally makes this dual approach difficult to implement. In the absence of a rectangular data array, Kuznets
argues that cross-sections could provide incorrect inferences
of past and future secular trends because they fail to take into
account technological innovations and changes in consumer
tastes, which cause divergences of secular from cross-section
trends. A theoretically correct regression must incorporate
these "innovational" factors or else run the risk of predicting
trends which differ from secular trends not only in magnitude
but also in direction. [1]

Perhaps the simplest way of incorporating innovational
factors into a cross-section regression is to include them as
period shift factors in the following manner:

$$y^{(c)} = X^{(c)'} M^{(c)} + t^{(c)} B_{(c)} + e^{(c)} \qquad (15)$$

$$y^{(s)} = X^{(s)'} M^{(s)} + t^{(s)} B_{(s)} + e^{(s)}, \qquad (16)$$

where the superscripts denote matrices and vectors, and the
subscripts denote scalars. The (c) scripts denote capitalist
variables and parameters; the (s) scripts denote socialist variables and parameters. The (') denotes matrix and vector trans-
position.

Equations (15) and (16) indicate that the variation of capitalist and socialist sector product shares ($y^{(i)}$) can be explained
by three factors: (a) by the variation in the cross-section independent variables ($X^{(i)}$), where $M^{(i)}$ measures the direction

---

*One could argue that given sufficient time, differences in
time series elasticities could explain intercountry variation
because base differences would become less significant.

and magnitude of this impact; (b) by the impact of different periods, i.e., by the change in periods ($t^{(i)}$), where $B_{(i)}$ measures the magnitude and direction of changes resulting from changes in $t^{(i)}$;* (c) by the impact of random shocks (e $^{(i)}$).

The normal cross-section coefficients ($M^{(i)}$) predict the structural pattern which would emerge in the long run if innovational changes did not occur ($t^{(i)} = 0$), or if these innovational changes had no significant effect upon the sector ($t^{(i)} \leq 0$, $B_{(i)} = 0$). In the latter case, the time series and cross-section patterns coincide, which is the normal assumption concerning cross-section patterns.

If, on the other hand, innovational changes do occur over time, and the period effect is not zero, the normal cross-section parameters are capable of explaining the intercountry structural variance at $t = 0$ but would be inaccurate in extrapolating past and future trends. The degree of error would depend on the magnitude of the period effect and the $t^{(i)}$ value.

The principal concern of this study is the socialist industrial development pattern vis-à-vis the capitalist industrial development pattern, which is essentially a dual question of whether $M^{(s)} = M^{(c)} \leq 0$, and whether $B_{(s)} = B_{(c)} \leq 0$. That is, we are asking, first, whether socialist industrial structures respond in the same way as capitalist economies, given a limited cross-section time horizon, to changes in independent variables and, second, whether socialist industrial structures respond in the same way as capitalist structures to innovational changes. The second, and broader, question unfortunately cannot be analyzed. There is, however, procedure for handling the first question--$M^{(s)} = M^{(c)} \leq 0$?[2]

The deviations of actual socialist industrial structures from their normal counterparts at different points in time, predicted from a nonsocialist cross-section, can be decomposed into three factors: The socialist structures differ from the normal structures because the socialist $M^{(s)}$ parameters differ from the nonsocialist $M^{(c)}$ parameters; because innovational changes affect the socialist structure $[t^{(s)} B_{(s)}]$; and

_____

*The variable t is measured relative to the cross-section period; that is, $t = 0$ when it corresponds to the cross-section period, $t < 0$ when it precedes the cross-section period, and $t > 0$ when it follows the cross-section period. The $B_{(i)}$ coefficient measures the direction and impact of the period effect, i.e., an upward or downward shift in the regression plane. If the period coefficient is positive, the sector is an "innovational" sector; if the period coefficient is negative, the sector is an "old" sector.

because of random error. On the other hand, the correction of the socialist structures for the period effect enables one to decompose the causes of the (corrected) deviations into parameter differences and random error alone, which greatly simplifies the problem.

Adjusting the actual socialist structure to eliminate the period effect is easy in concept but difficult to implement in practice. This is best illustrated with a practical example. In this chapter, we compare the actual USSR manufacturing structures at different points in time with their "normal" counterparts, predicted from a Western cross-section from the late 1950's and early 1960's.

Deviations of actual USSR late 1950's and early 1960's structures from "normal" cross-section structures are the result of random shocks and M coefficient differences, because there is no period effect ($t = 0$) in this instance.* However, deviations of actual 1925 and 1937 USSR manufacturing structures from their "normal" counterparts would be affected by the period effect, as well as by coefficient differences and random error, the effect of which could be expected to increase in magnitude as the distance between the cross-section period and the observation period increased.

If the sign (but not the magnitude) of the period effect were known, then additional information would be added. Assume that it is known that the metal products period effect is positive, i.e., that the metal products regression plane shifts upward over time, and that it is then shown that the 1937 deviation of the "normal" metal products share from the actual share ($y^{(s)} - {}^*y^{(s)}$) is positive. We can then conclude that the USSR coefficients differ significantly from the capitalist coefficients because the hypothetical period effect adjustment ($t < 0$, $B^{(s)} > 0$) would have made the deviation even larger. This conclusion rests, of course, on the assumption that the random error element does not dominate.

The real danger of attempting to infer parameter differences from comparisons of past USSR structures with normal cross-section structures arises either when a positive residual ($y - {}^*y > 0$) is combined with a negative period effect ($B^{(s)} < 0$) or when a negative residual is combined with a positive period effect. The former case would have the USSR (in 1937, for example) overproducing an "old" product, such as textiles,

_____

*We assume that the USSR in the postwar period has had equal access to innovational changes in technology and tastes. In other words, it is assumed that in any given year $t^{(c)} = t^{(s)}$.

relative to normal patterns. The latter case would have the
USSR (in 1937) underproducing an "innovational" product, such
as electrical machinery, relative to normal patterns. In both
cases, it is quite possible that any initial conclusion of significant parameter differences could be negated by the elimination
of period differences.

In this study, we use two approaches to this problem. The
first is intuition, which is used to determine the likely sign of
the period effect in particular sectors. For example, one can
readily predict that the textiles and leather products period
effects are negative and that the electrical products and chemicals period effects are positive. Second, we change the time
period of the cross-section parameters. In other words, we
compare the earlier USSR manufacturing structures with normal
counterparts derived from an earlier contemporaneous cross-
section.

USSR INDUSTRY PATTERNS

The primary Western cross-section employed in this
chapter to evaluate socialist industrialization patterns is the
one described in Chapter 5, which is composed of 41 observations from 29 nonsocialist economies in the 1953-65 period.
Normal regression equations are computed from this cross-
section for the aggregate industry sectors (industry and manufacturing) and for the manufacturing subsectors. These normal
equations are then employed to extrapolate the "normal" industrial structures of the USSR and of the Eastern European
countries, which are then contrasted with the actual industrial
structures of these countries. The normal regression equations
used in the extrapolations are given in Appendix C, Table 7.
The comparisons of actual and "normal" structures are given
in Figures 17 (USSR) and 18 (Eastern Europe). Figures 17
and 18 are computed from Appendix C, Tables 1-4.

Figures 17 and 18 deserve a word of explanation. They
contain the plotted deviations of the actual socialist sector
product shares from the "normal" Western product shares.
The zero lines represent the "normal" shares, and the con-
nected points represent the percentage point deviations of the
actual socialist sector product shares from the "normal"
shares. In the case of the manufacturing subsectors, three
sets of deviations are plotted because the extrapolation process
is carried out in three stages:

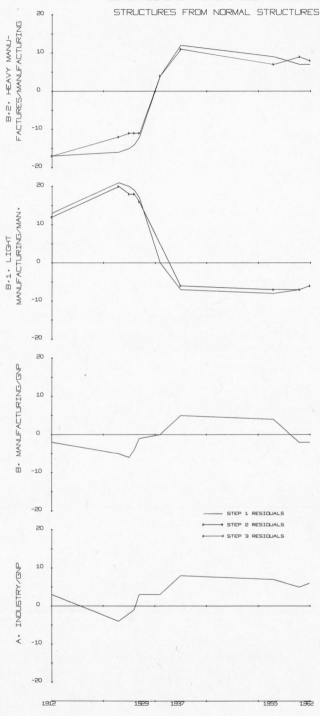

FIGURE 17
DEVIATIONS OF ACTUAL USSR INDUSTRIAL
STRUCTURES FROM NORMAL STRUCTURES

STEP 1 RESIDUALS
STEP 2 RESIDUALS
STEP 3 RESIDUALS

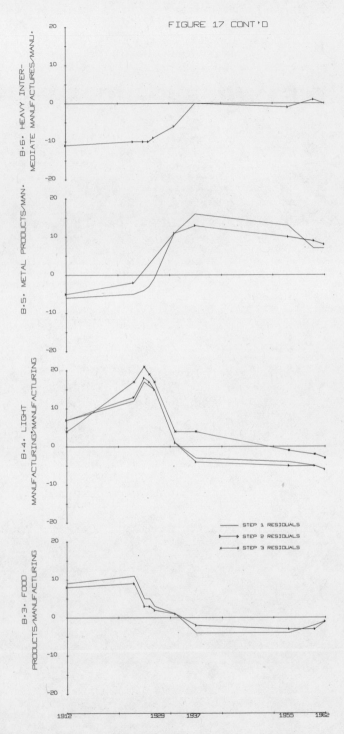

FIGURE 17 CONT'D

B·6· HEAVY INTER-MEDIATE MANUFACTURES/MANU.

B·5· METAL PRODUCTS/MAN.

B·4· LIGHT MANUFACTURING/MANUFACTURING

STEP 1 RESIDUALS
STEP 2 RESIDUALS
STEP 3 RESIDUALS

B·3· FOOD PRODUCTS/MANUFACTURING

*excluding food products

102

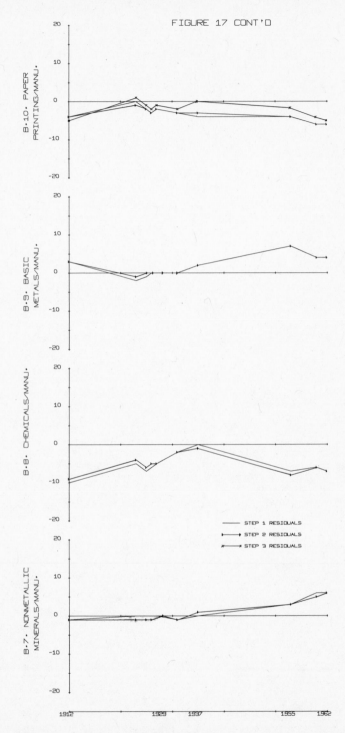

FIGURE 17 CONT'D

Source: Author's computations based on data in Table 1.

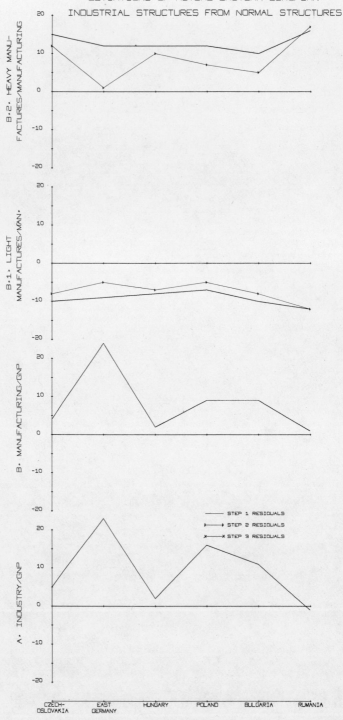

FIGURE 18

DEVIATIONS OF ACTUAL EASTERN EUROPEAN
INDUSTRIAL STRUCTURES FROM NORMAL STRUCTURES

STEP 1 RESIDUALS
STEP 2 RESIDUALS
STEP 3 RESIDUALS

B.2. HEAVY MANU-
FACTURES/MANUFACTURING

B.1. LIGHT
MANUFACTURES/MAN.

B. MANUFACTURING/GNP

A. INDUSTRY/GNP

CZECH-
OSLOVAKIA   EAST   HUNGARY   POLAND   BULGARIA   RUMANIA
             GERMANY

104

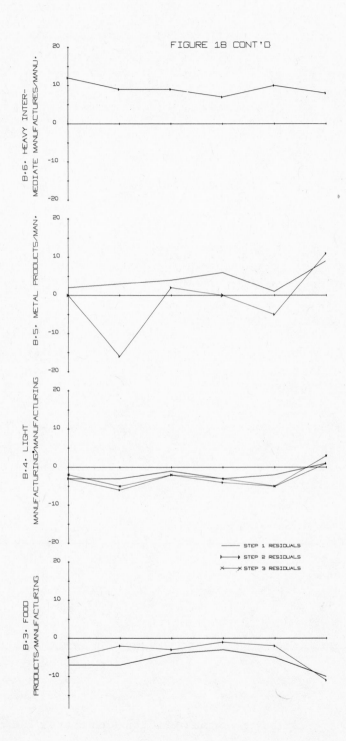

FIGURE 18 CONT'D

B·6· HEAVY INTER-MEDIATE MANUFACTURES/MANU.

B·5· METAL PRODUCTS/MAN·

B·4· LIGHT MANUFACTURING/MANUFACTURING

B·3· FOOD PRODUCTS/MANUFACTURING

STEP 1 RESIDUALS
STEP 2 RESIDUALS
STEP 3 RESIDUALS

FIGURE 18 CONT'D

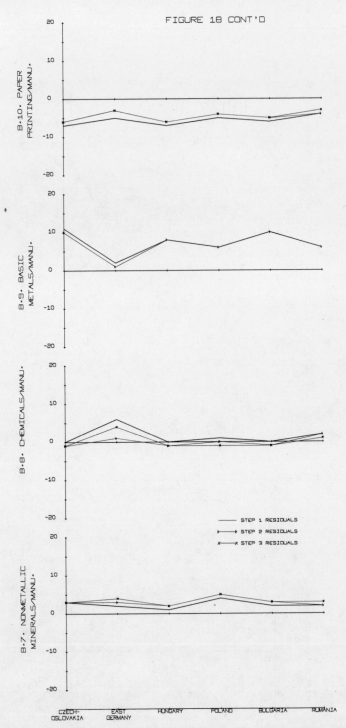

Source: Author's computations based on data in Table 1.

1.   The predicted socialist manufacturing structures are extrapolated, using the Western income, size and natural resource elasticities to compute "normal" structures, which are then compared with the actual USSR structures.

2.   MS is added to the three original independent variables and the "normal" structures are recomputed from the expanded coefficient set.

3.   A final step is added to the second regression set. For those sectors which yield significant trade orientation (V) coefficients, the trade orientation variable is added to the independent variable set of step 2.

This three-step arrangement was chosen because, as in covariance analysis, it is useful to preserve the distinction between environmental and explanatory variables. Assume that at the end of step 1, which takes into account the influence of the environmental variables (per capita income, population, natural resources), the actual USSR 1960 metal products value-added share exceeds the normal share by 50 percent. This means that the 1960 USSR metal products share is 50 percent larger than the normal share of a typical Western country at the same level of per capita income, size and natural resources. Steps 2 and 3 attempt to account for this gap by considering the impact of the explanatory variables (those variables which are correlated with the economic system) on the normal manufacturing structure. What portion of the 50 percent gap is accounted for by the fact that USSR planners opted for a large manufacturing sector relative to normal standards, or by the fact that the USSR chose to cut itself off from world markets, which forced Soviet planners to adopt an industrial structure which would provide self-sufficiency?

USSR INDUSTRY AND MANUFACTURING PATTERNS

In 1912, the actual 18 percent manufacturing ratio in the USSR was slightly below the ratio predicted for a typical Western country having the same per capita income, population and natural resources. (See Figure 17, parts A and B.) On the other hand, the 25 percent industry ratio (manufacturing plus construction) was three percentage points above the normal share. Throughout the entire NEP period, the actual USSR manufacturing and industry ratios were slightly below the normal ratios. From 1929 on, the actual USSR industry and manufacturing ratios were either equal to or exceeded the

normal ratios, attaining peaks of five and eight percentage
points above normal in 1937, both of which are roughly 20 percent larger than the normal ratios.

The postwar period witnessed a moderate trend towards
convergence of the USSR industry and manufacturing ratios
and the normal ratios. Between 1937 and the postwar period,
the deviations of the actual USSR industry ratios from the
normal industry ratios declined from a peak of eight percentage
points above normal (23 percent) to an average of around six
percentage points above normal (16 percent). On the other
hand, the average postwar manufacturing share of 29 percent
equaled the 1937 share. In 1937, the actual manufacturing
share was 17 percent above normal; the average postwar deviation of actual from normal manufacturing shares was zero,
a figure which masks a great deal of variation within the postwar period. In 1955, the manufacturing ratio was four percentage points above normal (13 percent), whereas in 1960 and
1962, the ratio was two percentage points (7 percent) below
normal.

As far as the aggregate industry and manufacturing sectors
are concerned, the period effect probably plays a minor role.
Chenery and Taylor have demonstrated the relative constancy
of industry cross-section coefficients over time,[3] and the postwar comparisons should provide accurate measures of deviations from normal because by definition the period effect plays
no role. For the earlier periods, one could probably classify
industry and manufacturing as "innovational" sectors on an intuitive basis, which means that the impact of the period effect
(if any) would be to lower the normal ratios, thereby increasing
the USSR positive deviations of the 1930's and reducing the
negative deviations of the 1920's.

USSR MANUFACTURING SUBSECTOR PATTERNS

The changes in the structure of the USSR manufacturing
sector between 1912 and 1962 were described in Chapter 3.
In this section, the deviations of the actual USSR manufacturing
structures from the "normal" patterns are described. (See
Figure 17, B1-B12.) As was indicated above, the "normal"
manufacturing patterns are estimated in three stages. The
Stage 1 results are as follows:

1. Prior to 1933, the USSR light manufactures share of
total manufacturing value added was markedly larger than the

normal share of a typical Western country having the same
per capita income, population and natural resources; after
1933, the USSR light manufactures shares were smaller than
the normal shares. In 1929, the actual USSR light manufactures
share was 61 percent and the predicted share was 44 percent,
leaving a residual of +17. In 1933, the actual USSR share of
42 percent was exactly equal to the normal share, and by 1937
the actual share of 33 percent was seven percentage points below the normal share. During the postwar period, actual USSR
light manufactures shares remained below normal, reaching a
low of eight percentage points below normal in 1955. Since
1955, the deviations of actual from normal shares have narrowed only marginally.

    2. The heavy manufactures residual pattern is the exact
opposite of the light manufactures pattern. In 1929, the actual
USSR heavy manufactures value-added share of 33 percent was
12 percentage points below the normal 45 percent share. In
1933, the USSR share of 51 percent exceeded the normal 47
percent share by four percentage points; by 1937, the residual
had widened to 12 percentage points. Throughout the postwar
period, the actual shares were significantly larger than the
predicted shares, although the postwar trend was towards convergence of actual USSR and normal shares. In 1955, the
actual share was 64 percent, and the predicted share was 55
percent; in 1962, the actual 68 percent share exceeded the
normal 61 percent share by seven percentage points.

    3. The same reversal of residual patterns between 1929
and 1933 can be observed for the major subsectors of heavy
and light manufactures. Prior to 1933, the actual USSR food
products value-added shares and light manufactures (excluding
food products) value-added shares were larger than the normal
predicted shares. In 1929, the food products value-added share
was 21 percent, three percentage points above the normal 18
percent share; in 1933, it was still slightly above normal, but
by 1937 food products was four percentage points below normal.
The postwar period witnessed a significant reduction in residuals until, in 1962, the USSR food products share was only
one percentage point below normal. The 1929 USSR light manufactures (excluding food products) value-added share of 39
percent was 15 percentage points above the 24 percent normal
share; by 1937, the 21 percent share was three percentage
points below the normal 24 percent share. The postwar trend
in this sector has been away from convergence.

    In 1929, the predicted metal products share of 16 percent
was one percentage point below the actual USSR share. In 1933,

the actual share of 30 percent exceeded the normal share by
11 percentage points; by 1937, the residual had been increased
to 16 percentage points above normal. The postwar period
witnessed a substantial reduction in these deviations. By 1960,
the USSR metal products sector was only seven percentage
points above normal. In the case of heavy intermediate manufactures, no radical reversal of residual patterns between
1929 and 1937 can be discerned; instead, the post-1929 period
witnessed a rapid convergence of actual and normal structures.
In 1929, the USSR heavy intermediate manufactures share was
nine percentage points below the normal share; in 1933, the
sector share was six percentage points below normal. After
1933, there were no significant differences between actual and
normal shares.

4.   The residual patterns at lower levels of aggregation
conform to the more highly aggregative patterns. For example,
prior to 1933, the textiles share was much larger than normal;
during the 1930's, the textiles share declined substantially
relative to the normal share. During the postwar period, the
textiles share equaled the normal share. Leather products
was above normal prior to 1933 and normal thereafter. Printing and paper was below normal both prior to 1933 and after
1933, the difference being a widening of deviations during the
latter period. The basic metals share was approximately
normal from 1927 to 1933; in 1933, it was two percentage
points above normal, rose to a peak of seven percentage points
above normal in 1955 and declined thereafter. The behavior
of the chemicals share was erratic. Between 1929 and 1937,
the chemical sector's value-added share changed from a position 5 percent below normal to exact normality, but during the
entire postwar period, the chemicals share was substantially
below normal.

5.   The largest negative USSR residuals occur in the relatively capital-intensive light industrial sectors, such as paper,
printing and food products. The less capital-intensive consumer
goods sectors, such as textiles, leather products and clothing,
fared much better relative to normal value-added shares.

Step 2 Residual Patterns

One should not accept residual patterns based upon per
capita income, population and natural resource differences
without further investigation, because it is possible that these
patterns can be explained by other factors which have not yet

been considered.   The step 2 residuals reflect the deviations
of actual USSR manufacturing subsector shares from the normal
shares of a typical Western country having the same per capita
income, population, natural resources and MS.   In other words,
the step 2 residuals test whether the step 1 residuals (which
omit MS) can be explained (i. e., made to disappear) by differences in the relative size of the USSR manufacturing sector
vis-à-vis normal levels.

The following step 2 results should be noted:

1.   The relative increase in the manufacturing sector
during the post-1929 period accounts for an insignificant portion
of the 1937-62 negative light manufactures gap.   The original
average light manufactures residual during this period is 7
percent below normal; the average residual after MS is approximately 6. 5 percent below normal.

2.   The average heavy manufactures share during the post-
1929 period is 7. 8 percentage points above normal at the end
of step 1.   The average USSR heavy manufactures share remains unchanged at the end of step 2, i. e., the relative size
of the manufacturing sector does not reduce the original gap.

3.   The original USSR food products sector is, on the
average, 2. 8 percentage points below the normal Western
share between 1937 and 1962; the average deviation is reduced
to 2. 3 percentage points below normal with the inclusion of
MS.

4.   The size of the USSR manufacturing sector during the
post-1929 period accounts for only a minor portion of the
above normal-USSR metal products deviations of step 1.   The
average USSR metal products share during this period is 10. 8
percentage points above normal (about 42 percent above normal)
at the end of step 1.   After MS is included, the average USSR
metal products share drops only marginally to 10. 2 percentage
points above the average normal share.

5.   The average USSR light manufactures (excluding food
products) value-added share during the post-1929 period is
3. 5 percentage points (about 11 percent) below the average
share at the end of step 1; the average deviation is essentially
unchanged when MS is taken into consideration.

Step 3 Residual Patterns

The step 3 residual patterns represent the deviations of
actual USSR sector value-added shares from the normal value-
added shares of a typical Western country having the same per

capita income, population, natural resources, manufacturing
ratio and trade orientation. Comparisons of USSR gaps, both
before and after entry of the trade orientation variable (V),
provide some measure of the impact of autarky on the USSR
industrial structure. *

TABLE 19

USSR Trade Orientation, 1912-62

Year	Actual X+M/GNP	Normal X+M/GNP	Trade Orientation
1912	21%	18%	+ 3%
1925	4%	18%	-14%
1927	5%	18%	-13%
1928	6%	18%	-12%
1929	6%	18%	-12%
1933	5%	18%	-13%
1937	1%	18%	-17%
1955	4%	17%	-13%
1960	5%	16%	-11%
1962	6%	16%	-10%

Notes: 1. Anti-logs from $\log (X+M/GNP) = 4.0 + .0155 \ln I - .2501 \ln N$
(6.85)   (.27)

2. The R^2 value is .37.

3. The number of observations is 85.

4. The sample encompasses both time series
and cross-sections.

Source: See Chapter 2.

---

*V is defined as the deviation of the normal ratio of ex-
ports plus imports to GNP (predicted by a regression of per
capita income and population on the trade ratio) from the actual
USSR ratio. The large negative USSR V values confirm a result noted by Pryor on a per capita basis; that is, the marked
socialist underutilization of trade. See Frederic Pryor, The
Communist Foreign Trade System, p. 27.

It is interesting to note that the Russian 1912 trade ratio
was slightly in excess of the potential ratio; thereafter, the
actual USSR ratios range from 63 percent below potential
(1962) to 95 percent below potential (1937).

Judging from the regressions of Appendix C, Table 7, and from the step 3 extrapolations of Figure 17, the underutilization of trade potential throughout the entire Soviet period had little impact on the structure of USSR industry. The majority of sectors yield V coefficients which are not significantly different from zero at a .75 level of significance. (See Appendix C, Table 7.)

A positive V coefficient means that an autarchy-oriented economy would tend towards a smaller value-added share in that particular sector than an economy at the same level of development which realizes its trade potential. For example, the positive paper and printing V coefficient indicates that underutilization of trade potential should explain a portion of the negative USSR gap in that sector.

The step 3 residual patterns are plotted in Figure 17. Extrapolations are made only for the four sectors (paper and printing, chemicals, nonmetallic minerals, and light manufactures excluding food products) which yield significant V coefficients. The impact of trade orientation upon the USSR structure of manufacturing is as follows:

1. In the majority of sectors, the residual patterns yielded by steps 1 and 2 are unaffected by trade orientation, because the insignificant V sector coefficients indicate a zero impact upon the normal extrapolated structures in those sectors.

2. Of those sectors which yield significant V coefficients, the entry of V into the calculation of normal values significantly narrows both the negative light manufactures (excluding food products) gap and the paper and printing gap. In the former sector, the average 1937-62 USSR gap of five percentage points below normal is reduced to .4 percentage points below normal, and in the latter sector, the original 1933-62 gap of 4.4 percentage points below normal is reduced to 2.6 percentage points below normal.

3. On the other hand, the entry of V significantly widens the original negative chemicals gap and positive nonmetallic minerals gap. The average 1937-62 nonmetallic minerals gap increases from 3.7 percentage points above normal to 4.8 percentage points above normal, and the average 1933-37 chemicals gap increases from 4.8 percentage points below normal to eight percentage points above normal.

THE PERIOD EFFECT AND RESIDUAL PATTERNS

The residual patterns of Figure 17 were derived under the assumption that long-run structural trends can be inferred from a single cross-section, i. e. , that regression planes do not shift over time. If one limits the scope of inquiry to the uniformity of USSR and Western short-run coefficients, the 1955, 1960 and 1962 USSR residuals are indicative of cross-section parameter differences and of random error effects, because they are contemporaneous with the cross-section observations. On the other hand, the earlier USSR residual patterns would be affected by shifts in regression planes.

If one could identify "innovational" and "old" sectors, the direction of the impact of the period effect upon the USSR residual patterns could be determined. It is, however, difficult to do so on an intuitive basis, especially if the sectors are highly aggregated. It is probably safe to classify metal products (engineering) as an "innovational" sector and food products and textiles as "old" sectors. If these two assumptions are correct, the cross-section would fail to predict the rapidity of the rise in metal products over time and would fail to predict the rapidity of the declines in food products and textiles over time. This means that the predicted normal metal products and food products and textiles shares will be respectively larger (or equal) and smaller (or equal) than the true normal values which include the period effect; therefore, the positive 1937 USSR metal products residual is probably an underestimation and the negative 1912 residual is an overestimation of the true metal products residuals, and the negative 1937 USSR food products residual is probably an underestimation and the positive 1912 residual is an overestimation of the true food products residuals, which means that the true USSR plan period residual pattern would be even more distinctive and the preplan pattern would be less distinctive in these two sectors, if the period effect had been eliminated. The same argument can be made concerning textiles.

This intuitive approach provides useful insights, but it is highly speculative in the absence of explicit information. As we noted above, another approach would be to eliminate the period effect by maintaining t = 0; that is, to recompute the USSR residuals from a new cross-section which is roughly contemporaneous with the individual USSR observations. For this purpose, we collected an additional sample composed of 19 observations from 14 countries from the 1937-39 prewar period. [4]

The normal structures derived from this new prewar cross-section must be regarded with a great deal of suspicion for two reasons. First, the sample size is quite small; second, the 1937-39 period is probably dominated by short-term disturbances emanating from the depression which practically destroy its usefulness in extrapolating normal structures. Nevertheless, despite all of the above reservations, the new USSR residual patterns for the prewar period are given in Appendix C, Table 8, and are commented upon below. MS data are not available in sufficient detail for this earlier period to permit the computation of three-stage residuals (as in Figure 17); instead, two residual sets are computed. The first gives normal structures defined on the basis of per capita income, population and natural resources; the second set adds trade orientation to the original list of variables. In view of the crude nature of the 1937-39 sample, the only appropriate question raised by the new residual set is whether it constitutes a contradiction of the USSR residual patterns derived from the postwar cross section.

A cursory examination of Appendix C, Table 8, reveals that the new step 1 pattern conforms quite closely to the pattern above. Prior to 1933, USSR light manufactures and light manufactures excluding food products both yielded value-added shares which exceeded the normal shares, whereas after 1933 the reverse was true. Prior to 1933, heavy manufactures and metal products yielded below-normal shares, whereas by 1937, both sectors yielded substantially above-normal shares. In 1929, food products was 10 percentage points above normal; by 1937 this residual had been reduced to two percentage points above normal. In 1929, heavy intermediate manufactures was 16 percentage points below normal; by 1937, this figure had been reduced to eight percentage points below normal.

The step 2 residual patterns of Appendix C, Table 8 which are not equivalent to the step 2 residual patterns of Appendix C, Table 2, are computed on the basis of per capita income, population, natural resources and trade orientation. They reconfirm the earlier results: the light manufacturing residuals move from above-normal to below-normal shares between 1929 and 1937, whereas the heavy manufacturing residuals move from below-normal to above-normal shares during the same period.

The rather obvious conclusion is that the basic features of the original USSR residual pattern are not altered by innovational shifts in regression planes. Whether or not innovational shifts did take place remains an open question far beyond the scope of this study. Such a question can be answered only

by comparing large cross-sections over longer periods of time.
As was noted above, the use of a depression-period cross-
section can in no way provide any definite answers. The important feature of the USSR industrial development pattern is
that it is so distinctive relative to normal patterns that extremely large changes in the definition of normal patterns are
required to negate its singularity.

One important lesson which the USSR development experience teaches should not be overlooked: The Czarist government, according to Gerschenkron,[5] exerted massive pressure
on the Russian economy in order to develop a top-heavy, producer goods-oriented economy; nevertheless, the discretionary
weapons employed generally worked through the market, e.g.,
tax benefits, government orders and profit guarantees. On the
other hand, Figure 17 indicates that the Russian economy in
1912 was still skewed in the direction of light manufactured
products and away from producer goods, despite the government's concerted efforts to the contrary. The vast transformation of the USSR economy relative to normal development
patterns had to await the advent of central planning, which to
a great extent abolished the market. The Russian experience
is perhaps indicative of the enormous institutional changes required to bring about radical structural change within an economy. A desire on the part of a socialist government or a
political dictatorship to alter the course of economic events
is not alone sufficient; instead, both the desire and the means
to implement (central command planning) must be combined.

Another point to be noted is the self-perpetuating nature
of the Soviet pattern, which is indicated by the lack of substantial convergence during the postwar period, for it might
be expected that the deviations of the Soviet pattern from the
normal pattern would be self-liquidating as the level of development increased.

EASTERN EUROPEAN AND "NORMAL"
MANUFACTURING STRUCTURES

In this section, we compare the actual postwar Eastern
European industrial structures with their "normal" counterparts in the same manner as the USSR structures in Figure 17
to determine how closely Eastern Europe parallels the Soviet
residual pattern.

Figure 18 plots the deviations of actual Eastern European ratios of manufacturing and industrial value-added shares from the normal ratios predicted by the nonsocialist sample. It is to be compared with Figure 17 for the USSR. Figure 18 can be summarized as follows.

In general, the Eastern European ratios of manufacturing and industrial value added to GNP also exceed their normal counterparts. Most notable are the East German, Polish, and Bulgarian manufacturing ratios, which exceed their normal counterparts by 24, nine and nine percentage points, respectively. The Czechoslovak and Hungarian manufacturing ratios exceed their normal counterparts by four and two percentage points respectively, and the Romanian manufacturing ratio is one percentage point above its normal ratio.

The Eastern European industrial value-added deviation pattern is quite similar to the above manufacturing pattern. In general, the Eastern European industry ratios exceed their normal counterparts, the largest positive deviations being recorded by East Germany, Poland, Bulgaria and Czechoslovakia. Only Romania yields a slightly below-normal industry ratio.

An interesting question is whether the Eastern European cross-section reveals any trend of convergence towards the normal Western pattern. Cross-section convergence would be indicated by large deviations at low levels of development and small deviations at high levels of development. No distinctive convergence trend can be discerned, however. Of the low-income countries, Bulgaria yields large and Romania yields small industry and manufacturing deviations. Of the high-income countries, East Germany yields extremely large deviations, Czechoslovakia yields moderate deviations, and Hungary yields small deviations.

Figure 18 (B1-B12) deals with the structure of manufacturing; it plots the deviations of actual Eastern European manufacturing subsector shares of total manufacturing value added from the normal shares. The normal share extrapolations have been carried out in three stages, as was done for the USSR in Figure 17.

Step 1 Residuals

1. In general, the actual Eastern European light manufactures shares tend to be less than their normal counterparts, whereas the actual Eastern European heavy manufactures

shares tend to exceed their normal counterparts. The average
light manufactures deviation is nine percentage points below
normal. These below-normal deviations are substantial,
ranging from a low of seven (Hungary) to a high of 12 (Romania)
percentage points below normal. The average heavy manufactures deviation is 12.5 percentage points above normal.
The deviations range from 10 (Hungary, Bulgaria) to 16 (Romania) percentage points above normal.

2. At lower levels of aggregation, the same general Eastern European residual pattern is maintained. The average
Eastern European food products deviation is 5.8 percentage
points below normal, the deviations ranging from 3 (Poland)
to 10 (Romania) percentage points below normal. The average
heavy intermediate manufactures share is nine percentage
points above normal, ranging from a low of six (Poland) to a
high of 12 (Czechoslovakia) percentage points above normal.
The average metal products deviation is 3.8 percentage points
above normal, with deviations varying from a low of one (Bulgaria) to a high of nine (Romania) percentage points above normal. The average light manufactures (excluding food products)
deviation is 1.8 percentage point below normal. Romania
yields an above-normal share, but the rest of the Eastern European countries yield below-normal shares.

3. At an even lower level of aggregation, it is interesting
to note the consistently large Eastern European basic metals
shares relative to predicted shares: the average Eastern European basic metals deviation is seven percentage points above
normal. On the other hand, the paper and printing share is
consistently below normal. The nonmetallic minerals share
is consistently above normal. A surprising feature of Figure
18, which parallels the USSR experience, is the solid array
of above-normal textiles shares in postwar Eastern Europe.

                        Step 2 Residuals

In terms of the overall Eastern European deviations, the
inclusion of MS has the following impact:

1. About 20 percent of the original average light manufactures deviation is explained and about 33 percent of the original average heavy manufactures deviation is explained. The
average light manufactures deviation declines from -nine to
-7.2 percentage points, and the average heavy manufactures
deviation declines from +12.5 to +8.3 percentage points. The
most radical impact is felt in those countries in which the

relative size of the manufacturing sector deviated widely from the size expected for the level of development. Within Eastern Europe, the most drastic changes therefore occur in the East German, Polish and Bulgarian deviations (as might be expected from Figure 18 B). The original East German light manufactures and heavy manufactures deviations change from -nine percent and +12 percent, respectively, to -5 percent and +1 percent, respectively. The Polish deviations change from -7 percent and +12 percent to -5 percent and +7 percent, and the Bulgarian deviations change from -10 percent and +10 percent to -8 percent and +5 percent, respectively.

    2. At a lower level of aggregation, the inclusion of the manufacturing ratio explains about 33 percent of the original -5.8 percent average food products deviation (the average deviation declines to -3.8 percent), the impact varying quite radically within the sample. The original Polish and Bulgarian food products deviations narrow from -2 percent and -5 percent, respectively, to 0 percent and -2 percent, respectively. The East German deviation changes from -7 percent to -2 percent. On the other hand, the Romanian food products deviation widens.

    The entry of MS has no impact on the original heavy intermediate manufactures residual pattern. The average Eastern European deviation remains constant at +9 percent. On the other hand, it effects major changes in the metal products deviation pattern. The average Eastern European metal products deviation changes from +3.8 percent to -1.8 percent, owing to the negative deviations yielded by East Germany and Bulgaria, both of which have large manufacturing sectors relative to their level of per capita income, population and natural resources. The impact on the light manufactures (excluding food products) residual pattern is worthy of note: the average deviation widens from -1.8 percent to -3.2 percent, with only the Czechoslovakian and Romanian deviations remaining constant.

Step 3 Residuals

    The Eastern European countries, with the exception of Bulgaria, failed to utilize fully their trade potential. The individual Eastern European V values are computed from the normal regression equation given in Table 14. * Step 3

*	Actual Trade Ratio	Potential	Deviation (V)
Poland 1963	20%	26%	- 6%
Hungary 1963	34%	35%	- 1%

residuals are again computed only for those sectors which yield
significant V coefficients.

In general, trade orientation has little explanatory value
as far as the Eastern European residual pattern is concerned.
Only in the case of light manufactures (excluding food products)
does the entry of the trade orientation variable result in a significant narrowing of deviations, from an average of -3.2 percent
to an average of -2.2 percent. In other cases, deviations were
either unaffected (chemicals), became wider (nonmetallic minerals) or were slightly narrowed (paper and printing).

Turning to the question of convergence within the manufacturing sector, no clear cross-section convergence pattern can
be discerned from the Eastern European residual patterns.
Of the low-income countries, Romania's heavy and light manufactures residuals are large, whereas Bulgaria's residuals
are average and small. Of the more highly developed countries,
East Germany's heavy and light manufactures residuals are
small, and Hungary's and Czechoslovakia's residuals are average and large. As was noted above, a cross-section convergence pattern would be indicated by a combination of large
low-income deviations and small high-income deviations.

In sum, the Eastern European deviations from the normal
patterns have been shown to parallel the USSR deviations,
which again confirms the striking similarity between the patterns of industrialization in the Soviet Union and in Eastern
Europe. This similarity is most noteworthy in view of the size
and resource differences between these two areas.

East Germany 1963	29%	31%	- 2%
Czechoslovakia 1965	30%	32%	- 2%
Romania 1958	16%	33%	-17%
Bulgaria 1963	46%	37%	+ 9%

The generally negative Eastern European deviations confirm
the marked underutilization of trade potential by the CMEA
nations noted by Pryor in his investigation of a 1955 Eastern
European cross-section. See Frederic Pryor, The Communist
Foreign Trade System. The actual trade ratios are computed
from the Ernst ratio of imports to GNP (Maurice Ernst, "The
Postwar Economic Growth in Eastern Europe," p. 900) and
from the ratio of imports to exports (from the various national
statistical yearbooks). The 1955 East German ratio includes
reparations. See Heinz Köhler, Economic Integration in the
Soviet Bloc, pp. 328-29.

NOTES

1. Kuznets, <u>Modern Economic Growth</u>, pp. 432-36.

2. First $M^{(c)}$ is estimated, using the least squares method:

$$\hat{M}^{(c)} = (X^{(c)'} X^{(c)})^{-1} X^{(c)'}_y{}^{(c)} .$$

This provides an unbiased estimate of $M^{(c)}$, which is used to compute

$$*_y (s) = X^{(s)'} \hat{M}^{(c)} ,$$

which is the predicted socialist structure over time, computed under the assumption that the socialist sector responds in exactly the same manner as the capitalist sector to changes in independent variables. The $*_y{}^{(s)}$ is termed the "normal" structure.

A comparison of the actual socialist structures with the "normal" structures involves the following operation (from equation (16) in text and the equation predicting the socialist structure over time):

$$y^{(s)} - *_y{}^{(s)} = X^{(s)'} (M^{(s)} - \hat{M}^{(c)}) + t^{(s)} B_{(s)} + e^{(s)} .$$

Thus, the deviation of the actual socialist structure from the "normal" capitalist structure is explained by three factors: (a) the difference in socialist and capitalist cross-section coefficients ($M^{(s)} - \hat{M}^{(c)}$); (b) the socialist period effect, $t^{(s)} B_{(s)}$; and (c) the random error effect ($e^{(s)}$).

Of primary concern is the first factor, the difference between socialist and capitalist structural parameters, which are would like to infer from the deviations of actual socialist structures from "normal" structures. Inference is made difficult because the above deviations could have been caused by a combination of random error and the period effect and not by real differences in structural parameters.

Conceptually, the period effect can be eliminated by correcting the actual socialist structure to eliminate the period effect in the following manner:

$$[_y{}^{(s)} -_t{}^{(s)} B_{(s)}] - *_y{}^{(s)} = X^{(s)}(M^{(s)} - M^{(c)}) + e^{(s)} .$$

After correction of the actual socialist structure for the
period effect, deviations of actual socialist structures from
normal structures can be attributed to two factors: the difference between socialist and capitalist cross-section coefficients and random error.

3. H. Chenery and L. Taylor, "Development Patterns:
Among Countries and Over Time," p. 402.

4. Most of the observations are drawn from United
Nations, The Growth of World Industry, 1938-1961. The
German, US, Canadian and UK observations are from Appendix
B. In many cases, the UN data were corrected for incomplete
coverage by using more comprehensive labor force data.

5. Alexander Gerschenkron, "The Rate of Industrial
Growth in Russia Since 1885."

CHAPTER 7 POSTWAR WESTERN AND SOCIALIST CROSS-SECTIONS: A COMPARATIVE APPRAISAL

Perhaps the most informative comparison of socialist and Western industrialization patterns is to contrast directly the socialist and Western cross-section regression parameters, as outlined in Chapter 1. In this brief chapter, we regress two separate cross-sections--one socialist and the other the nonsocialist cross section which was used in Chapter 6-- to derive two sets of income, population, resource and relative industrialization elasticities. These two cross-sections are roughly contemporaneous, so their elasticity differences should reflect actual differences in cross-section parameters independent of period effects. (See Chapter 6.)

We should add one precautionary note before proceeding to discuss the regression equations. In the socialist postwar cross-section, we have included 10 observation: two observations for the USSR (1955, 1962), East Germany (1955, 1963) and Hungary (1957, 1963) and one observation each for Czechoslovakia, Bulgaria, Romania and Poland. In other words, we are dealing with a limited number of degrees of freedom, which might possibly prejudice the outcome. The reader must therefor decide how much weight he is willing to attribute to this small sample of socialist countries. This criticism applies less to the Chow tests and dummy variables given in this chapter than to the actual regression coefficients.

We summarize the two cross-section regressions in Table 20, which deserves a word of explanation. The two regression coefficient sets are recorded in the first five columns. We have supplied two different socialist R elasticities. The first is derived using estimates of natural resource endowments based on prewar Eastern European trade structures, assuming that natural resources remain constant over time. The second (in parentheses) uses the actual postwar Eastern European trade structures to compute natural resource endowments.

TABLE 20

Normal Regression Equations, Manufacturing Subsectors,
Postwar Socialist and Nonsocialist Cross-Sections

Sector	Regression Coefficients for:					R^2	S.E.	Socialist Dummy	Chow Test
	Inter-cept	Log I	Log N	Log R	Log MS				
Light Manufactures									
Socialist	2.16	-.473	.017*	-.042* (-.58)	.127*	.88	.06	-.160	3.50
Nonsocialist	.09	-.137	-.101	.053	-.163	.77	.15	(2.92)	
Heavy Manufactures									
Socialist	-2.57	.266	.027*	-.010* (.033)	-.135	.82	.05	.128	2.96
Nonsocialist	-1.35	.111	.095	-.005	.304	.77	.16	(2.23)	
Food Products									
Socialist	1.72	-.504	-.029*	.042* (-.029)*	.314*	.65	.17	-.240	3.56
Nonsocialist	-.87	-.153	.182	.074	-.491	.78	.27	(2.44)	
Light Manufactures (excl. food)									
Socialist	1.32	-.452	.050*	-.095 (-.081)	.015*	.77	.10	-.088*	
Nonsocialist	-.47	-.091	-.027*	.047	.268	.13	.21	(1.17)	
Metal Products									
Socialist	-3.84	.322	.095	-.084* (-.024)*	-.133*	.81	.10	.072*	3.22
Nonsocialist	-2.26	.258	.062	-.053	.780	.84	.23	(.83)	
Heavy Intermediate									
Socialist	-2.72	.212*	-.043*	-.021* (.078)	-.149*	.65	.06	.215	3.57
Nonsocialist	-1.64	-.039*	.123	-.035	-.016*	.43	.22	(2.69)	

124

Textiles

	(1)	(2)	(3)	(4)	(5)	(6)	(7)	(8)	(9)	(10)
Textiles										
Socialist	2.66	-.715	.007*	-.072*	(.047)*	.117*	.89	.09	.430	1.45**
Nonsocialist	.42	-.486	.032*	.052*		-.031*	.39	.59	(2.18)	
Nonmetallic Minerals										
Socialist	-7.32	.664	-.136*	.111*	(.118)*	-.406*	.40	.30	.498	7.61
Nonsocialist	-4.41	.038*	.029*	-.049*		-.774	.23	.48	(2.98)	
Chemicals										
Socialist	2.73	-.644	.080*	-.161*	(-.228)*	.673	.65	.20	-.075*	1.80**
Nonsocialist	-1.39	-.118	.106	-.010*		.245	.49	.22	(.90)	
Basic Metals										
Socialist	-9.19	.915	-.162*	.061*	(.181)	-1.043	.71	.27	.600	1.27**
Nonsocialist	-4.70	.150*	.349	-.202		.249*	.31	1.07	(1.52)	
Paper, Printing										
Socialist	1.07	-.702	.260	-.314*	(-.054)*	.525	.92	.10	-.954	22.75
Nonsocialist	-5.35	.334	.021*	-.051		-.362	.46	.30	(8.65)	
Manufacturing										
Socialist	-3.07	.263*	.038*	-.099*	(-.102)*		.42	.28	.163	2.25**
Nonsocialist	-2.76	.155	.107	-.072			.60	.21	(2.15)	
Industry										
Socialist	-3.17	.303*	.051*	-.071*	(-.066)*		.46	.23	.178	3.60
Nonsocialist	-2.40	.144	.075	-.078			.66	.16	(3.05)	

*Insignificant at .10.
**Insignificant at .05.

Sources: Author's computations based on data in Tables 1, 10, and statistical appendix (available from author).

Each measure suffers from a different deficiency. The prewar R measures are subject to improper adjustment owing to a wide margin of error in prewar Eastern European per capita income. The postwar measures, on the other hand, perhaps do not reflect comparative advantage owing to the peculiarities of trade among socialist countries. By definition, R is independent of the other variables, so the other coefficients are unaffected by having two different R values.

Turning first to the question of elasticity differences (as opposed to intercept differences) between the socialist and Western cross-sections, we note that in the majority of sectors the two cross-sections represent two distinct populations. The Chow test, which tests the significance of differences between coefficient sets, is significant (at the .05 level of significance) for light manufactures, heavy manufactures, food products, metal products, heavy intermediate manufactures, nonmetallic minerals, paper and printing and total industry. The remaining sector coefficients-- light manufactures (excluding food products), textiles, chemicals, basic metals and manufacturing--are not significantly different according to the Chow test.

The individual regression coefficients indicate interesting distinctions: In general, the income elasticities of both cross-sections are of the same sign but the absolute values are markedly different. For example, the socialist light manufacturing income elasticity (-.473) is over three times larger (in absolute value) than the nonsocialist elasticity (-.137). The same is true of most of the other sectors: the socialist heavy manufactures elasticity is more than double the nonsocialist elasticity, the food products elasticity is over four time the nonsocialist income elasticity, etc. The generally larger (in absolute value) socialist income elasticities indicate that the expected structural transformation per percentage increase in per capita income is much larger in socialist than in nonsocialist countries.

The socialist population elasticities are almost uniformly insignificant at the .10 level of significance. The only exceptions are metal products and paper and printing, both of which yield significant population elasticities. On the other hand sector population elasticities are generally significant in the Western cross-section. This lack of significance indicates rather clearly the unimportant role which scale factors have played in socialist countries in the determination of sectoral production patterns. This conclusion is especially striking in view of the major importance of scale factors in the West.

One can draw a similar conclusion concerning the role of natural resource endowments in determining sectoral producttion patterns in socialist countries. In general, the socialist R elasticities are insignificant (although the postwar R values tend to be slightly more significant than the prewar R values). It is especially noteworthy that the significant socialist R elasticities invariably differ in sign from the nonsocialist R elasticities. For example, the light manufactures R elasticity is negative, whereas the nonsocialist R elasticity is positive. The same is true of light manufactures (excluding food products), heavy intermediate manufactures and basic metals. In other words, the socialist economies developed their industrial structures with little regard to natural resource endowments.

One can note similar discrepancies concerning the role of the relative level of industrialization (MS) in determining sectoral production patterns. The socialist MS elasticity is generally less significant than its Western counterpart, and one can note discrepancies of significant coefficients (heavy manufactures, paper and printing).

The broad overall conclusion is that the socialist countries adopted their uniform socialist pattern of industrialization without considering the scale and resource requirements which had proved so significant in the development of Western industrialization patterns. Small and natural resource-rich socialist countries adopted industrialization patterns suited to large, natural resource-poor countries. The implication of such policies remain to be investigated.

The socialist and nonsocialist regression intercepts also differ significantly. The direction and significance of these intercept differences is indicated by the socialist dummy and its t value (in parenthesis). In the majority of cases, the socialist dummy is significant at the .10 level of significance, which confirms the significance of socialist and Western intercept differences. As one might expect from the earlier chapters, the socialist dummy coefficients are positive in the case of the heavy manufacturing sectors, manufacturing and industry and negative in the case of the light manufacturing sectors.

Table 20 dealt with individual industrial sectors. Table 21 deals with the overall homogeneity of all manufacturing sectors simultaneously. In earlier sections we established the overall heterogeneity of Western and socialist manufacturing structures by comparing separate USSR and Eastern European structures with Western structures. The postwar socialist cross-section is a combination of USSR and Eastern

TABLE 21

Unadjusted and Adjusted Postwar Socialist and Postwar Western Group Means and F Statistic

	Unadjusted Group Mean			Adjusted Group Mean		
	Socialist	Western	D	Socialist	Western	D
1. Food Prods.	12%	20%	-8%	15%	19%	-4%
2. Light Mfg. (excl. Food)	20%	22%	-2%	19%	22%	-3%
3. Metal Prods.	32%	27%	+5%	30%	27%	+3%
4. Heavy Inter-mediate Mfg.	28%	23%	+6%	27%	23%	+4%
Average Absolute Deviation		5.3%				3.5%
F Statistic					$F_{(4, 45)} =$	2.53*

*Significant at .05.

Source: Author's computations based on data in Tables 1, 10 and statistical appendix.

European structures, so one would expect the covariance results to conform to the results previously established for the USSR and Eastern Europe separately.

Adjustment for per capita income, population, natural resource and MS differences reduces the unadjusted average absolute deviation of socialist from non-socialist group means from 5.3 percent to 3.5 percent, i.e., approximately 34 percent of the original gap is explained by differences in the independent variables. Nevertheless, the remaining group differences are still significant at the .95 level of significance, which means that the overall socialist and nonsocialist cross-section structural differences are significant.

CHAPTER **8** THE SOURCES OF
INDUSTRIAL GROWTH
IN THE USSR AND
EASTERN EUROPE

Having established that the centrally planned socialist
pattern of industrialization differs significantly from the Western pattern, we shall now consider the sources of industrialization in the USSR and postwar Eastern Europe. In other words,
we are interested in the respective roles played by domestic
final and intermediate demand, on the one hand, and by the
foreign export and import sectors on the other hand, in im-
plementing the vast structural transformations which occurred
in the centrally planned socialist economies during the course
of the industrialization, and in whether the sources of industrialization were similar in East and West.

If all sectors grew at an equal pace, structural change
would not occur because sector shares of total product would
remain constant. Structural change occurs because certain
sectors expand more rapidly than total product, thereby increasing their shares of GNP.

The gross output of a given sector can be decomposed in
the following manner:

$$X = D + W + E - M, \qquad (17)$$

where X is the gross output, D is the final domestic demand,
W is the intermediate demand, E is the export demand and M
is the import demand.

Sector supply (S) and sector demand (Q) are defined in the
following manner:

$$S = X + M \qquad (18)$$

$$Q = D + W + E. \qquad (19)$$

Manipulating the above definitions, it can be shown (see
Appendix D) that the change in the sector gross output <u>share</u>
of GNP $[\Delta(X/Y)]$ can be "explained" by three broad factors:

129

$$\Delta(X/Y) = u_1 \Delta \left[\frac{D+W}{Y}\right] + u_1 \Delta \left[\frac{E}{Y}\right] + (u_2 - u_1)S_2/Y_2, \qquad (20)$$

where Y is GNP and u_i is the ratio of sector gross production to sector supply in year i (X_i/S_i).

In other words, equation (20) indicates that a given sector can increase (decrease) its gross product share for three reasons: (a) because sector final and intermediate demand have increased (decreased) their GNP share $\{\Delta [(D+W)/Y] \neq 0\}$, assuming that this change is not offset by import substitution or expansion, i.e., that u_i is constant over time; (b) because sector export demand has increased or decreased its GNP share $[\Delta(E/Y) \neq 0]$, again assuming that this change is not offset by import substitution; and (c) because import substitution or expansion has taken place $(u_2 - u_1 \neq 0)$, i.e., because a larger or smaller portion of total sector supply is produced domestically in period 2 than in period 1. [1]

MEASURING THE SOURCES OF SOCIALIST INDUSTRIALIZATION

In order to measure the sources of industrialization, one must have base and terminal year measures of all the variables given in formula (20). The sector value-added estimates have been described in Chapter 2. Export and import data are generally available for socialist countries; therefore the sole difficulty lies in the computation of sector net to gross product ratios, which are required to convert the value added data into gross production data. [2]

In the next two sections, we compute the sources of long-term industrial growth of sector gross output shares in the USSR and in three Eastern European countries (Czechoslovakia, Hungary and Bulgaria) according to formula (20). The USSR base year is 1912, and the terminal year is 1960; for the three Eastern European countries, selected prewar years are employed as base years and the 1960's are used as terminal years.

SOURCES OF INDUSTRIALIZATION IN THE USSR

Equation (20) is computed in Table 22 for seven USSR manufacturing subsectors and for total manufacturing: Column 1

gives the change in the sector's gross output share of GNP
between 1912 and 1960. Column 2 indicates the change in share
attributed to changes in domestic demand, assuming no import
substitution. The figures in parentheses represent the percentages of the total change explained by the particular factor.
Column 3 is the change in share attributed to the expansion (+)
or contraction (-) of export demand, assuming no import substitution. Column 4 is the share change attributed to import
substitution. Column 5 is that portion of the change in gross
output typically explained in nonsocialist economies by import
substitution. [3]

Several features of Table 22 are worthy of noting. First,
between 28 percent and 43 percent of the 67 percentage point
share increase of the USSR manufacturing sector is explained
by import substitution. The typical Western figure is 50 percent; therefore, import substitution played a less important
relative role in the USSR than in the West.

On the other hand, expansion of domestic demand accounts
for between 66 percent and 75 percent of the manufacturing share
expansion. The comparable Western figure is less than 32
percent. In the USSR, export contraction exerted downward
pressure on the manufacturing share, offsetting the domestic
demand expansion by from -3 percent to -8 percent.

Chenery notes that in the course of Western industrialization, import substitution played a larger relative role in producer goods sectors than in consumer goods sectors, as is
evidenced by the large portions of the metal products, basic
metals, nonmetallic minerals and chemicals share expansions
explained by import substitution and by the small portion of
the food products expansion explained by import substitution
in the West.

The USSR industrialization experience is to a great extent
the reverse of this trend. Only 32 percent of the metal products share increase is explained by import substitution;
whereas 66 percent is explained by domestic demand expansion
(variant 1). The same is true of basic metals: expansion of
domestic and export demand accounts for about 78 percent of
the total share increase, with import substitution accounting
for the remainder. Import substitution accounts for between
11 percent and 14 percent of the nonmetallic minerals expansion, whereas it typically accounts for about 30 percent in
nonsocialist economies. A possible exception is chemicals,

TABLE 22

Sources of Increase of Gross Production, USSR, 1912 and 1960

Variant 1. 8 Percent Return to Capital

	(1)	(2)	(3)	(4)	(5)
	$\Delta(X/Y)$	$u_1\Delta[(D+W)/Y]$	$u_1\Delta(E/Y)$	$(u_2-u_1)S_2/Y_2$	Chenery Ratio
1. Food Products	+5.6% (100)	+4.5% (80)	-1.8% (-32)	+2.8% (50)	(9)
2. Textiles, Clothing, Leather Products	+19.7% (100)	+17.3% (88)	-.8% (-4)	+3.5% (18)	(42)
3. Paper, Printing	+1.2% (100)	+.3% (25)	0% (0)	+.9% (75)	(31)
4. Chemicals	+3.9% (100)	+2.4% (62)	-.1% (-03)	+1.6% (41)	(50)
5. Nonmetallic Minerals	+4.4% (100)	+3.9% (89)	0% (0)	+.5% (11)	(31)
6. Basic Metals	+8.3% (100)	+6.3% (76)	+2% (2)	+1.8% (22)	(55)
7. Metal Products	+23.6% (100)	+15.6% (66)	+.4% (2)	+7.5% (32)	(86-94)
8. Manufacturing	+66.7% (100)	+50.3% (75)	-2.1% (-3)	+18.6% (28)	(50)

Variant 2. 20 Percent Return to Capital

1. Food Products	+1.8% (100)	+1.2% (67)	-1.8% (-100)	+2.4% (133)	(9)
2. Textiles, Clothing, Leather Products	-1.6% (100)	-1.3% (81)	-1.2% (75)	+1.1% (-69)	(42)
3. Paper, Printing	+.8% (100)	+.1% (13)	0% (0)	+.7% (87)	(31)
4. Chemicals	+1.5% (100)	+.5% (33)	-.1% (-7)	+1.1% (73)	(50)
5. Nonmetallic Minerals	+3.7% (100)	+3.2% (86)	0% (0)	+.5% (14)	(31)
6. Basic Metals	+5.2% (100)	+3.8% (73)	+.2% (+4)	+1.2% (23)	(55)
7. Metal Products	+20.5% (100)	+13.4% (65)	+.4% (2)	+6.7% (33)	(86-94)
8. Manufacturing	+31.9% (100)	+20.9% (66)	-2.5% (-8)	+13.7% (43)	(50)

Source: Author's computations based on data in Table 1 in Appendix D.

which does not seem to differ radically from the Western pattern. *

Food products is the sole final consumer goods sector analyzed. Import substitution plays a major role in this sector, accounting for between 50 percent and 133 percent of the share expansion, in comparison with the 9 percent Chenery figure.

It should be stressed that the relative unimportance of import substitution vis-à-vis domestic demand in the USSR does not imply the absolute unimportance of this factor in the course of USSR industrialization. Import substitution alone calls for a 19 percentage point increase in the manufacturing gross output share, which is quite substantial. The point is that the expansion of domestic demand was so substantial that it swamped the import substitution effect.

Insofar as the absolute expansion of the USSR manufacturing sector outpaced the typical Western expansion, no conclusions can be drawn concerning the absolute role of import substitution in the USSR vis-à-vis the West. Comparable figures are not available, but the absolute role of import substitution in the USSR must have been great owing to the autarkic nature of Soviet trade policy.

SOURCES OF INDUSTRIALIZATION
IN EASTERN EUROPE

In order to compare the causes of industrialization in Eastern European with the Soviet experience, equation (20) is computed and recorded in Table 23 for three Eastern European countries: Czechoslovakia (1929 and 1965), Hungary (1937 and 1963) and Bulgaria (1936 and 1963). The interpretation of Table 23 is the same as that of Table 22.

---

*A qualitative remark is in order at this point: If the above analysis had been carried out using an immediately preplan period year as a base, the impact of import substitution would have been negligible in all sectors, owing to the exceedingly low trade volumes which followed the Revolution and Civil War. For this reason, the USSR import substitution figures of Table 22 differ from the standard concept, which involves a reduction of the portion of total supply imported from one period to the next. Import substitution in the USSR must be understood in a different sense, as a failure to return to previously established trade ratios.

TABLE 23

Sources of Increase of Gross Production, Manufacturing,
Czechoslovakia, Hungary, Bulgaria

Czechoslovakia, 1929 and 1965

		(1)	(2)	(3)	(4)
		$\Delta(X/Y)$	$u_1\Delta[(D+W)/Y]$	$u_1\Delta(E/Y)$	$(u_2-u_1)S_2/Y_2$
1.	Food Products	-1.3%	-1.7%	-2.0%	+2.5%
		(100)	(130)	(154)	(-192)
2.	Textiles, Clothing Leather	-14.6%	-9.7%	-7.0%	+2.0%
		(100)	(66)	(48)	(-14)
3.	Paper, Printing	+.8%	+1.1%	-.4%	+.1%
		(100)	(138)	(-50)	(13)
4.	Chemicals	+4.5%	+2.2%	0	+2.3%
		(100)	(49)		(51)
5.	Nonmetallic Minerals	+.5%	+1.1%	-1.1%	+.5%
		(100)	(220)	(-220)	(100)
6.	Basic Metals	+11.0%	+4.6%	-.2%	+7.1%
		(100)	(42)	(-2)	(60)
7.	Metal Products	+16.7%	+12.1%	+4.6%	0
		(100)	(72)	(28)	
8.	Manufacturing	+17.6%	+9.7%	-6.2%	+14.5%
		(100)	(55)	(-35)	(82)

Hungary, 1937 and 1963
Variant 1. 8 Percent Return on Capital

		(1)	(2)	(3)	(4)
1.	Food Products	+10.1%	+9.9%	+1.4%	-1.1%
		(100)	(98)	(14)	(-11)
2.	Textiles, Clothing, Leather	+8.0%	+5.0%	+.7%	+2.3%
		(100)	(63)	(9)	(29)
3.	Paper, Printing	-.7%	-1.1%	0	+.4%
		(100)	(157)		(-57)
4.	Chemicals	+9.9%	+5.7%	+.3%	+3.8%
		(100)	(58)	(3)	(38)
5.	Nonmetallic Minerals	+2.9%	+3.1%	0	-.2%
		(100)	(107)		(-7)
6.	Basic Metals	+12.1%	+8.4%	+.1%	+3.4%
		(100)	(70)	(1)	(28)
7.	Metal Products	+29.0%	+18.5%	+3.1%	+6.4%
		(100)	(64)	(11)	(23)
8.	Manufacturing	+71.3%	+49.5%	+5.6%	+15.1%
		(100)	(69)	(8)	(21)

134

Variant 2. 20 Percent Return on Capital

		(1)	(2)	(3)	(4)
1.	Food Products	+2.4% (100)	+2.4% (100)	+1.4% (58)	-1.4% (-58)
2.	Textiles, Clothing, Leather	+4.4% (100)	+2.3% (52)	+.7% (16)	+1.4% (32)
3.	Paper, Printing	-1.4% (100)	-1.6% (114)	0	+.2% (-14)
4.	Chemicals	+6.3% (100)	+3.8% (60)	+.3% (5)	+2.2% (35)
5.	Nonmetallic Minerals	+1.9% (100)	+2.1% (111)	0	-.2% (-11)
6.	Basic Metals	+6.9% (100)	+4.8% (70)	+.1% (2)	+2.0% (28)
7.	Metal Products	+21.4% (100)	+13.5% (63)	+3.1% (15)	+4.8% (22)
8.	Manufacturing	+41.9% (100)	+27.3% (65)	+5.6% (13)	+9.0% (22)

Bulgaria, 1936 and 1963

Variant 1. 8 Percent Return on Capital

		(1)	(2)	(3)	(4)
1.	Food Products	+22.3% (100)	+19.9% (89)	+2.0% (9)	+.4% (2)
2.	Textiles, Clothing, Leather	+18.7% (100)	+15.2% (81)	+1.3% (7)	+2.2% (12)
3.	Paper, Printing	+.7% (100)	+.4% (57)	0	+.3% (43)
4.	Chemicals	+8.6% (100)	+3.9% (45)	-.1% (-1)	+4.8% (56)
5.	Nonmetallic Minerals	+2.0% (100)	+1.6% (80)	0	+.4% (20)
6.	Basic Metals	+9.6% (100)	+.6% (6)	0	+9.0% (94)
7.	Metal Products	+18.4% (100)	+3.2% (17)	+.4% (2)	+14.8% (80)
8.	Manufacturing	+80.3% (100)	+44.8% (56)	+3.6% (5)	+31.9% (40)

(Continued)

TABLE 23--Continued

Variant 2. 20 Percent Return on Capital

	(1)	(2)	(3)	(4)
1. Food Products	+10. 1% (100)	+7. 8% (77)	+2. 0% (20)	+. 3% (3)
2. Textiles, Clothing, Leather	+12. 7% (100)	+11. 1% (87)	+1. 3% (10)	+. 3% (2)
3. Paper, Printing	+. 2% (100)	+. 1% (50)	0	+. 1% (50)
4. Chemicals	+6. 4% (100)	+3. 0% (47)	-. 1 (-2)	+3. 5% (55)
5. Nonmetallic Minerals	+1. 7% (100)	+1. 4% (82)	0	+. 3% (18)
6. Basic Metals	+6. 4% (100)	+. 4% (6)	0	+6. 0% (94)
7. Metal Products	+14. 1% (100)	+2. 3% (16)	+. 4% (3)	11. 4% (81)
8. Manufacturing	+51. 6% (100)	+26. 1% (51)	+3. 6% (7)	+21. 9% (42)

Source: Table 1 in Appendix D

The sources of industrialization were not uniform in the three countries, a result not unexpected in view of the widely divergent levels of development which the three countries had attained prior to World War II.

The Czechoslovak pattern is quite unusual. Import substitution was the primary source of industrial expansion, accounting for about 82 percent of the 18 percentage point share increase of the manufacturing sector. Total demand (domestic final and intermediate demand and export demand) played a less significant role, accounting for the remainder. Total demand, however, is the sum of two offsetting factors: Domestic demand expansion accounted for 55 percent of the manufacturing expansion, which was cancelled to a great extent by export demand contraction. This indicates that Czechoslovak industrialization would have been much more rapid if the export sector had maintained its prewar levels, in view of the rapid expansion of domestic demand and the rapid rate of import substitution.

The Hungarian experience reveals a different picture. Depending upon the variant chosen, import substitution accounted for only 21-22 percent of the expansion of the manufacturing sector. The principal source of industrialization was the expansion of domestic demand, which accounted for between 65 and 69 percent of the manufacturing share expansion. A less significant role was played by export expansion, which accounted for between 8 and 13 percent of the manufacturing expansion.

Domestic demand expansion also dominates Bulgarian industrialization. Domestic demand accounts for between 51 and 56 percent of the manufacturing share expansion, whereas import substitution accounts for between 40 and 42 percent. Export expansion is relegated to a minor role, accounting for from 5 percent to 7 percent of the manufacturing share expansion.

It is interesting to note the factors behind the expansion of the metal products (engineering) sector in the three countries studied, insofar as metal products was the most rapidly expanding sector in all three countries. In Czechoslovakia, there was no import substitution in the metal products sector; rather, all share increases were accounted for by domestic demand (72 percent) and export demand (28 percent). At the other extreme, 80 percent of the expansion of metal products in Bulgaria was accounted for by import substitution, the other 20 percent being accounted for almost entirely by domestic demand. In Hungary, import substitution accounted for only 23 percent of the metal products expansion, with domestic demand (about 63 percent) and export demand (between 11 and 15 percent)

accounting for the rest. These results, combined with the
USSR results, suggest the magnitude of the expansion of the
engineering sectors in the course of socialist industrialization.

SUMMARY

In broad terms, the sources of industrialization of the
centrally planned socialist economies have been rather similar:
The expansion of domestic demand in accordance with centrally
planned production targets has been the principal source of
socialist industrialization. The sole exception to this rule is
Czechoslovakia, where import substitution outweighed domestic
demand expansion; nevertheless, even in Czechoslovakia, domestic demand expansion played a much more important
relative role than was typical in the course of Western industrialization. The socialist experience is in marked contrast
with the Western pattern, which was dominated by import substitution, especially in the investment goods sectors. Export
expansion (Hungary and Bulgaria) and export contraction (USSR
and Czechoslovakia) played relatively minor roles in the socialist industrialization process.
    The above comparison of sources of growth in socialist
and capitalist countries reveals a basic distinction between
the two industrialization patterns. In the West, structural
charge was primarily a response to changing supply conditions,
augmented by income effects from the demand side, especially
for the producer goods sectors. In the centrally planned socialist economies, the radical restructuring of domestic demand
in accordance with planners' preferences determined the direction of structural change, especially in the producer goods
sectors.

NOTES

1. Formula (20) was derived in ratio form from the
definitions in Hollis Chenery, "Patterns of Industrial Growth. "

2. The centrally planned socialist countries studied in
this section are the USSR, Czechoslovakia, Hungary and Bulgaria. These countries recommend themselves because presocialism industrial data are available and because they were

not subject to significant territorial changes at the end of World
War II, as were Poland and East Germany.

Two methods have been employed to compute the net
to gross product ratios of the USSR and postwar Eastern European countries. The first was to take actual sector value added
(net of turnover taxes plus subsidies) and divide by sector gross
product (also net of turnover taxes plus subsidies). The basic
drawbacks of this approach are twofold: Data on indirect taxation and subsidies are generally insufficient; and insofar as
market prices do not include a return to capital, the resulting
ratios diverge from the theoretically correct ratios. However,
both the numerator and the denominator suffer from this defect,
it is possible that the errors will cancel. The 1965 Czechoslovak sector value added to gross product ratios were computed
in this manner from the data in Milos Stadnik, Some Problems
of Economic Growth in Czechoslovakia.

The second method was to take the ratios of wage costs
to value added, which were derived in the course of computing
value added, and divide them by the ratios of wage costs to
total costs. This method recommends itself insofar as the data
necessary for the computations are generally available and insofar as the first component imputes a return to capital. The
drawbacks are twofold: The choice of the imputed rate of return to capital affects the eventual outcome; and the numerator
includes an imputed return to capital but a portion of the denominator (the cost of intermediate products) does not. In order
to compensate for these drawbacks, two variants have been
computed, one imputing an 8 percent return and the second a
20 percent return to capital, on the assumption that the true
net to gross ratios lie between these two extremes. This
second method was used to compute USSR 1960, Hungarian
1963 and Bulgarian 1963 ratios.

The USSR 1912, Czechoslovak 1929, Hungarian 1937
and Bulgarian 1936 ratios were derived from official gross and
net product data. The data are recorded in Appendix D, Table 2.

3.   Chenery, op. cit., pp. 641-43. In some sectors, the
Chenery figures were aggregated using the 1960 USSR value
added structure as weights.

CHAPTER **9** SOCIALIST
INDUSTRIALIZATION:
A SUMMARY
APPRAISAL

Chapters 1-8 examined the socialist pattern of industrialization, as represented by the USSR historical pattern and by
the postwar socialist cross-sectional pattern, and the nonsocialist (Western) pattern of industrialization, as represented
by US, UK, German and Canadian time series patterns and by
two Western cross-sectional patterns. The series of covariance
and regression residual tests revealed rather conclusively
the heterogeneous nature of the USSR historical pattern and
the postwar Eastern European cross-sectional pattern vis-à-vis
the historical Western patterns and the two nonsocialist cross-
sectional patterns. At the same time, structural differences
between the USSR and Eastern European patterns were shown
to be insignificant.

Prior to the beginning of the plan era, the structure of the
USSR manufacturing sector was skewed quite heavily in the
direction of light manufactures, which in 1929 was approximately 28 percent above the normal level expected of a country
with the same income, population and natural resource levels.
The same picture held for the major subsectors of light manufacturing: food products was approximately 15 percent and
light manufacturing (excluding food products) was some 40
percent above normal. At the same time, heavy manufacturing
was approximately 36 percent below normal; the largest de-
ficit relative to normal shares was in heavy intermediate manufacturing, which was about 50 percent below normal.

Within eight years, this pattern had been reversed. The
magnitude of the structural transformations which occurred
within the manufacturing sector during the initial plan periods
is illustrated by the fact that by 1937 heavy manufacturing had
attained a share 20 percent above the normal share expected
of a Western country with identical income, population and
natural resource endowments. The rapid increase of heavy

140

manufacturing was spearheaded by metal products, which was
37 percent above normal in 1937. The decline of light manufacturing between 1929 and 1937 was equally dramatic. Relative to normal patterns, light manufacturing had dropped to
a value-added share 21 percent below normal by 1937.

In 1929, the manufacturing sector's share of total product
was 21 percent, which was slightly less than the normal ratio
expected for that level of development. By 1937, the USSR
ratio had risen to 29 percent, which was 5 percentage points,
above the normal 24 percent ratio.

The trends established during the 1930's carried over
into the postwar period. Despite rising per capita income,
the structure of the USSR manufacturing sector remained
skewed in the direction of heavy manufactures, relative to
normal structures, throughout the postwar period. The 1960's,
however, revealed some weak signs of convergence of the
USSR and normal patterns. The ratio of manufacturing to
GNP declined from its 1937 peak of 29 percent to 28 percent,
which was slightly below the normal 30 percent share. The
deviations of USSR heavy manufactures and metal products
shares from normal shares narrowed slightly during the postwar period. On the other hand, the light manufactures sector
exhibited no tendency towards convergence.

Comparisons of long-term USSR, US, Canadian and UK
industrial structure trends in terms of income elasticities indicated that the precipitous decline of the USSR light manufactures share was not matched by the historical experience
of these four industrialized Western countries, although all
four yielded declining light manufactures shares. The same
is true for the rise of the heavy manufactures and metal products shares in the USSR, although the prewar German trends
intersect the USSR trends at high income levels. The German
trends, however, represent hypothetical extrapolations of
pre-World War II elasticities, so it is difficult to compare the
two at high income levels. The distinctive feature of the USSR
historical industrial development pattern was the USSR's
ability to attain extremely high heavy manufactures shares
and low light manufactures shares at relatively low levels of
per capita income.

Another feature of the USSR development pattern was the
rapid increase of value added per worker in heavy industries
relative to value added per worker in light industries during
the 1930's. The emergence of large intersectoral value added
per worker differentials reflects the Soviet investment policy
during this period, which resulted in the allocation of investment goods to the heavy industrial sector on a priority basis.

The postwar Eastern European industrialization pattern
paralleled that of the USSR during its plan period quite closely.
Homogeneity tests reveal remarkable similarities between
USSR and Eastern European structures, with the possible
exception that the Eastern Europeans tended to place more
emphasis on heavy intermediate manufactures within the heavy
manufactures sector, whereas the Soviets concentrated more
on engineering output (relative to normal shares).

Comparisons of prewar and postwar (socialist) Eastern
European industrial structures reveal marked structural
changes between the two periods which cannot be explained by
changes in the level of development. The same is true of comparisons of prewar Eastern European industrial structures
and preplan USSR structures in terms of value-added shares
and labor force shares; however, comparisons of postwar
Eastern European and USSR plan structures show that structural
differences were virtually eliminated in the postwar period.

Cross-sectional elasticities derived from separate postwar socialist and nonsocialist samples yield additional insights
into the socialist pattern of industrialization. In general,
structural responses to changes in per capita income levels
were broadly similar for both samples, although the socialist
sector income elasticities are much larger in terms of absolute
values. However, structural changes occurred within the
socialist sample with little regard to scale requirements and
natural resource endowments, as is shown by conflicting scale
and resource elasticities between the two samples. This is
probably the result of the general autarky policy employed
throughout the socialist bloc to regulate the rate of import
substitution. Comparisons of actual trade ratios with potential
trade ratios reveal the marked underutilization of trade potential
throughout the socialist bloc.

An examination of the sources of industrialization in the
USSR and Eastern Europe reveals broad uniformities within
the socialist bloc. In all cases, the prime moving force behind socialist industrialization was the expansion of domestic
demand, which relegated import substitution to a secondary
role. Only in Czechoslovakia did import substitution outweigh
domestic demand as a source of industrialization. Despite
efforts to establish a common market within the socialist
bloc, export expansion generally played a negative or insignificant role as a source of industrialization bloc. It is interesting to note the minor role played by import substitution
in the expansion of the metal products sector (with the exception of Bulgaria), in view of its importance in nonsocialist

countries.   These facts do not, however, deny the important
absolute role played by import substitution, owing to the
autarkic trade policy.   The point is that the expansion of
domestic demand was great enough to overwhelm the import
substitution effect.

CONSEQUENCES OF SOCIALIST INDUSTRIALIZATION

The goals of socialist industrialization most generally
cited are (1) to achieve rapid growth of total product and increases in the standard of living; (2) to increase military
capacity; (3) to bring about independence from capitalist markets; and (4) to provide an industrial base sufficient to support
the industrialization efforts of less advanced socialist economies,
thus allowing them to remain independent of capitalist markets.[1]
Let us examine socialist industrialization in light of these
objectives.

One of the most basic characteristics of the industrial
development pattern chosen by the socialist central planners
of the USSR and Eastern Europe to achieve these objectives is
the marked predominance of the heavy industrial sector over
the light industrial sector relative to the role played by these
sectors elsewhere.   The reason for this choice has already
been discussed.   It is a generally accepted principle in the
socialist world that the rates of growth of total output and military power are positively correlated with the proportion of
total resources which an economy devotes to heavy industry,
and if the economy is to remain independent of outside influences,
these heavy industrial resources must be produced domestically,
not imported.

In a closed economy in which capital is the only limiting
factor, factor supply and consumption are independent and
capital cannot be transferred between the producer and consumer goods sectors, it can be demonstrated in terms of
abstract growth models that the rates of growth of investment,
consumption and total product, in the long run, approach the
ratio of the output of the investment goods sector ploughed
back into the investment goods sector to the (constant) capital
coefficient of the investment goods sector.[2]

Insofar as sector capital coefficients are determined primarily by the state of technology, the crucial policy variable
under the control of planners is the percentage of investment
goods allocated to (reinvested in) the investment goods sectors.

In determining the optimal reinvestment ratio, socialist planners must choose between a series of consumption, investment
and total product streams over time. A high ratio yields low
consumption levels in early years that is offset by high rates
of growth of consumption in later years, whereas a low ratio
yields high consumption levels in early years coupled with
moderate rates of growth of consumption in later years. The
ratio actually chosen by socialist planners would reflect their
time preferences concerning present and future consumption
as well as the relative weights attached to consumer and producer goods.

It would be foolhardy to attempt to describe socialist industrial growth patterns in terms of an abstract growth model
which reduces to one policy variable because the assumptions
upon which the model is based do not correspond to reality.
Labor, especially skilled labor, has been a limiting factor;
the supply of labor and consumption are related; labor can be
substituted for capital; and capital can be transferred among
major sectors. Nevertheless, the model serves a useful
purpose in that it describes the type of thinking which went into the formation of planners' preferences.

Socialist planners opted for high ratios of investment
goods ploughed back into the investment goods sector relative
to the ratio chosen by market forces in the West. As was
noted in Chapter 6, the high ratio was implemented by ploughing
back the output of the investment goods sector at the expense
of capital-intensive light industrial sectors, such as food
products, paper and printing. Measured according to normal
shares, the anticonsumer goods bias of socialist planners was
felt primarily in those consumer goods sectors which tended
to absorb large amounts of capital; labor-intensive consumer
goods sectors, such as textiles, clothing and leather products,
fared much better relative to normal levels. This policy is
indicative of the low relative shadow price imputed by socialist
planners to labor relative to capital.

As a result of the above policy, the socialist economies
were able to generate relatively high ratios of investment to
GNP, the major portion of this investment being produced
domestically. Not only were the socialist heavy manufactures
to GNP ratios high by normal standards (Chapter 6), but the
socialist investment ratios were also extremely high by international standards.* One may well ask whether this policy
enabled the socialist economies to achieve their objectives.

---

*We compared the socialist investment ratios with the
ratios of 18 industrialized Western Countries. The Western

The long-term USSR growth rates of total product and the post-war growth rates in Eastern Europe are quite high. The long-term USSR 1928-40, 1950-58 growth rate of total product of 5.2 percent is rapid but has been exceeded over long periods in other countries.[3] The average postwar rate of growth of total product in Eastern Europe of 5.1 percent was roughly matched by the average growth rate in postwar Western Europe.[4] Owing to the relatively poor performance of agriculture and services in the socialist countries, inter-country comparisons on the basis of growth rates of industrial production would yield generally higher rates for the socialist countries. To what extent can these high growth rates be attributed to socialist industrialization policy?

We performed an extremely rough (and inadequate) test of the relationship between economic structure, investment ratios and long-term, growth rates by regressing and correlating long-term growth rates against the investment ratio and the respective heavy and light manufactures shares of total product.

Our sample included 26 observations of investment ratios, industrial production structures and long-term growth rates (annual rates over a seven - to 10-year period, depression years not included). Ten of the observations were for socialist economies. Only industrialized countries were included in the sample to avoid the impact of massive foreign aid on growth rates.

The correlation and regression results are as follows:

1. The cross-correlation coefficient of growth rates and investment ratios is + .75, which is significant at .05.

2. The cross-correlation coefficient of growth rates and the ratios of heavy manufactures to light manufactures is + .56, which is also significant at .05.

3. The cross-correlation coefficient of investment ratios and the GNP shares of heavy manufactures is + .31, which is insignificant at .05. This means that the GNP share of heavy manufactures is not a simple surrogate for the investment ratio.

---

sample included the high postwar Japanese, West German and Norwegian ratios. The average socialist ratio is 27.8 percent of GNP; the average Western ratio is 20.8 percent of GNP; and the overall average is 22.9 percent of GNP. The $F_{(1,23)}$ ratio of 6.30 is significant at .02, which demonstrates the significance of group differences.

4.   The regression of light manufactures' GNP shares and heavy manufactures' GNP shares on growth rates yields the following regression equation:

growth rate = 4.36 -.155 light manufacturing
share +.107 heavy manufacturing share.   (21)

Both coefficients are significant at .95 and the coefficient of determination is .36.

The above regression and correlation results support the general validity of the socialist industrialization model as far as growth rates are concerned. More rigorous tests of the impact of the structure of production on growth rates would involve a limited sample of essentially closed economies or covariance adjustments for the impact of imports of invest- ment goods upon growth rates.

Granted the crude nature of the above empirical tests, coupled with the complex nature of growth rates which generally are heavily influenced by technological factors, the significance of the correlation coefficients and the portion of variance ex- plained by investment ratios and by heavy manufacturing ratios is surprising. The lack of significant correlation between the investment ratio and the GNP share of heavy manufactures, along with the significant correlation of the GNP share of heavy manufactures and growth rates, provides some evidence that the growth impact of domestically produced capital equipment is perhaps different from the growth impact of imported capital equipment, possibly because of external effects on technology and on the labor force which arise in the course of domestic production. A more convincing demonstration of this phenomenon would be desirable insofar it is a possible argument in favor of autarky.

Even though one can demonstrate a general correlation between the rate of growth of GNP, on the one hand, and the structure of the final use of GNP (the investment ratio) and the structure of output (the heavy industry ratio), on the other hand, an evaluation of Soviet and Eastern European industria- lization policies in terms of the growth objective remains far beyond the scope of this study. The relationship between growth rates and investment ratios is by nature complex, depending not only on the investment ratio per se, but also on the com- position of investment.* In order to be able to evaluate the

---

*The 1955 US and USSR investment figures indicate the complexities of the problem. In 1955, about 36 percent of total US gross fixed investment and about 13 percent of total USSR gross fixed investment were devoted to residential con- struction. See Economic Report of the President, 1968, p.

relationship of growth and industrialization policy in the USSR
and in Eastern Europe, one must be able to designate some
optimal growth rate which should accompany a whole complex
of variables, such as investment rates, investment distributions and inter-sectoral production structures. Of course,
not enough is known about the above relationships to make
such a determination.

One can only indicate that ceterus paribus, the USSR and
Eastern European policy of gearing the industrial structure
to generate high investment ratios contributed to the high GNP
growth rates. Whether these rates were in any way optimal
is a completely different question. *

Although this study, does not permit a more precise evaluation of socialist industrialization policy in terms of the growth
objectives, it is nevertheless within the scope of this study
to investigate the impact of socialist industrialization policy
on the final use distribution of GNP, i.e., on consumption.

A closed economy, which devotes the major portion of its
resources to the current production of investment goods de-
presses base year consumption standards. A great deal of
attention has been devoted to the rates of growth of per capita

---

210; Richard Moorsteen and Raymond Powell, The Soviet
Capital Stock, 1928-1962, pp. 325, 329. If residential construction has a low growth impact, one can expect higher
growth rates for the USSR even if the overall investment
ratios were equal.

*According to Moorsteen and Powell, the Soviet regime
in 1929 had decided upon the route of growth which it wished
to follow but found itself faced with a transformation function
ill-suited to the achievement of these goals. The First Five-
Year Plan can therefore be viewed as a vast reshaping of the
Soviet transformation function in order to approach the "turnpike" of rapid growth. The results of this study seem to
confirm this point of view: The vast transformations of the
USSR industrial structure took place primarily between 1929
and 1937; thereafter, the structure more or less reproduced
itself. It is an interesting exercise to extrapolate the Soviet
growth patterns under the assumption that a particular base
structure is a necessary precondition for rapid secular growth.
If one assumes that the 1937 structure was the required
structure for turnpike growth, one can conclude that the USSR
would have attained the turnpike well after 1962 for the 1962
normal USSR structure is essentially equivalent to the 1937,
actual USSR structure, (Appendix C, Table 2). See Moorsteen
and Powell, The Soviet Capital Stock, 1928-1962, pp. 299-301.

consumption and the ratio of consumption to GNP in socialist economies, [5] and this study does not have anything vitally new to offer. The reason for reopening the whole question of consumption ratios is to determine the impact of socialist production patterns on consumption levels and to examine the socialist data for signs of convergence towards nonsocialist consumption proportions.

In a centrally planned socialist economy, the ratio of consumption to total product is essentially a policy variable, in the same manner as the investment ratio. The central plan determines the investment ratio (in a closed economy) by determining the volume of investment goods to be produced; conversely, the central plan determines the consumption ratio by determining the volume of consumption goods to be produced. Once these fixed volumes of consumption goods are produced, demand and supply can be equated either by adjusting indirect taxation rates (so that changing retail prices eliminate excess demand and supply) or by direct or de facto physical rationing.* Indeed, the policy of maximizing the expansion of the investment goods sector depends to a great extent upon the ability of the central authority to create savings equal to the physical capacity to invest.

It is true that the consumption ratio cannot be strictly determined by central planners insofar as consumer demand can be satisfied by individuals and production units outside of the planners' competence, such as individual services, handicraft production, and agricultural produce from private plots. Nevertheless, forms of fiscal and social discrimination and administrative regulations can be employed to minimize this lack of direct control.

An important feature of the Soviet industrialization model is its conclusion that although high investment rates necessarily result in a sacrifice of base year consumption, at some time in the future the high investment ratio consumption path must intersect and surpass the alternative low investment path.

---

*It is also possible to control personal disposable incomes by direct taxation, social insurance payments, government bond purchases and wage policy. All were tried in the USSR, but major reliance was placed on indirect taxation and rationing. As a result, the planning decision to devote the major portion of output to investment was implemented on the consumption side by placing enormous tax burdens on the Soviet population. In the late 1930's, about 70 percent of consumer money income was taxed away. See Franklyn Holzman, Soviet Taxation, pp. 2-8, 251-52.

The following is taken from the official Soviet political economy textbook:

> The creation of a heavy industry within a short period of time forced the population of the Soviet Union to make heavy sacrifices. Because the Soviet state had to allocate a huge volume of its resources to the development of heavy industry, the Soviet state was forced to limit the production of mass consumer goods, which made it difficult to meet the growing needs of the workers and hindered the increase in real wages. But at the same time, socialist industrialization created the necessary basis for the rapid growth of consumption in the future in that it equipped all branches of industry and agriculture with modern technology. [6]

One of the results derived from the earlier analysis of the USSR production residuals over time and from the Eastern European cross-section residuals is that there has been relatively little convergence towards nonsocialist production patterns. Therefore, it is of interest to determine whether this phenomenon is true for the demand side also, in view of what was said above.

To compare socialist and Western consumption patterns and to investigate the convergence of consumption patterns, we computed some simple quadratic regressions of per capita income (and per capita income squared) on the GNP shares of personal consumption expenditures and of personal consumption expenditures plus communal services (government expenditures minus administration and defense) for a cross-section of Western and socialist countries. The cross-section data are recorded in Appendix E.

In the course of modern economic growth, the share of personal consumption declines owing to the increase of total government expenditures and of gross investment. The trend in total consumption expenditures (including government consumption expenditures for health, education and welfare) is also downward because the moderate increases in the share of government consumption expenditures over time are more than offset by the decline in the share of private consumption expenditures. [7] Our cross-section regressions on personal consumption expenditures and communal services conform to these historical trends. The nonsocialist cross-section regressions of per capita income on the GNP shares of personal consumption expenditures (PCE), communal services (CS) and total consumption expenditures (TCE) yield negative, positive and negative income coefficients, respectively.

Before turning to the cross-section results, we would like to note the degree to which socialist planners have been able to determine consumption levels by controlling the structure of output and the rate of import substitution. Table 24 gives the indexes of the relative change in the light manufactures share of GNP and the index of the relative change in the share of personal consumption expenditures of GNP in four socialist countries and five nonsocialist industrialized countries. The calculations were made from data in Appendix E.

The outstanding feature of Table 24 is the greater degree of (positive) correlation between changes in the light manufactures share of GNP and changes in the personal consumption expenditures share of GNP in socialist countries. The correlation coefficients between the two indexes are +.89 for the four socialist countries and -.33 for the five nonsocialist countries.

TABLE 24

Index of Change in the Light Manufactures GNP Share
and Index of Change in the GNP Share of Personal
Consumption Expenditures, Selected Socialist and
Nonsocialist Economies

		PCE ÷ GNP	Light Mfg: ÷ GNP
1.	USSR 1962 (1928=100)	77	71
2.	East Germany 1963 (1936=100)	81	74
3.	Czechoslovakia 1965 (1929=100)	59	53
4.	Hungary 1963 (1936=100)	77	82
5.	US 1950-59 (1929-38=100)	82	93
6.	UK 1950-58 (1900-14=100)	85	80
7.	Canada 1950-59 (1890-1910 =100)	77	94
8.	Germany 1891-1913 (1871-90=100)	94	98
9.	Japan 1950-59 (1934-36= 100)	91	52

Sources: Socialist PCE data from Appendix E. Non-socialist data from Kuznets, Modern Economic Growth, pp. 238-239; K. Okhawa, The Growth Rate of the Japanese Economy Since 1878, p. 242.

The relatively low correlation between the light manufactures share of GNP and the personal consumption expenditures share of GNP in nonsocialist countries is explained in part by their tendency to substitute high-income elasticity services, such as recreation, private education and personal care, for manufactured consumer products and by import substitution and expansion in the consumer goods sphere. In the socialist countries, import substitution has been controlled administratively and therefore has not responded to income-import elasticities. Also, the bulk of consumer purchases in socialist countries of services was concentrated in low-elasticity sectors, such as housing, light and water, whereas high income-elasticity services, such as domestic service and financial services, were either nonexistent or were provided outside of the framework of the market economy. For this reason, no upward trends were generated in the service sector to counter the declining manufactured consumer goods shares.

Granted the positive correlation in socialist countries between the relative decline in manufactured consumer goods and the decline in personal consumption ratios, one can expect extremely rapid declines in consumption ratios relative to normal nonsocialist trends because of the extreme nature of the relative decline of manufactured consumer goods in socialist countries compared with normal industrialization patterns. In the following section we compare shares of personal consumption expenditures (PCE ÷ GNP) and of personal consumption expenditures and government communal services combined (TCE ÷ GNP) in four socialist countries over time with their so-called "normal" counterparts, derived from cross-section quadratic regressions with per capita income as the independent variable from a sample of 23 nonsocialist economies, taken from Appendix E.

Socialist consumption gaps are defined as negative deviations of actual consumption shares from the normal shares predicted by the regression parameters; such a gap would be indicated by a nonrandom array of socialist negative deviations from predicted values. The sum of capitalist deviations is zero as a result of the least-squares method of estimation. Actual and normal Russian PCE/GNP, CS/GNP and TCE/GNP values from 1928 to 1962 are computed in Table 25. Actual and normal consumption shares are also given for Hungary (1936, 1955, 1964), Poland (1956, 1964), Czechoslovakia (1929, 1956, 1964) and East Germany (1936, 1955, 1964). With the exception of Poland, precentrally planned socialism consumption ratios are given to provide historical perspective. The Russian and postwar Eastern European consumption ratios are drawn from independent Western studies which employ factor cost concepts.[8]

TABLE 25

Actual and Normal Ratios of Personal Consumption Expenditures (PCE), Communal Consumption Expenditures (CS), and Total Consumption Expenditures (TCE) to GNP, USSR and Eastern Europe. Selected Years

		PCE/GNP Actual	PCE/GNP Normal	D	CS/GNP Actual	CS/GNP Normal	D	TCE/GNP Actual	TCE/GNP Normal	D
USSR	1928	65	69	-4	4	5	-1	69	74	-5
	1937	53	67	-14	10	5	+5	63	72	-9
	1955	49	64	-15	9	7	+2	58	71	-13
	1962	50	62	-12	8	7	+1	58	69	-11
Hungary	1936	65	68	-3	-	-	-	-	-	-
	1955	51	68	-17	11	3	+8	62	71	-9
	1964	50	64	-14	-	-	-	-	-	-
Poland	1956	57	67	-10	4	5	-1	61	72	-11
	1964	53	64	-11	-	-	-	-	-	-
Czechoslovakia	1929	75	68	+7	-	-	-	-	-	-
	1956	44	63	-19	7	7	0	51	70	-19
	1964	40	61	-21	-	-	-	-	-	-
East Germany	1936	61	65	-4	-	-	-	-	-	-
	1955	43	64	-21	12	6	+6	55	70	-15
	1964	39	61	-22	-	-	-	-	-	-

Sources: Actual consumption ratios and per capita income estimates are from Appendix E. The normal ratios are calculated from the following normal regression equations:

$$PCE/GNP = 75.6 - .0176I + .0000050I^2$$
$$CS/GNP = -2.1 - .0072I + .0000026I^2$$
$$TCE/GNP = 77.7 - .0104I + .0000024I^2$$

The R^2 values are .33, .26, and .22, respectively.

The standard errors are 6.7, 2.2 and 6.7, respectively.

The number of observations is 23.

The t values are insignificant because of the almost perfect correlation between income (I) and income squared (I^2).

The per capita income coefficients are all significant at the .05 level of significance when the quadratic term is omitted.

The following features of Table 25 should be noted:

1. The centrally planned socialist PCE ratios are, without exception, well below the normal predicted ratios during both the mid-1950's and mid-1960's. The smallest socialist deviation is the 1956 Polish deviation of -10 percentage points; the largest is the -22 percentage point East German deviation of 1964.

2. The centrally planned socialist CS ratios (available only for the mid-1950's) are generally above the normal predicted ratios, with the exception of Poland in 1956, which is two percentage points below normal. The USSR in 1928 yields a CS ratio five percentage points above the normal ratio; the USSR CS ratio is two percentage points above normal in 1962. The largest CS deviations are yielded by East Germany (1955) and Hungary (1955), which are six and eight percentage points above the normal ratios, respectively.

3. The generally above-normal socialist CS ratios are not sufficient to eliminate or substantially reduce the socialist private consumption gaps. The socialist TCE ratios of the mid-1950's are all negative, ranging from a low of nine percentage points below normal in the USSR (1937) and Hungary (1955) to a high of 19 percentage points below normal in Czechoslovakia (1956).

4. The prewar (nonsocialist) Eastern European PCE ratios and the 1928 (socialism without central planning) USSR PCE and TCE ratios are closer to their normal counterparts than are the centrally planned socialist ratios. The USSR 1928, Hungarian 1936 and East German 1936 ratios are only five percentage points, three percentage points and four percentage points below their counterparts, and the 1929 Czechoslovak ratio is seven percentage points above its normal counterpart; these negative deviations are all less than the standard error.

5. The examination of socialist PCE and TCE consumption gaps over time for the USSR from 1937 to 1962, for Eastern Europe from the mid-1950's to the mid-1960's and for a postwar cross-section of socialist economies fails to reveal definite trends of convergence of the socialist consumption ratios towards the normal ratios as per capita income increases. The 1937 USSR PCE ratio was 14 percentage points below its normal counterpart. The Hungarian PCE consumption gap dropped from 17 to 14 percentage points below normal between 1956 and 1964, whereas the Polish, Czechoslovak and East German PCE consumption gaps widened from 10 to 11, 19 to 21 and 21 to 23 percentage points below normal, respectively.

Cross-section convergence would be indicated by a combination of small deviations for the high per capita income socialist countries and large deviations for the low per capita income socialist countries. In the present sample, the average mid-1950's high income PCE deviation is 18 percentage points below the average normal counterpart, whereas the average low income deviation is 13.5 percentage points below normal.[*] The average mid-1960's high income PCE deviation is still 18 percentage points below normal, and the average low income PCE deviation is 12.5 percentage points below normal. The same is true of the mid-1950's TCE deviations: the average high income deviation is 16 percentage points and the average low income deviation is 10 percentage points below the normal average figure.

Thus the socialist cross-section fails to reveal consumption convergence patterns towards the normal Western pattern, which is an expected result in view of the absence of convergence trends on the production side.

Table 25 examined consumption gaps in relative terms, i.e., in terms of personal and total consumption shares of total product. If, by adopting low consumption ratios, the socialist economies were able to generate rates of growth of total product sufficiently high to create a nonrandom distribution of per capita income in favor of the socialist economies, the relative consumption gap might disappear in absolute terms (consumption per capita in dollar values). Table 26 gives the extrapolations of socialist per capita PCE and TCE in 1960 dollars (Appendix E).

As was true in the case of the PCE and TCE ratios, the absolute socialist per capita PCE and TCE (in dollar values) exhibit no cross-section tendency towards convergence. The high income socialist countries (Czechoslovakia, East Germany and postwar USSR) yield larger negative deviations than the lower income socialist countries (Hungary and Poland). The same is true for the USSR over time in absolute terms. In

---

[*] The high per capita income countries are USSR, East Germany and Czechoslovakia. The low per capita income countries are Hungary and Poland. See Appendix E.

It is unfortunate that factor cost estimates of Bulgarian and Romaninan consumption ratios have not been made by Western analysts. The inclusion of these two countries would not only enlarge the socialist sample but would also increase the per capita income variation within the socialist cross-section. The absence of cross-section convergence would have been more convincing had the sample included Bulgaria and Romania.

TABLE 26

Actual Socialist Per Capita PCE (1960 $)
and Normal Per Capita PCE Plus
Actual Socialist Per Capita TCE (1960 $)
and Normal TCE (1960 $)

		Actual PCE	Normal PCE	D	Actual TCE	Normal TCE	D
USSR	1928	269	298	-29	284	329	-45
	1937	311	380	-69	373	422	-49
	1955	420	493	-73	500	546	-46
	1958	505	554	-49	583	612	-30
	1962	600	667	-67	696	736	-40
Hungary							
	1955	430	481	-51	516	533	-16
	1964	489	555	-66	---	---	---
Poland							
	1956	341	384	-43	366	426	-60
	1964	456	496	-40	---	---	---
Czechoslovakia							
	1956	415	532	-117	484	589	-105
	1964	560	802	-242	---	---	---
East Germany							
	1955	398	521	-123	503	577	-74
	1964	527	770	-243	---	---	---

Sources: PCE and TCE data from Appendix E.   The
normal regression equations used for purposes of extrapolation

$$PCE \ \$ = 224.7 + .1576I + .1767I^2$$
$$\qquad\qquad (2.49) \qquad (6.62)$$

The R^2 value is .95 and the standard error is 97.7.
$$TCE \ \$ = 246.0 + .1852I + .18691I^2$$
$$\qquad\qquad (2.52) \qquad (6.05)$$
The R^2 value is .94 and the standard error is 113.0.

1928, the USSR PCE gap was -$29; in 1962, the gap was -$67.
In percentage terms (D ÷ PCE), the USSR residual has declined
since 1937 but has risen slightly since 1928. The absolute
Eastern European residuals increased between the mid-1950's
and mid-1960's, with the exception of Poland.

Tables 25 and 26 indicate a rather substantial socialist
consumption gap, which persists into the 1960's and ranges
from a low of 11 percent to a high of 22 percent of GNP on a
relative basis and from a low of $40 to a high of $243 on a
per capita basis. In other words, socialism has served as a
kind of tax on the population to limit consumption below those
levels which would have obtained under a market system. The
term "consumption gap" could be criticized because the term
carries with it a negative connotation. It could just as well be
argued that the socialist consumption pattern should be accepted
as the standard, which means that the capitalist countries have
"investment gaps" and "consumption surpluses" which should
be eliminated. In fact, some prominent Western economists
stress the existence of "investment gaps" in the US economy. [9]

In sum, as far as the first (dual) goal of growth and
consumer welfare is concerned, socialist industrialization
possibly aided in the achievement of the growth objective, but
the long-run consumer welfare benefits which socialist theoret-
icians expected are still to be derived, especially if one judges
socialist consumption standards according to "normal" Western
standards. A less equivocal answer cannot be given because
of the complexity of the growth equation.

As far as the second goal of socialist industrialization
is concerned, the results are fairly obvious. Inasmuch as
military hardware is generally produced by the metal products
(engineering) sector, it is to be expected that of two economies
with identical income, population and natural resources, the
one devoting more of its resources to the metal products sector would be capable of generating a greater military potential
than the other. The fact that the USSR in 1960 devoted roughly
the same proportion of GNP (valued at factor cost) to defense
expenditures (broadly defined) as the US, although the US
GNP was roughly twice that of the USSR, is perhaps indicative
of this relationship. [10] In view of the high priority placed by
socialist planners on an independent capacity to produce militar
hardware, socialist industrialization was quite successful.

The third goal of socialist industrialization--the attain-
ment of independence from capitalist markets--has been
achieved to a great extent. After 1928, foreign trade fell to
a negligible portion of GNP in the Soviet Union and has remaine

insignificant ever since. The foreign trade proportions of the
Eastern European countries in the postwar period reveal a
marked underutilization of trade potential relative to normal
standards, despite the availability of a socialist bloc with
which to trade. Chapters 5 and 6 indicated the lack of specializa-
tion of production structures within the socialist bloc by
pointing out the basic similarity between the Eastern European
and Soviet industrial structures in the postwar period despite
a prewar heritage of structural diversity. So, curiously enough,
it seems that independence from both capitalist and socialist
economies has become a built-in objective of socialist industrialization.

As far as the fourth objective of socialist industrialization is concerned--the provision of an industrial base to support less advanced socialist economies--an answer can be
obtained only by a careful examination of Soviet aid to the less
developed socialist world, in particular to China, North Vietnam,
North Korea and Cuba, to determine how much the effectiveness
of such aid has been hampered by the lack of industrial capacity.
Such a question is beyond the scope of this study.

THE RELEVANCE OF THE SOCIALIST
INDUSTRIALIZATION PATTERN TO
DEVELOPING ECONOMIES

Most developing economies have instituted economic planning to direct the economic development of their country and,
in this sense, these economies must make the practical choice
of which industrialization pattern they should follow. In making
such a decision, they have almost an infinity of choices. They
can adopt the industrialization pattern of the capitalist West--
relying on private enterprise with minimal government inter-
ference, comparative advantage in foreign markets with eventual
import substitution, private agriculture and indicative (as
opposed to command) planning. In such a system, the pattern
of industrialization would be determined by the free interplay
of sectoral income elasticities, economies of scale and sectoral
import substitution patterns. If they adopt the Western path,
sectoral planning would be based on the "normal" Western
pattern (as indicated by the cross-section income, population
and resource elasticities derived in this and other studies),
and the objective of planning would then be to close gaps between actual and such normal patterns.

At the other extreme, developing economies could choose the socialist pattern of industrialization, with its emphasis on social ownership in industry and agriculture, forced import substitution under a foreign trade monopoly and negation of consumer preferences via command planning and indirect taxation. In making this choice, sectoral planning would be based upon the "normal" socialist pattern of industrialization as indicated by the socialist income, population and resource elasticities shown in Chapter 7.

Third, they could choose to combine features of both indus-trialization patterns, which would involve, for practical plan-ning purposes, taking weighted averages of the two polar "normal" patterns. An infinity of choices would then be availabl insofar as an infinity of weighting schemes would be available.

The decision facing the developing economies is a real one. It is therefore relevant to consider the relevance of the socialist industrialization model to the developing world. Typically, the applicability of the Soviet model to the circum-stances of underdeveloped countries is discounted because the USSR in 1928 was at a much higher level of development than the present-day underdeveloped countries. USSR 1928 per capita income was well above \$300 (1960 US \$), the transpor-tation system had already been developed, the USSR had al-ready experienced rapid industrial growth and the agricultural sector was capable of producing a marketed surplus.[11] On the negative side, the overwhelming majority of the Russian population was illiterate and lived in rural areas with high rates of infant mortality.

When speaking of the Soviet model, one may wish to differentiate between the socialist industrialization model and the socialist agricultural model (collectivization with forced state deliveries). The following comments refer in-itially to the socialist industrialization model.

The socialist industrialization model might commend it-self to nations having the following characteristics: (1) per capita income levels roughly comparable to the initial USSR levels of the late 1920's (over \$250); (2) fairly large populations; (3) low foreign exchange earning capacities either now or in the future, coupled with a lack of access to foreign aid; (4) extreme political stability; and (5) interest in the development of an independent military capacity.

The minimum per capita income requirement plus the political stability requirement would make the reductions in living standards, which are the concomitants of large heavy industrial shares at low per capita income levels, feasible.

The large population requirement ensures that the developing economy will not be saddled with advanced sectors which can be supported only by large-scale internal markets. The third and fifth characteristics provide the rationale for adopting the socialist industrialization model in the first place. The aid and trade path is certainly less painful in terms of domestic austerity than the socialist autarky model; nevertheless, the growing dissatisfaction with real (or imagined) losses of primary exports earnings could perhaps induce certain countries to experiment with the socialist elasticities.

Adoption of the socialist industrial sector expansion paths would require the use of USSR historical elasticities or of socialist cross-section elasticities to define "normal" industrial structures, which could be compared with the initial industrial structure in order to pinpoint which sectors should be accorded highest priority. A sectoral plan would be established on the basis of the actual and normal share comparisons, which would be implemented by using tax credits, subsidies, government enterprise, investment controls, foreign exchange controls etc.

Whether or not the socialist industrialization pattern can be employed to industrialize a developing economy successfully is an open question. Several points are evident, however. Indiscriminate imitation of the socialist industrialization model without regard to scale requirements and natural resource endowments (as done in Eastern Europe) can lead to poor results. Second, developing countries traditionally do not possess the political stability required to implement the austerity measures. Third, it is questionable whether socialist industrialization can be implemented without resorting to Soviet-type central planning, as was indicated by the Czarist Russian experience. The inefficiencies of command-type central planning have been well documented, and one may well ask whether poor countries can afford the inefficient use of scarce resources.

Fourth, it is questionable whether socialist industrial goals can be implemented in a predominantly agricultural economy independently of agriculture, i.e., whether the socialist industrialization model can be adopted by developing economies without also adopting some form of socialist ownership in agriculture. The Soviets learned during the 1920's that the one required the other. A review of the "scissors crisis" and "goods famine" will perhaps convince the reader of this interrelationship. [12] It is notable that wholesale collectivization was to a great extent avoided in Eastern Europe and was approached with extreme caution initially in Communist

China, in view of the Soviet experience. Nevertheless, the
more ambitious the industrialization goals, the more dependent
the industrial sector becomes on the agricultural sector in
the initial stages of industrialization, when agriculture still
dominates. An industrialization program geared towards the
production of producer goods in such a country will eventually
run up against the resistance of the private peasantry (unless
consumer goods are imported). To what extent agriculture
restricts the realm of choice of industrialization patterns in
developing countries remains to be investigated. If it turns
out that the adoption of the socialist industrialization model
is contingent upon the collectivization of agriculture, it is then
an open question whether developing economies can "afford"
socialist industrialization.

Even as it is difficult to attach normative significance
to the Western "normal" structures, so is it difficult to discuss
the normative implications of "normal" socialist industrialization patterns, for this involves the choice between planners'
preferences and consumer preferences. More importantly, one
should concentrate on the derivation of alternative patterns
in order to broaden the realm of choice facing planners. It
should be stressed that the choice of industrialization patterns
is not purely a mechanical choice of different sets of elasticity
coefficients. To make the correct choice, planners must
consider not only the direct effects but also the indirect effects
of their industrialization policies on human incentives, political
institutions, international relations and a multitude of other
factors.

AREAS FOR FURTHER RESEARCH

The scope of this study could be extended in two directions
when (and if) further data are made available. First, time
series patterns of the individual Eastern European countries
throughout the entire postwar period could be analyzed on an
individual basis in the same fashion as were the USSR long-
term trends. Meaningful combinations of cross-section and
time series data could be effected, thereby increasing the size
of the socialist sample, the small size of which was the greates
limiting factor in the current study. Second, more developing
socialist economies should be studied to determine whether
they are adopting the socialist industrialization pattern as
defined in this study and, if so how successful their industrialization efforts have been relative to those of the noncentrally

planned developing economies. Countries which should be included in this extension are Communist China, Cuba, North
Korea, North Vietnam, and Albania. Insofar as one of the
primary reasons for studying Soviet-type economies is their
relevance to development problems, a study of this sort is
essential.

A second major area for further research is that of
evaluating the effectiveness of the two polar industrialization
models. In order to do so further research must be undertaken
to define optimal patterns for given investment and consumption
levels and production patterns. Until such models are developed,
an interim approach may be to compare the overall performances
of those Western countries which deviate most widely from
the normal Western pattern in the direction of the socialist
pattern with the performances of the socialist economies.
This approach permits one to evaluate socialist and nonsocialist
economies on an equal footing, leaving the economic system
as the distinguishing feature. Performance differences can
then be attributed to the system as such because the economies
are alike in other respects.

NOTES

1. Politische Ökonomie, pp. 371-75.

2. Evsey Domar, Essays in the Theory of Economic Growth,
pp. 223-61. Domar's essay is an elaboration of Fel'dman's
model of Soviet economic growth, developed by Fel'dman in
the late 1920's as a theoretical planning model for the State
Planning Commission. The principal results are

$$I = I_o e^{(a/v_1)t}$$

$$C = C_o + (\frac{1-a}{a})v_1/v_2(e^{(a/v_1)t}-1)$$

$$Y = Y + [(\frac{1-a}{a}) v_1/v_2 +] (e^{(a/v_1)t}-1),$$

where I is investment, C is consumption, Y is total product,
a is the proportion of output of the investment goods sector
reallocated to the investment goods sector, V_1 is the capital-
output ratio in the investment goods sector and V_2 is the

capital-output ratio in the consumer goods sector. The o refers
to the base year values. The Polish economist Sulmicki,
using a very similar model, suggests entering two constraints
into the Fel'dman model. The first constraint involves the
setting of a minimum C value, below which the supply and
productivity of labor are seriously impaired. The second
constraint is the maximum period of sacrifice, which the consumer must suffer before C again reaches a suitable level.
See Pawel Sulmicki, "Some Observations on the Rate of Growth
of National Product."

3. Kuznets, "A Comparative Appraisal," in Bergson and
Kuznets, eds., Economic Trends in the Soviet Union, p. 335.

4. M. Ernst, "The Postwar Economic Growth in Eastern
Europe," p. 880.

5. S. Kuznets, "A Comparative Appraisal," pp. 358-64;
Ernst, op, cit., pp. 885-89.

6. Politische Ökonomie, p. 383.

7. S. Kuznets, Modern Economic Growth, pp. 234-43;
Kuznets, "A Comparative Appraisal," pp. 358-60.

8. Abram Bergson, Real SNIP, pp. 128, 130, 143;
Abraham Becker, Soviet National Income and Product, 1958-
1962, p. 37. Thad Alton, Czechoslovak National Income and
Product, 1947-1948 and 1955-1956, p. 87; Alton, Hungarian
National Income and Product in 1955, p. 80; Alton, Polish
National Income and Product in 1954, 1955 and 1956, p. 82;
Wolfgang Stolper, The Structure of the East German Economy,
p. 436.

9. John Kenneth Galbraith, The Affluent Society.

10. S. Cohn, "The Gross National Product in the Soviet
Union," p. 72; A. Bergson, Real SNIP, p. 342. Comparisons
of this sort can be questioned on the grounds of significant
differences in relative Soviet and US prices. The purchasing
power of the ruble relative to the dollar is substantially lower
for consumer goods and services than for investment and
defense goods. See Philip Hansen, The Consumer in the
Soviet Economy, pp. 88-90.

11.   Oleg Hoeffding, Soviet State Planning and Forced Industrialization as a Model for Asia.

12.   Maurice Dobb, Soviet Economic Development Since 1917, Chs. 5-7.

APPENDIXES

APPENDIX   A   SOCIALIST
MANUFACTURING VALUE-
ADDED DATA

The following is a brief summary of the derivation of
USSR and Eastern European manufacturing value added. (The
actual calculations are given in a statistical appendix, which
is available upon request from the author.)

RUSSIAN AND USSR MANUFACTURING VALUE ADDED

1. 1912 Manufacturing Value Added. The employment
and gross and net production data used in estimating 1912
manufacturing value added are from Svod statističeskikh
dannykh po fabrično-zavodskoi promyšlennost' c 1887 po 1926
god. Since the above source covers only census (large-scale)
industry, value added in noncensus (small-scale) industry
must be estimated separately.

For census industries, only gross production figures are
available for 1912; therefore the 1915 sector ratios of net to
gross production were applied to the 1912 gross production
figures, assuming that these ratios had not changed between
1912 and 1915.

To estimate value added in noncensus industries, the
following procedure was adopted: The ratios of branch value
added per person in noncensus branches to value added per
person in census branches in 1924 were computed first. Second, the ratios of branch employment in non-census branches
to employment in census branches in 1913 were calculated.
Under the assumption that the 1924 value added per employee
ratios are indicative of 1912 relationships, 1912 noncensus
value added was computed according to the formula $V^s_i = kV^l_i$
(N^s_i/N^l_i), where V^s_i is the noncensus value added of branch i
in 1912, V^l_i is the 1912 value added in branch i (census branches), N^s_i is the 1913 noncensus branch i employment, N^l_i
is 1913 census branch i employment. Also used is $k = (V^s_i/v^l_i)$, where v^s_i is the 1924 value added per worker in branch i

(noncensus) and v^1_i is 1924 value added per worker in branch i (census). The 1913 ratios are from Nutter, The Growth of Industrial Production in the Soviet Union, Table C-1.

Total 1912 value added is the sum of value added in the census branches and value added in the noncensus branches.

2. 1925 Manufacturing Value Added. More direct methods can be employed to estimate 1925 manufacturing value added because net production data are available for both census and noncensus branches in Statsprav 1927. The calculations were made quite simply by multiplying branch gross production (net of indirect taxes) in census and noncensus industries by the ratio of net production to gross production in census and noncensus industries.

3. 1927, 1928 and 1929 Manufacturing Value Added. Manufacturing value added in the years 1927, 1928 and 1929 are taken directly from G. W. Nutter's The Growth of Industrial Production in the Soviet Union. Nutter computes net production in census and noncensus industries separately by deducting material costs from gross production (net of indirect taxes).

4. 1933 and 1937 Manufacturing Value Added. The 1933 and 1937 data are computed by extrapolating the 1928 figures with the appropriate constant price production indexes from Nutter.

5. 1955 Manufacturing Value Added. The paucity of data for 1955 made it necessary to estimate the 1955 manufacturing value-added structure by extrapolating the 1960 value-added structure to 1955, using appropriate production indexes found in the Index of Civilian Industrial Production in the USSR, 1950-1961, published by the Central Intelligence Agency.

6. 1960 and 1962 Manufacturing Value Added. The calculations of USSR manufacturing value added in 1960 and 1962 are based upon capital stock and depreciation data in the Narodnoe Khoziastvo SSSR (Narkhoz), on labor force data and wage data in the Current Economic Indicators for the USSR and the Soviet Economic Performance, both published by the Joint Economic Committee of Congress. Branch value added in both years is computed as the sum of industrial branch wage bills, industrial branch depreciation charges and imputed branch capital services. Capital stock is valued at 1955 replacement costs.

EASTERN EUROPEAN VALUE-ADDED DATA

The industrial data published by the socialist countries
of Eastern Europe are generally sufficient to allow the estimation of industrial value-added structures. The data vary from
barely sufficient (Romania) to detailed (Hungary). All the
countries surveyed publish rather detailed industrial branch
labor force distributions, along with direct wage bill data or
average annual earnings of workers and employees, which
can be used to estimate branch wage bills. In addition, all
of the countries surveyed publish detailed depreciation charges,
broken down by industrial branches. All of the countries (with
the exception of Romania) have made and published capital
stock surveys, broken down by industrial branches, during
the 1960's.

1. Polish Manufacturing Value Added, 1963. Industrial
branch value added is computed as the sum of industrial branch
wage bills, depreciation charges and imputed capital services
on the basis of data in Rocznik Statystyczny Przemyslu, 1945-
1965 and Rocznik Dochodu Narodowego, 1960-1965. Private
industry accounts for less than 0.50 percent of gross industrial production; therefore it is ignored.

2. Bulgarian Value Added, 1963. Bulgarian manufacturing
value added in 1963 is estimated in the same manner as Polish
value added: as the sum of branch wage bills, depreciation
charges and imputed capital services. Since Statističeskii
Godišnik na Narodna Republika B'lgaria, 1964 gives only the
capital stock of state enterprises, equal capital intensity in
state and cooperative enterprises at the branch level is assumed for the purpose of estimating capital services in cooperative enterprises. The private sector accounts for 0.60
percent of gross industrial production; therefore its impact
upon the industrial structure is assumed to be negligible.

3. Hungarian Value Added, 1957 and 1963. On the basis
of information in the Statistical Yearbook of the Hungarian
Central Statistical Office (1957 and 1963 editions, in English),
manufacturing value added was estimated as the sum of branch
wage bills, depreciation charges and imputed capital services.
Capital services in cooperative industries were computed by
assuming equal capital intensity per florint of wage bill in
state and cooperative enterprises.

4. East German Value Added, 1955 and 1963. East Germany
manufacturing value added in 1955 and 1963 was estimated on

the basis of labor force and wage data from <u>Statistisches Jahrbuch der DDR</u> (1956 and 1964 editions) and from the capital
stock estimates at 1962 replacement cost of the Deutsches Institut für Wirtschaftsforschung (West Berlin). In addition,
depreciation charges are given in the <u>Statistisches Jahrbuch</u>.
Branch value added is computed as the sum of wage bills,
depreciation charges and capital services. Value added of
the (less than marginal in 1955) handicraft sector is estimated
on the basis of employment.

  5. Czechoslovak Value Added, 1965. Czechoslovak manufacturing value added in 1965 is estimated as the sum of wage
bills, depreciation charges and capital services in the socialist sector at the industrial branch level on the basis of data in
<u>Statistička Ročenka ČSSR, 1967.</u>

  6. Romanian Value Added, 1958. The value-added estimates cited are the Montias-Lee 1958 value-added weights for
their index of industrial production from Montias' <u>Economic
Development in Communist Rumania,</u> adjusted somewhat to
conform more closely with the ISIC system of industrial classification. The Montias-Lee value-added estimates are not
exactly comparable with the other Eastern European value-
added estimates because they exclude capital services; Romanian value added is defined to include only wage bills and
depreciation charges.

  This means that the value-added shares of the more
heavily capitalized industries will be understated relative to
other Eastern European countries. It was decided, nevertheless, to include the Montias-Lee estimates because wage bills
plus depreciation charges do provide useful approximations
of value added. Those interested in more information on the
Montias-Lee estimates should consult J. M. Montias, <u>Econo-
mic Development in Communist Rumania,</u> pp. 251-53, and
Pong Lee's interesting analysis of the structure of Rumanian
industry on the basis of normal industrial structures, "Structural Change in Rumanian Industry, 1938-1963."

B
MANUFACTURING SUBSECTOR
PERCENTAGES OF MANUFACTURING
VALUE ADDED: UNITED KINGDOM,
GERMANY, CANADA, UNITED STATES

TABLE 1

Subsector Percentages of Manufacturing
Value Added, United Kingdom, 1907-65

		1907	1924	1930	1935	1953	1958	1960	1963	1965
a.	Food Products (ISIC 20-22)	19	17	18	17	10	12	11	12	11
b.	Textiles (ISIC 23)	17	17	11	12	9	8	7	7	6
c.	Clothing, Footwear (ISIC 24)	9	11	10	7	5	4	4	4	4
d.	Wood Products (ISIC 25, 26)	4	3	4	4	4	3	3	3	3
e.	Paper Products (ISIC 27)	1	4	5	3	3	3	3	3	3
f.	Printing (ISIC 28)	6	4	4	7	4	5	5	5	5
g.	Leather Products (ISIC 29)	1	1	1	1	1	1	1	1	1
h.	Chemicals, Rubber, Coal, Oil Products (ISIC 30-32)	7	7	8	9	11	10	11	12	13
i.	Nonmetallic Minerals (ISIC 33)	3	4	5	5	4	4	4	4	4
j.	Basic Metals (ISIC 34)	10	8	6	7	9	8	9	8	8
k.	Metal Products (ISIC 35-38)	22	21	25	28	38	40	39	40	39
l.	Miscellaneous Manufactures (ISIC 39)	2	3	3	2	3	3	3	4	4
	Total	100	100	100	100	100	100	100	100	100
m.	Manufacturing ÷ GNP	26	30	31	28	34	35	37	36	36
n.	Industry ÷ GNP	29	33	35	32	40	41	43	42	42

Sources: M. A. Flux, "Gleanings from the Census of Production Report," pp.
557-85: Phyllis Deane and W. A. Cole, British Economic Growth, 1688-
1959, United Nations, pp. 174-75; The Growth of World Industry, pp. 454-
60.

TABLE 2

Subsector Percentages of Manufacturing
Value Added, Germany, 1873-1936

		1873	1881	1893	1900	1905	1913	1926	1930	1936
a.	Food Products (ISIC 20-22)	27	29	20	24	23	19	17	17	15
b.	Textiles (ISIC 23)	26	24	27	20	20	17	12	11	11
c.	Clothing, Footwear (ISIC 24)	8	7	7	6	6	5	4	4	4
d.	Wood Products (ISIC 25, 26)	5	5	5	4	4	4	5	4	4
e.	Paper Products (ISIC 27)	1	1	1	2	2	2	3	3	3
f.	Printing (ISIC 28)	2	3	3	5	4	3	5	5	3
g.	Leather Products (ISIC 29)	3	3	3	2	2	2	2	2	1
h.	Chemicals, Rubber, Coal, Oil Products (ISIC 30-32)	3	4	5	5	6	7	9	12	13
i.	Nonmetallic Minerals (ISIC 33)	7	6	9	8	8	7	7	6	6
j.	Basic Metals (ISIC 34)	5	7	7	8	9	12	8	7	9
k.	Metal Products (ISIC 35-38)	10	9	12	15	15	19	26	28	30
l.	Miscellaneous Manufactures (ISIC 39)	3	3	3	2	3	2	3	2	3
	Total	100	100	100	100	100	100	100	100	100
m.	Manufacturing ÷ GNP	27	27	31	32	33	35	38	36	39
n.	Industry ÷ GNP	30	30	34	37	38	41	45	42	46

Sources: 1936, Die Deutsche Industrie, pp. 44-55; other years, Walther Hoffmann, Das Was
der deutschen Wirtschaft seit der Mitte des 19. Jahrhunderts, pp. 389-95.

TABLE 3

Subsector Percentages of Manufacturing
Value Added, Canada, 1891-1962

		1891	1901	1911	1923	1926	1928	1938	1953	1958	1960	1962
a.	Food Products (ISIC 20-22)	15	18	20	20	29	23	19	15	17	17	16
b.	Textiles (ISIC 23)	20	20	4	6	4	5	9	4	4	4	4
c.	Clothing, Footwear (ISIC 24)	11	11	13	11	8	9	11	5	5	5	5
d.	Wood Products (ISIC 25, 26)	17	15	18	10	7	9	9	7	6	6	7
e.	Paper Products (ISIC 27)	8	1	2	4	9	9	7	9	9	10	9
f.	Printing (ISIC 28)	3	4	4	7	5	6	6	5	5	5	5
g.	Leather Products (ISIC 29)	2	3	3	3	1	1	1	--*	--	--	--
h.	Chemicals, Rubber, Coal, Oil Products (ISIC 30-32)	5	5	4	10	7	9	8	11	11	11	11
i.	Nonmetallic Minerals (ISIC 33)	5	3	1	5	4	4	2	3	4	4	4
j.	Basic Metals (ISIC 34)	5	6	9	4	7	11	6	8	11	12	10
k.	Metal Products (ISIC 35-38)	9	10	14	12	18	15	12	32	25	24	27
l.	Miscellaneous Manufactures (ISIC 39)	5	2	3	2	1	2	2	3	4	2	3
	Total	100	100	100	100	100	100	100	100	100	100	100
m.	Manufacturing ÷ GNP	24	21	23	24	24	23	28	28	26	26	27
n.	Industry ÷ GNP	28	25	28	30	29	28	31	34	33	32	32

*-- denotes less than 1 percent (rounded).

Sources: Dominion Bureau of Statistics, Census of Manufactures, selected years; O. J. Firestone, Canada's Economic Development, 1867 to 1953, p. 254; United Nations, The Growth of World Industry, pp. 52-58.

173

TABLE 4

Subsector Percentages of Manufacturing
Value Added, United States, 1870-1963

		1870	1899	1904	1909	1919	1925	1939	1954	1958	1960	1963
a.	Food Products (ISIC 20-22)	17	20	19	19	14	14	16	12	13	13	12
b.	Textiles (ISIC 23)	9	9	8	8	8	7	7	4	4	3	3
c.	Clothing, Footwear (ISIC 24)	12	10	11	11	10	10	7	4	5	5	5
d.	Wood Products (ISIC 25, 26)	14	12	11	11	7	8	5	4	4	4	4
e.	Paper Products (ISIC 27)	1	2	2	2	2	3	4	4	4	4	4
f.	Printing (ISIC 28)	4	6	7	7	5	7	7	6	6	6	6
g.	Leather Products (ISIC 29)	4	2	2	2	2	1	1	1	1	1	--*
h.	Chemicals, Rubber, Coal, Oil Products (ISIC 30-32)	5	5	7	7	10	10	12	12	14	14	14
i.	Nonmetallic Minerals (ISIC 33)	4	4	5	5	3	5	4	3	4	4	4
j.	Basic Metals (ISIC 34)	10	9	8	8	8	8	9	9	8	8	8
k.	Metal Products (ISIC 35-38)	18	18	20	20	30	27	25	36	34	35	36
l.	Miscellaneous Manufactures (ISIC 39)	3	1	1	1	1	1	4	4	4	5	5
	Total	100	100	100	100	100	100	100	100	100	100	100
m.	Manufacturing ÷ GNP	14	18	18	19	22	22	24	29	27	28	28
n.	Industry ÷ GNP	20	23	23	23	25	26	27	33	32	33	32

*-- denotes less than 1 percent (rounded).

Sources: U. S. Bureau of the Census, Census of Manufactures, 1870; Solomon Fabricant, The Output of Manufacturing Industries, 1899-1937, pp. 605-40; United Nations, The Growth of World Industry, pp. 461-68.

174

C

ACTUAL AND NORMAL
ASPECTS OF MANUFAC-
TURING: RUSSIA-USSR,
EASTERN EUROPE,
CROSS-SECTION

TABLE 1

Actual and Normal USSR Industry (IS) and
Manufacturing (MS) Shares of GNP, 1912-62

	(1) Actual MS	(2) Normal MS	(3) D	(4) Actual IS	(5) Normal IS	(6) D
1912	18	20	-2	25	22	+3
1925	17	22	-5	21	25	-4
1927	17	23	-6	24	26	-2
1928	18	22	-4	24	25	-1
1929	21	22	-1	28	25	+3
1933	23	23	0	29	26	+3
1937	29	24	+5	35	27	+8
1955	31	27	+4	37	30	+7
1960	27	29	-2	38	33	+5
1962	28	30	-2	39	33	+6

Notes: 1. The column 2 normal shares are the anti-logs from
$\ln MS = -2.76 + .1547 \ln I + .1068 \ln N - .0719 \ln R.$
$\qquad (4.18) \qquad (4.58) \qquad (2.93)$

2. The column 5 normal shares are the anti-logs from
$\ln IS = -2.40 + .1440 \ln I + .0751 \ln N - .0780 \ln R.$
$\qquad (5.18) \qquad (4.29) \qquad (4.23)$

3. The R^2 value and standard error of the MS regression are .60 and .21.

4. The R^2 value and standard error of the IS regression are .66 and .16.

Source: Author's computations based on data in Table 1.

TABLE 2

Actual (A) and Normal (P) USSR Manufacturing Structures, Selected Years

Step 1. Normal Structures with Respect to Per
Capita Income, Population and Natural
Resources Percent of Manufacturing Value Added

	Light Manufactures			Heavy Manufactures			Food Products			Light Mfg. (excl. food)		
	A	P	(A-P)	A	P	(A-P)	A	P	(A-P)	A	P	(A-P)
1912	61	48	+13	23	40	-17	30	21	+ 9	32	25	+ 7
1925	65	44	+21	29	45	-16	29	18	+11	36	24	+12
1927	63	43	+20	31	46	-15	22	17	+ 5	41	24	+17
1928	63	44	+19	31	45	-14	23	18	+ 5	40	24	+16
1929	61	44	+17	33	45	-12	21	18	+ 3	39	24	+15
1933	42	42	0	51	47	+ 4	17	16	+ 1	25	24	+ 1
1937	33	40	- 7	63	49	+12	12	16	- 4	21	24	- 3
1955	28	36	- 8	64	55	+9	9	13	- 4	19	23	- 4
1960	26	33	- 7	67	60	+ 7	9	11	- 2	17	22	- 5
1962	26	32	- 6	68	61	+ 7	10	11	- 1	16	22	- 6

Step 2. Normal Structures with Respect to Per
Capita Income, Population Natural Resources
and Manufacturing Share of GNP.

	A	P	(A-P)	A	P	(A-P)	A	P	(A-P)	A	P	(A-P)
1912	61	49	+12	23	40	-17	30	22	+ 8	32	25	+ 7
1925	65	45	+20	29	41	-12	29	20	+ 9	36	23	+13
1927	63	45	+18	31	42	-11	22	19	+ 3	41	23	+18
1928	63	45	+18	31	42	-11	23	20	+ 3	40	23	+17
1929	61	45	+16	33	44	-11	21	19	+ 2	39	24	+15
1933	42	42	0	51	47	+ 4	17	16	+ 1	25	24	+ 1
1937	33	39	- 6	63	52	+11	12	14	- 2	21	25	- 4
1955	28	35	- 7	64	57	+ 7	9	12	- 3	19	24	- 5
1960	26	33	- 7	67	58	+ 9	9	12	- 3	17	22	- 5
1962	26	32	- 6	68	60	+ 8	10	11	- 1	16	22	- 6

Metal Products			Heavy Intermediate Manufactures			Textiles			Nonmetallic Minerals		
A	P	(A-P)	A	P	(A-P)	A	P	(A-P)	A	P	(A-P)
9	15	- 6	14	25	-11	24	14	+10	3	4	-1
12	17	- 5	18	28	-10	21	14	+ 7	4	4	0
14	18	- 4	17	27	-10	25	13	+12	4	4	0
14	17	- 3	17	27	-10	25	13	+12	4	4	0
16	17	- 1	18	27	- 9	24	13	+11	4	4	0
30	19	+11	21	27	- 6	15	11	+ 4	3	4	-1
37	21	+16	26	26	0	12	10	+ 2	4	4	0
39	26	+13	26	27	- 1	8	8	0	6	3	+3
38	31	+ 7	29	28	+ 1	7	7	0	9	3	+6
39	32	+ 7	28	28	0	7	7	0	9	3	+6
9	14	- 5	14	25	-11	24	14	+10	3	4	-1
12	14	- 2	18	28	-10	21	14	+ 7	4	5	-1
14	14	0	17	27	-10	25	13	+12	4	5	-1
14	14	0	17	27	-10	25	13	+12	4	5	-1
16	16	0	18	27	- 9	24	13	+11	4	4	0
30	19	+11	21	27	- 6	15	11	+ 4	3	4	-1
37	24	+13	26	26	0	12	10	+ 2	4	3	+1
39	29	+10	26	27	- 1	8	8	0	6	3	+3
38	29	+ 9	29	28	+ 1	7	7	0	9	4	+5
39	31	+ 8	28	28	0	7	7	0	9	3	+6

(Continued)

177

TABLE 2--Continued

	Chemicals			Basic Metals			Paper, Printing			Leather		
	A	P	(A-P)	A	P	(A-P)	A	P	(A-P)	A	P	(A-P)
1912	4	14	-10	7	4	+3	2	6	-4	1	1	0
1925	10	15	-5	4	6	-2	5	5	0	3	1	+2
1927	8	15	-7	5	6	-1	4	6	-2	3	1	+2
1928	9	15	-6	5	5	0	3	6	-3	3	1	+2
1929	9	14	-5	5	5	0	4	6	-2	3	1	+2
1933	12	14	-2	6	6	0	3	6	-3	2	1	+1
1937	14	14	0	8	6	+2	3	7	-4	1	1	0
1955	7	14	-7	14	7	+7	3	7	-4	1	1	0
1960	8	14	-6	13	9	+4	2	8	-6	1	1	0
1962	7	14	-7	13	9	+4	2	8	-6	1	1	0
1912	4	13	-9	7	4	+3	2	6	-4	1	1	0
1925	10	14	-4	4	5	-1	5	6	-1	3	1	+2
1927	8	14	-6	5	5	0	4	6	-2	3	1	+2
1928	9	14	-5	5	5	0	3	6	-3	3	1	+2
1929	9	14	-5	5	5	0	4	6	-2	3	1	+2
1933	12	14	-2	6	6	0	3	6	-3	2	1	+2
1937	14	15	-1	8	6	+2	3	6	-3	1	1	0
1955	7	15	-8	14	7	+7	3	7	-4	1	1	0
1960	8	14	-6	13	9	+4	2	8	-6	1	1	0
1962	7	14	-7	13	9	+4	2	8	-6	1	1	0

Step 3. Normal Structures with Respect to Per Capita
Income, Population, Natural Resources,
Manufacturing Share of GNP and Trade
Orientation.

Light Mfg. (excl. food)			Nonmetallic Minerals			Chemicals			Paper, Printing		
A	P	(A-P)	A	P	(A-P)	A	P	(A-P)	A	P	(A-P)
32	28	+ 4	3	5	-2	4	11	-9	2	7	-5
36	19	+17	4	3	+1	10	17	-7	5	4	+1
41	20	+21	4	4	0	8	16	-8	4	5	-1
40	21	+19	4	4	0	9	15	-6	3	5	-2
39	22	+17	4	3	+1	9	15	-6	4	5	-1
25	21	+ 4	3	3	0	12	17	-5	3	5	-2
21	17	+ 4	4	1	+3	14	22	-8	3	3	0
19	20	- 1	6	2	+4	7	17	-10	3	5	-2
17	19	- 2	9	3	+6	8	16	-8	2	6	-4
16	19	- 3	9	3	+6	7	16	-9	2	7	-5

Note: The A column gives the actual subsector shares of total manufacturing value added; the P column gives the normal USSR shares; the (A-P) column gives the difference between the actual share and the normal share. The regression coefficients used for extrapolation are given in Table 7. It should be noted that the step 3 residuals are computed only if the sector trade orientation coefficients are significant. The predicted shares are the antilogs of the predicted shares in natural logarithmic form. Alternative calculations have been carried through using subsector shares of GNP as the dependent variable. They are recorded in Table 8.

Source: Author's computations based on data in Table 1.

TABLE 3

Actual and Normal Ratios of Manufacturing and
Industry Value Added to GNP, Eastern
Europe, Postwar Years

	Actual Manufacturing	Normal Manufacturing	D	Actual Industry	Normal Industry	D
Poland 1963	33%	24%	+ 9%	45%	29%	+16%
Hungary 1963	28	26	+ 2	35	33	+ 2
East Germany 1963	52	28	+24	57	34	+23
Czechoslovakia 1965	32	28	+ 4	40	35	+ 5
Romania 1958	22	21	+ 1	25	26	- 1
Bulgaria 1963	31	22	+ 9	39	28	+11

Source: Author's computations based on data in Table 10.

TABLE 4

Actual and Normal Eastern European Manufacturing Structures

Step 1 Residuals.	Normal Structures with Respect to Per Capita Income, Population, Natural Resource Endowments										

	Light Manufactures			Heavy Manufactures			Food Products			Light Manufactures (excl. food)		
	A	P	(A-P)	A	P	(A-P)	A	P	(A-P)	A	P	(A-P)
Poland 1963	34	39	- 5	59	49	+10	14	16	- 2	20	22	- 3
Hungary 1963	31	39	- 8	61	49	+12	13	17	- 4	19	20	- 1
East Germany 1963	27	36	- 9	65	53	+12	9	15	- 7	18	21	- 3
Czechoslovakia 1965	27	37	-10	68	53	+15	9	16	- 7	18	21	- 3
Romania 1958	34	46	-12	58	42	+16	11	21	-10	23	22	+ 1
Bulgaria 1963	35	45	-10	52	42	+10	16	21	- 5	19	21	- 2
Average Deviation		-9.0			+12.5			-5.8			-1.8	

	Metal Products			Heavy Intermediate Mfg.			Textiles		
	A	P	(A-P)	A	P	(A-P)	A	P	(A-P)
Poland 1963	29	25	+ 4	30	24	+ 6	11	7	+ 4
Hungary 1963	31	27	+ 4	30	21	+ 9	10	6	+ 4
East Germany 1963	34	31	+ 3	31	22	+ 9	9	5	+ 4
Czechoslovakia 1965	34	32	+ 2	34	22	+12	9	5	+ 4
Romania 1958	28	19	+ 9	30	22	+ 8	12	9	+ 3
Bulgaria 1963	21	20	+ 1	30	20	+10	12	7	+ 6
Average Deviation		+3.8			+9.0			+4.2	

	Nonmetallic Minerals			Chemicals			Basic Metals			Paper, Printing			Leather		
	A	P	(A-P)	A	P	(A-P)	A	P	(A-P)	A	P	(A-P)	A	P	(A-P)
Poland 1963	8	4	+4	12	11	+1	11	6	+ 5	3	8	-5	1	1	0
Hungary 1963	6	5	+1	10	10	0	14	6	+ 8	2	9	-7	1	1	0
East Germany 1963	6	4	+2	17	11	+6	8	6	+ 2	4	9	-5	1	1	0
Czechoslovakia 1965	7	4	+3	10	10	0	17	6	+11	3	10	-7	1	1	0
Romania 1958	7	5	+2	13	11	+2	10	4	+ 6	3	7	-4	2	1	+1
Bulgaria 1963	7	5	+2	10	10	0	14	4	+10	2	8	-6	1	1	0
Average Deviation		+2.3			+1.5			+7.0			-5.7			+.2	

(Continued)

TABLE 4--Continued

Step 2 Residuals. Normal Structures with Respect to Per Capita Income,
Population, Natural Resources and Ratio
of Manufacturing to GNP

	Light Manufactures			Heavy Manufactures			Food Products			Light Manufactures (excl. food)		
	A	P	(A-P)	A	P	(A-P)	A	P	(A-P)	A	P	(A-P)
Poland 1963	34	37	- 3	59	54	+ 5	14	14	0	20	24	- 4
Hungary 1963	31	38	- 7	61	51	+10	13	16	- 3	19	21	- 2
East Germany 1963	27	32	- 5	65	64	+ 1	9	11	- 2	18	24	- 6
Czechoslovakia 1965	27	35	- 8	68	56	+12	9	14	- 5	18	21	- 3
Romania 1958	34	46	-12	58	41	+17	11	22	-11	23	22	+ 1
Bulgaria 1963	35	43	- 8	52	47	+ 5	16	18	- 2	19	24	- 5
Average Deviation		-7.2			+8.3			-3.8			-3.2	

	Metal Products			Heavy Intermediate			Textiles		
	A	P	(A-P)	A	P	(A-P)	A	P	(A-P)
Poland 1963	29	31	- 2	30	24	+ 6	11	7	+ 4
Hungary 1963	31	29	+ 2	30	21	+ 9	10	6	+ 4
East Germany 1963	34	50	-16	31	22	+ 9	9	5	+ 4
Czechoslovakia 1965	34	34	0	34	22	+12	9	5	+ 4
Romania 1958	28	17	+11	30	22	+ 8	12	9	+ 3
Bulgaria 1963	21	26	- 5	30	20	+10	12	7	+ 5
Average Deviation		-1.8			+9.0			+4.0	

	Nonmetallic Minerals			Chemicals			Basic Metals			Paper, Printing			Leather		
	A	P	(A-P)	A	P	(A-P)	A	P	(A-P)	A	P	(A-P)	A	P	(A-P)
Poland 1963	8	3	+5	12	12	0	11	6	+ 5	3	7	- 4	1	1	0
Hungary 1963	6	4	+2	10	11	- 1	14	6	+ 8	2	8	- 6	1	1	0
East Germany 1963	6	3	+3	17	13	+ 4	8	7	+ 1	4	7	- 3	1	1	0
Czechoslovakia 1965	7	4	+3	10	11	- 1	17	7	+10	3	9	- 6	1	1	0
Romania 1958	7	5	+2	13	11	+ 2	10	4	+ 6	3	7	- 4	2	1	+1
Bulgaria 1963	7	4	+3	10	11	- 1	14	4	+10	2	7	- 5	1	1	0
Average Deviation		+3.0			+.5			+6.7			-4.7			+.2	

Step 3 Residuals. Normal Structures with Respect to Per Capita Income, Population, Natural Resources, Ratio of Manufacturing to GNP and Trade Orientation

	Light Manufactures (excl. food)			Nonmetallic Minerals			Chemicals			Paper, Printing		
	A	P	(A-P)	A	P	(A-P)	A	P	(A-P)	A	P	(A-P)
Poland 1963	20	23	- 3	8	3	+ 5	12	13	- 1	3	7	- 4
Hungary 1963	19	20	- 1	6	4	+ 2	10	11	- 1	2	8	- 6
East Germany 1963	18	23	- 5	6	2	+ 4	17	13	+ 4	4	7	- 3
Czechoslovakia 1965	18	20	- 2	7	4	+ 3	10	11	- 1	3	9	- 6
Romania 1958	23	20	+ 3	7	4	+ 3	13	12	+ 1	3	6	- 3
Bulgaria 1963	19	24	- 5	7	4	+ 3	10	11	- 1	2	7	- 5
Average Deviation			-2.2			+3.3			+.2			-4.5

Note: The A column gives the actual subsector shares of total manufacturing value added; the P column gives the normal USSR shares; the (A-P) column gives the difference between the actual share and the normal share. The regression coefficients used for extrapolation are given in Table 7. It should be noted that the step 3 residuals are computed only if the sector trade orientation coefficients are significant. The predicted shares are the anti-logs of the predicted shares in natural logarithmic form. Alternative calculations have been carried through using subsector shares of GNP as the dependent variable. They are recorded in Table 8.

Source: Author's computations based on data in Table 10.

TABLE 5

Actual and Normal USSR Manufacturing Structures, GNP Shares
(with Respect to Per Capita Income, Population and Natural Resources), 1912-62

	Light Manufactures			Heavy Manufactures			Food Products		
	A	P	(A-P)	A	P	(A-P)	A	P	(A-P)
1912	11.1	9.5	+ .6	4.2	8.0	-3.8	5.4	4.1	+1.3
1925	10.9	9.7	+1.2	5.0	10.0	-5.0	4.9	3.9	+1.0
1927	10.9	9.7	+1.2	5.4	10.4	-5.0	3.8	3.9	- .1
1928	10.9	9.7	+1.2	5.5	10.0	-4.5	4.0	3.9	+ .1
1929	12.4	9.7	+2.7	6.8	9.8	-3.0	4.4	3.9	+ .5
1933	9.7	9.7	0	11.8	10.8	+1.0	3.9	3.8	+ .1
1937	9.6	9.7	- .1	18.4	11.6	+6.8	3.5	3.7	- .2
1955	8.6	9.7	-1.1	19.7	14.6	+5.1	2.8	3.5	- .7
1960	7.0	9.7	-2.7	18.0	17.6	+ .4	2.3	3.3	-1.0
1962	7.3	9.7	-2.4	18.9	18.4	+ .5	2.7	3.3	- .6

	Light Mfg. (excl. food)			Metal Products			Heavy Intermediate Manufactures		
1912	5.7	5.0	+ .7	1.6	2.9	-1.3	2.6	5.0	-2.4
1925	6.1	5.4	+ .7	2.0	3.7	-1.7	3.0	6.1	-3.1
1927	7.2	5.5	+1.7	3.4	4.0	- .6	3.0	6.2	-3.2
1928	7.0	5.4	+1.6	2.4	3.8	-1.4	3.0	6.0	-3.0
1929	8.1	5.4	+2.7	3.2	3.7	- .5	3.6	5.9	-2.3
1933	5.8	5.5	+ .3	7.0	4.3	+2.6	4.9	6.2	-1.3
1937	6.1	5.7	+ .4	10.8	4.9	+5.9	7.5	6.2	+1.3
1955	5.8	6.2	- .4	11.9	7.0	+4.9	7.9	7.2	+ .5
1960	4.7	6.6	-1.9	10.3	9.1	+ .8	7.9	8.1	- .2
1962	4.6	6.7	-2.1	11.0	9.8	+1.3	7.9	8.3	- .4

	Chemicals			Nonmetallic Minerals			Basic Metals		
	A	P	(A-P)	A	P	(A-P)	A	P	(A-P)
1912	.8	2.7	-1.9	.5	.8	- .3	1.3	.8	+ .5
1925	1.7	3.3	-1.6	.6	.9	- .3	.7	1.3	- .6
1927	1.4	3.3	-1.9	.7	.9	- .2	.9	1.4	- .5
1928	1.5	3.3	-1.8	.7	.8	- .1	.9	1.3	- .4
1929	1.8	3.2	-1.4	.8	.8	0	1.0	1.2	- .2
1933	2.8	3.3	- .5	.7	.9	- .2	1.3	1.5	- .2
1937	4.2	2.3	+1.9	1.2	.9	+ .3	2.2	1.5	+ .7
1955	2.0	3.7	-1.7	1.7	.9	+ .8	4.1	2.2	+1.9
1960	2.0	4.1	-2.1	2.3	1.0	+1.3	3.5	3.0	+ .5
1962	2.1	4.2	-2.1	2.4	1.0	+1.4	3.5	3.2	+ .3

	Paper, Printing		
1912	.3	1.1	- .8
1925	.9	1.3	- .3
1927	.6	1.3	- .7
1928	.6	1.2	- .6
1929	.7	1.2	- .5
1933	.8	1.4	- .6
1937	.8	1.5	- .7
1955	.8	1.9	-1.1
1960	.6	2.3	-1.7
1962	.7	2.4	-1.7

Source: Author's computations based on data in Table 1.

TABLE 6

Actual and Normal Eastern European Manufacturing Structures,
GNP Shares (with Respect to Per Capita Income, Population and Natural Resources)

	Light Manufactures			Heavy Manufactures			Food Products		
	A	P	(A-P)	A	P	(A-P)	A	P	(A-P)
Poland 1963	11.2	9.8	+ .4	20.0	11.6	+8.4	4.5	4.2	+ .3
Hungary 1963	8.8	10.2	-1.4	17.1	12.9	+4.2	3.6	4.4	- .8
Romania 1958	6.8	10.0	-3.2	11.6	9.2	+2.4	2.1	4.6	-2.5
GDR 1963	13.9	10.0	+3.9	23.8	14.9	+8.9	4.5	4.1	+ .4
Czechoslovakia 65	8.7	10.0	-1.3	21.5	15.2	+6.3	2.9	4.1	-1.2
Bulgaria 1963	11.0	10.8	+ .2	16.1	9.4	+6.7	5.1	4.8	+ .3

	Light Mfg. (excl. food)			Metal Products			Heavy Intermediate Manufactures		
Poland 1963	6.7	5.4	+1.3	9.6	5.6	+4.0	10.1	5.5	+4.6
Hungary 1963	5.2	5.4	- .2	8.8	7.0	+1.8	8.4	5.6	+2.8
Romania 1958	4.7	4.9	- .2	5.6	4.1	+1.5	6.0	4.8	+1.2
GDR 1963	9.4	5.8	+3.6	18.0	8.6	+9.4	16.1	6.2	+9.9
Czechoslovakia 65	5.8	5.8	0	10.6	9.0	+1.6	10.8	6.2	+4.6
Bulgaria 1963	6.0	4.8	+1.2	6.7	4.5	+2.8	9.5	4.6	+4.9

	Chemicals			Nonmetallic Minerals			Basic Metals		
	A	P	(A-P)	A	P	(A-P)	A	P	(A-P)
Poland 1963	4.0	2.8	+1.2	2.6	1.0	+1.6	3.5	1.2	+2.3
Hungary 1963	2.9	2.7	+ .2	1.7	1.2	+ .5	3.8	1.3	+2.5
Romania 1958	2.6	2.4	+ .2	1.5	1.0	+ .5	1.9	.8	+1.1
GDR 1963	9.1	3.0	+6.1	3.0	1.2	+1.8	3.9	1.6	+2.3
Czechoslovakia 65	3.3	3.0	+ .3	2.1	1.2	+ .9	5.5	1.7	+3.8
Bulgaria 1963	3.0	2.3	+ .7	2.3	1.1	+1.2	4.2	1.7	+2.5

	Paper, Printing		
Poland 1963	1.1	1.9	- .8
Hungary 1963	.7	2.5	-1.8
Romania 1958	.6	1.5	- .9
GDR 1963	2.0	2.6	- .6
Czechoslovakia 65	1.1	2.7	-1.6
Bulgaria 1963	.7	1.7	-1.0

Source: Author's computations based on data in Table 1.

TABLE 7

Normal Regression Equations, Manufacturing Subsectors, 1953-65 Cross-Section

(shares of manufacturing)

			Regression Coefficients with Respect to				
	Inter-cept	Log I	Log N	Log R	Log MS	Log V	R^2	S.E.
Light Manufactures								
Step 1	.537	-.1622 (5.97)	-.1180 (6.88)	.0647 (3.59)	--	--	.76	.15
Step 2	.088	-.1371 (4.20)	-.1006 (4.74)	.0531 (2.68)	-.1626 (1.36)	--	.77	.15
Step 3	V coefficient highly insignificant							
Heavy Manufactures								
Step 1	-2.183	.1576 (5.23)	.1273 (6.70)	-.0664 (3.32)	--	--	.73	.17
Step 2	-1.350	.1106	.0948	-.0045	.3039	--	.77	.16
Step 3	V coefficient highly insignificant							
Food Products								
Step 1	.487	-.2286 (4.61)	-.2345 (7.49)	.1092 (3.32)	--	--	.74	.28
Step 2	-.868	-.1527	-.1821	.0739	-.4912	--	.78	.27
Step 3	V coefficient highly insignificant							
Light Manufactures (excl. food)								
Step 1	-1.204	-.0499 (1.30)	-.0018 (.07)	.0276 (1.08)	--	--	.07	.21
Step 2	-.465	-.0913 (2.00)	-.0268 (.90)	.0468 (1.69)	.2679 (1.60)	--	.13	.21
Step 3	-.5415	-.0918 (2.08)	-.0165 (.57)	.0647 (2.28)	.2303 (1.42)	.1635 (1.92)	.21	.21

	Inter-cept	Log I	Log N	Log R	Log MS	Log V	R^2	S.E.
Metal Products								
Step 1	-4.410	.3781 (7.74)	.1453 (4.72)	-.1093 (3.37)	--	--	.75	.28
Step 2	-2.259	.2575 (5.31)	.0621 (1.97)	-.0532 (1.81)	.7796 (4.39)	--	.84	.23
Step 3	V coefficient highly insignificant							
Heavy Intermediate Manufactures								
Step 1	-1.593	-.0411 (1.08)	.1213 (5.04)	-.0334 (1.32)	--	--	.43	.22
Step 2	-1.636	-.0386 (.82)	.1230 (4.03)	-.0345 (1.21)	-.0159 (.09)	--	.43	.22
Step 3	V coefficient is highly insignificant							
Textiles								
Step 1	.508	-.4912 (4.79)	.0291 (.45)	.0537 (.79)	--	--	.39	.58
Step 2	.422	-.4864 (3.85)	.0321 (.40)	.0515 (.67)	-.0312 (.07)	--	.39	.59
Step 3	V coefficient is highly insignificant							
Nonmetallic Minerals								
Step 1	-2.2712	-.0814 (.93)	-.1106 (1.99)	.0070 (.12)	--	--	.14	.50
Step 2	-4.406	.0382 (.37)	-.0289 (.42)	-.0486 (.78)	-.7737 (2.06)	--	.23	.48
Step 3	-4.552	.0373 (.37)	-.0084 (.13)	-.0146 (.23)	-.8452 (.28)	.3107 (1.61)	.28	.47

(Continued)

189

TABLE 7--Continued

	Inter-cept	Log I	Log N	Log R	Log MS	Log V	R^2	S.E.
Chemicals								
Step 1	-2.062	-.0796	.1323	-.0281	--	--	.46	.23
		(2.01)	(5.29)	(1.07)				
Step 2	-1.385	-.1176	.1060	-.0104	.2452	--	.49	.22
		(2.48)	(3.43)	(.36)	(1.41)			
Step 3	-1.305	-.1170	.0953	-.0291	.2845	-.1706	.54	.21
		(2.56)	(3.15)	(.99)	(1.69)	(1.94)		
Basic Metals								
Step 1	-5.390	.1883	.3757	-.2194	--	--	.31	1.07
		(1.00)	(3.18)	(1.77)				
Step 2	-4.704	.1498	.3492	-.2015	.2485	--	.31	1.07
		(.65)	(2.33)	(1.44)	(.30)			
Step 3	V coefficient highly insignificant							
Paper, Printing								
Step 1	-4.354	.2777	-.0175	-.0248	--	--	.42	.31
		(5.15)	(.52)	(.69)				
Step 2	-5.352	.3337	.0211	-.0508	-.3620	--	.46	.30
		(5.20)	(.51)	(1.30)	(1.54)			
Step 3	-5.484	.3329	.0387	-.0203	-.4263	.2794	.53	.28
		(5.52)	(.97)	(.52)	(1.92)	(2.41)		
Leather Products								
Step 1	-3.663	-.2052	.0063	.0547	--	--	.04	.96
		(1.45)	(-06)	(.49)				
Step 2	-4.308	-.1691	.0312	.0379	-.2338	--	.04	.98
		(.81)	(.23)	(.30)	(.31)			
Step 3	V coefficient highly insignificant							

Note: Step 1 degrees of freedom=37.
  Step 2 degrees of freedom = 36.
  Step 3 degrees of freedom = 35.

Normal Regression Equations, Manufacturing Subsectors, 1953-65 Cross-section

(shares of GNP)

	Intercept	Log I	Log N	Log R	R^2	S.E.
Light Mfg.	2.383	-.0073 (.18)	-.0117 (.45)	-.0068 (.04)	.01	.23
Heavy Mfg.	-.337	.3125 (5.61)	.2335 (6.65)	-.1379 (3.73)	.74	.32
Food Products	2.334	-.0737 (1.48)	-.1282 (4.07)	.0376 (1.13)	.39	.28
Light Mfg. (excl. food)	.6427	.1050 (1.75)	.1081 (2.85)	-.0440 (1.10)	.29	.34
Metal Products	-2.5632	.5330 (6.95)	.2516 (5.20)	-.1808 (3.55)	.74	.44
Heavy Intermediate Mfg.	.254	.1138 (2.16)	.2275 (6.85)	-.1050 (3.00)	.65	.30
Textiles	1.860	-.3040 (3.42)	.2062 (3.66)	-.0816 (1.38)	.40	.51
Nonmetallic Minerals	-.425	.0735 (.88)	-.0043 (.08)	-.0645 (1.16)	.05	.47
Chemicals	-.215	.0753 (1.25)	.2385 (6.28)	-.0996 (2.50)	.59	.34
Basic Metals	-3.966	.3636 (2.25)	.5583 (5.48)	-.2723 (2.54)	.57	.92
Paper, Printing	-2.507	.4326 (7.50)	.0888 (2.44)	-.0964 (2.52)	.67	.33
Leather Products	-2.480	.0699 (.64)	.0429 (.62)	.0191 (.26)	.03	.62

Source: Author's computations (statistical appendix is available upon request from the author).

TABLE 8

Actual and Normal USSR Manufacturing Structures,
Derived from a 1937-39 Cross-Section

Step 1. Normal Structures with Respect to Per
Capita Income, Population and Natural
Resources (percent of manufacturing
value added)

	Light Manufactures			Heavy Manufactures			Food Products		
	A	P	(A-P)	A	P	(A-P)	A	P	(A-P)
1912	61	49	+12	23	43	-20	30	14	+16
1925	65	45	+20	29	50	-21	29	12	+17
1927	63	45	+18	31	52	-21	22	11	+11
1928	63	45	+18	31	51	-20	23	11	+14
1929	61	44	+17	33	51	-18	21	11	+10
1933	42	42	0	51	55	- 4	17	10	+ 7
1937	33	40	- 7	63	57	+ 6	12	10	+ 2

Step 2. Normal Structures with Respect to Per
Capita Income, Population, Natural
Resources and Trade Orientation

	A	P	(A-P)	A	P	(A-P)	A	P	(A-P)
1912	61	47	+14	23	23	0	30	32	- 2
1925	65	52	+13	29	41	-12	29	21	+ 8
1927	63	50	+13	31	40	- 9	22	21	+ 1
1928	63	49	+14	31	36	- 5	23	23	0
1929	61	48	+13	33	35	- 2	21	23	- 2
1933	42	48	- 6	51	41	+10	17	20	- 3
1937	33	53	-20	63	56	+ 7	12	16	- 4

192

	Light Manufactures (excl. food)			Metal Products			Heavy Intermediate Manufactures		
	A	P	(A-P)	A	P	(A-P)	A	P	(A-P)
1912	32	38	- 6	9	14	- 5	14	28	-14
1925	36	38	- 2	12	15	- 3	18	34	-16
1927	41	38	+ 3	14	16	- 2	17	34	-17
1928	40	38	+ 2	14	16	- 2	17	34	-17
1929	39	38	+ 1	16	16	0	18	34	-16
1933	25	37	-12	30	18	+12	21	35	-14
1937	21	36	-15	37	21	+16	26	34	- 8
1912	32	40	- 8	9	14	- 5			
1925	36	32	+ 4	12	15	- 3			
1927	41	32	+ 9	14	16	- 2			
1928	40	34	+ 6	14	16	- 2			
1929	39	34	+ 5	16	16	0			
1933	25	32	- 7	30	18	+12			
1937	21	25	- 4	37	21	+16			

Note: The heavy intermediate manufactures step 2 residuals are not computed because the V coefficient is highly insignificant.

Source: Author's computations based on data in Table 1.

193

FORMULAS FOR
MEASURING CAUSES OF
INDUSTRIALIZATION;
DATA FOR ESTIMATING
TABLES 23 AND 24

FORMULAS FOR MEASURING THE SOURCES OF INDUSTRIALIZATION

S = Total supply of sector i
Q = Total demand for sector i
D = Final domestic demand for sector i
E = Export demand for sector i
W = Intermediate domestic demand for sector i
X = Gross domestic production of sector i
Y = GNP
r = V/X
V = Value added of sector i

(1) $S = Q$

(2) $S = X + M$

(3) $Q = D + W + E$

(4) $X + M = D + W + E$

(5) $X = D + W + E - M$

(6) $\Delta X = X_2 - X_1$

(7) $= Q_2 (X_2/S_2) - Q_1 (X_1/S_1)$

(8) $= Q_2 (X_1/S_1) + X_2 - Q_1(X_1/S_1) - S_2 (X_1/S_1)$

(9) $= (X_1/S_1)\Delta Q + (X_2/S_2 - X_1/S_1)S_2$

Let $u = X/S$

(10) $\Delta \; X = u_1 \Delta Q + (u_2 - u_1) S_2$

(11) $\qquad = u_1 \Delta (D + W) + u_1 \Delta E + (u_2 - u_1) S_2$

(12) $\Delta \; (X/Y) = (X + \Delta X)/(Y + \Delta Y) - X/Y$

(13) $\qquad = \Delta X/(Y + \Delta Y) + X/(Y + \Delta Y) - X/Y$

(14) $\qquad = \dfrac{u_1 \Delta (D+W+E) + (u_2 - u_1) S_2}{Y + \Delta Y} + \dfrac{u_1 \; (D+W+E)}{Y + \Delta Y}$

$$- \dfrac{u_1 \; (D+W+E)}{Y}$$

(15) $\qquad = u_1 \left[\dfrac{D+W+E + \Delta (D+W+E)}{Y + \Delta Y} - \dfrac{D+W+E}{Y} \right] + \dfrac{(u_2 - u_1) S_2}{Y + \Delta Y}$

(16) $\Delta \left[\dfrac{D+W+E}{Y} \right] = \dfrac{D+W+E + \Delta (D+W+E)}{Y + \Delta Y} - \dfrac{D+W+E}{Y}$

(17) $\Delta (X/Y) = u_1' \left[\dfrac{D+W+E}{Y} \right] + (u_2 - u_1) \dfrac{S_2}{Y_2}$

Sources: 1-11 from H. B. Chenery, S. Shishido and T. Watanabe, "The Pattern of Japanese Growth, 1914-1954," pp. 104-108; and from S. R. Lewis and R. Soligo, Growth and Structural Change in Pakistan's Manufacturing Industry, 1954-1964, pp. 11-14.

TABLE 1

Data for Estimating Tables 23, 24

USSR 1912, 1960

	r_1	r_2	r^1_2	m_1	m_2	e_1	e_2	x_1	x_2	x^1_2
1. Food Products	.31	.10	.12	2.7	.2	2.2	.1	17.4	23.0	19.2
2. Textiles, Clothing, Leather	.32	.12	.13	1.9	.6	1.7	.3	14.4	34.1	12.8
3. Paper, Printing	.48	.33	.44	.6	.0	.0	.0	.6	1.8	1.4
4. Chemicals	.31	.26	.37	1.1	.1	.5	.4	4.2	8.1	5.7
5. Nonmetallic Minerals	.57	.43	.50	.1	.0	.0	.0	.9	5.3	4.6
6. Basic Metals	.50	.32	.45	.6	.3	.2	.4	2.6	10.6	8.1
7. Metal Products	.54	.38	.43	1.5	.8	.0	.6	3.5	27.1	24.8

Czechoslovakia 1929, 1965

	r_1	r_2	r^1_2	m_1	m_2	e_1	e_2	x_1	x_2	x^1_2
1. Food Products	.31	.22	--	6.5	2.4	3.4	.4	13.2	6.5	--
2. Textiles, Clothing, Leather	.35	.44	--	8.2	.9	10.7	1.5	25.7	11.1	--
3. Paper, Printing	.57	.38	--	.2	.2	.6	.2	2.1	2.9	--
4. Chemicals	.46	.39	--	2.0	.9	.9	.9	3.7	8.2	--
5. Nonmetallic Minerals	.84	.70	--	.7	.2	2.1	.7	2.6	3.1	--
6. Basic Metals	.57	.42	--	2.0	1.5	1.9	1.5	1.9	12.9	--
7. Metal Products	.57	.42	--	1.8	4.9	2.1	7.5	9.3	26.0	--

Hungary 1936, 1963

	r_1	r_2	r^1_2	m_1	m_2	e_1	e_2	x_1	x_2	x^1_2
1. Food Products	.34	.14	.20	.5	2.0	1.8	3.2	15.6	25.7	18.0
2. Textiles, Clothing, Leather	.42	.28	.36	2.7	2.3	1.0	1.9	8.1	16.1	12.5
3. Paper, Printing	.57	.32	.48	.6	.0	.0	.0	2.6	1.9	1.2
4. Chemicals	.45	.25	.37	1.2	2.9	.1	.7	1.3	11.2	7.6
5. Basic Metals	.36	.24	.35	.8	1.8	.6	.7	4.2	16.3	11.1
6. Nonmetallic Minerals	.64	.49	.69	.0	.2	.0	.0	.6	3.5	2.5
7. Metal Products	.57	.28	.37	1.1	4.8	1.1	5.8	2.1	31.1	23.5

Bulgaria 1936, 1963

	r_1	r_2	r^1_2	m_1	m_2	e_1	e_2	x_1	x_2	x^1_2
1. Food Products	.23	.13	.19	.2	.0	1.6	3.6	16.1	38.4	26.2
2. Textiles, Clothing, Leather	.30	.20	.22	1.6	3.0	.6	2.2	7.3	26.0	20.0
3. Paper, Printing	.40	.41	.58	.3	.2	.0	.0	.8	1.5	1.0
4. Chemicals	.65	.32	.41	1.6	2.2	.6	.4	1.1	9.7	7.5
5. Nonmetallic Minerals	.35	.60	.65	.2	.0	.0	.0	1.7	3.7	3.4
6. Basic Metals	.43	.44	.65	2.5	1.9	.0	.4	.2	9.8	6.6
7. Metal Products	.39	.35	.45	3.5	1.8	.0	1.8	1.0	19.4	15.1

Notes: r_1 is the ratio of net to gross product in the initial period.
r_2 is the ratio of net production to gross production in the terminal period. 8 percent return to capital is assumed.
r^1_2 is the ratio of net to gross product in the terminal period. 20 percent return to capital is assumed.

m_1 and m_2 are the ratios of sector imports in the initial and terminal periods to GNP.
e_1 and e_2 are the ratios of sector exports in the initial and terminal period to GNP.
x_1 is the ratio of sector gross product to GNP in the initial period.
x_2 is the ratio of sector gross product to GNP in the terminal period, computed from r.
x^1_2 is the ratio of sector gross product to GNP, computed from r^1_2.

(Continued)

197

TABLE 1--Continued

Sources: USSR 1913: The r_1 figure is the 1913 ratio of net product to gross product in factory industry from statistical appendix. The m_1 figure is the product of the 1913 sector share of total imports (Ministerstvo Vnesnei Torgovli SSSR, Vnešniaia Torgovlia SSSR za 1918-1940 g.g.) and the 1913 ratio of total imports to GNP, from F. Holzmann, Soviet Taxation, pp. 288-90. The e_1 figure is computed in the same manner. The x_1 figures are computed by applying the r_1 figures to the value added data of Statistical appendix.

USSR 1960: The r_2 figure is the ratio of wages to value added, from Statistical appendix, divided by the 1963 ratio of wage costs to total costs, from Narodnoe Khoziastvo SSSR 1963 (p. 135). The r_2^1 figure is the ratio of wages to value added computed under the assumption of a 20 percent return to capital. The m_2 and e_2 figures are computed as the product of sector shares of total imports and exports from Ministerstvo Vnesnei Torgovli SSSR, Vnešniaia Torgovlia za 1959-1963 g.g. and the ratios of total exports and imports to GNP. The GNP figure is from Abraham Becker, Soviet National Income and Product, 1958-1962, Part I, p. 14. The x_2 and x^1_2 figures are computed by applying the r_2 and $r1_2$ figures to the value added data of Statistical appendix.

Czechoslovakia 1929: The r_1 figure is taken directly from Stadnik, Statistical Appendix. The m_1 and e_1 figures are estimated from League of Nations, International Trade and Balance of Trade Yearbook, 1927-1929, p. 230 and from United Nations National Income Statistics, 1938-1948, p. 230. x_1 was computed by applying r_1 to the value added data of Table 11, using Stadnik's estimate of the 1929 ratio of manufacturing to GNP.

Czechoslovakia 1965: r_2 is taken directly from Stadnik, Some Problems of Economic Growth in Czechoslovakia, after netting out indirect taxes. m_2 and e_2 are computed as the product of sector shares of total imports and exports from Statistička Ročenka ČSSR 1967 (Table 17-8) and the ratios of exports and imports to GNP, from Ernst, "The Postwar Economic Growth in Eastern Europe" (p. 900). x_2 is computed from the value added data of Table 10.

198

Hungary 1937: r_1 is the 1937 ratio of net to gross product in factory industry from Ungarns Industrie und Handel im Jahre 1937. m_1 and e_1 are computed from the same source (pp. 36-37) and from United Nations, National Income Statistics, 1938-1948 (p. 231). x_1 is computed from Table 11, using 21 percent as the ratio of manufacturing to GNP. This figure was decided upon by taking the UN ratio and assuming that the excluded services were roughly equal to the Netherlands proportions.

Hungary 1963: r_2 and r^1_2 are computed as the ratios of wages to value added (under alternative assumptions of 8 percent and 20 percent returns to capital) from Statistical appendix divided by the ratio of wage costs to total costs from Hungarian Statistical Yearbook 1963, pp. e_2 and m_2 are computed as the product of sector shares of total exports and imports from United Nations, Yearbook of International Trade Statistics, 1963, p. 313, times the ratio of exports and imports to GNP from Ernst, "The Postwar Economic Growth in Eastern Europe." x_2 and x^1_2 are computed by applying r_2 and r^1_2 to the value added data of Statistical appendix.

Bulgaria 1936: r_1 is the ratio of net product to gross product in factory industry from Statističeski Godišnik na Tsarstvo B'lgaria, pp. 390-411. m_1 and e_1 are derived as the ratio of sector imports and exports (from the same source, pp. 498-501) to GNP from United Nations, National Income Statistics, 1938-1948, p. 229. x_1 is derived from the value-added data of Table 10. Manufacturing is computed as 8 percent of GNP from net product data in United Nations, National Income Statistics, 1938-1948 and Statistiteski Godišnik.

Bulgaria 1963: r_2 and r^1_2 are computed as the ratios of wages to value added (under alternative assumptions of 8 percent and 20 percent returns to capital) from Statistical appendix divided by the ratio of wage costs to total costs from Statistiteski Godišnik na Narodna Republika B'lgaria 1964, pp. 131-32. e_2 and m_2 are derived in the same manner and from the same sources as Hungary 1963. x_2 and x^1_2 are derived by applying r_2 and r^1_2 to the value-added data of Table 10.

199

APPENDIX **E** PERSONAL CONSUMPTION EXPENDITURES,
GOVERNMENT COMMUNAL SERVICES AND
TOTAL CONSUMPTION EXPENDITURES,
SOCIALIST AND NONSOCIALIST COUNTRIES,
SELECTED YEARS

PERSONAL CONSUMPTION EXPENDITURES (PCE),
GOVERNMENT COMMUNAL SERVICES (CS), AND
TOTAL CONSUMPTION EXPENDITURES (TCE),
SOCIALIST AND WESTERN COUNTRIES, SELECTED YEARS

		(1) PCE ÷ GNP	(2) CS ÷ GNP	(3) TCE ÷ GNP	(4) Per Capita Income (1960 $)
1. Hungary	1955	51.3	10.3	61.6	838
	1964	50.			978
2. Poland	1956	56.5	4.2	60.7	604
	1964	53.			861
3. Czechoslovakia					
	1956	43.8	7.3	51.1	947
	1964	40.			1401
4. East Germany	1955	43.1	11.4	54.5	924
	1964	39.			1351
5. USSR	1937	52.5	10.5	63.0	593
6.	1955	48.6	9.2	57.8	865
7.	1958	51.0	7.9	58.9	990
8.	1962	50.1	8.0	58.1	1198
9. Australia	1960	63.0	4.6	67.6	1624
10. Brazil	1953	70.0	1.0	71.0	156
11. Canada	1953	62.0	3.3	65.3	1487
12.	1958	64.0	3.3	67.7	1503
13.	1964	63.0	4.3	67.3	1631
14. Chile	1964	80.0	4.2	84.2	439
15. Denmark	1964	64.0	8.5	72.5	1340
16. Finland	1964	59.0	9.1	68.1	1109
17. Germany	1960	57.0	5.3	62.3	1879
18. Israel	1964	71.0	5.8	76.8	603
19. Japan	1953	61.0	8.0	69.0	263
20.	1958	62.0	4.5	66.5	353
21.	1964	52.0	4.5	56.5	697
22. Mexico	1960	82.0	2.1	84.1	322
23. Netherlands	1964	58.0	8.2	66.2	1252
24. Norway	1964	56.0	5.0	61.0	1424
25. Spain	1964	70.3	3.0	73.3	399
26. UK	1953	67.0	10.0	77.0	1240
27.	1964	65.0	10.8	75.8	1524
28. Sweden	1964	57.0	6.0	63.0	1847
29. US	1953	62.0	4.8	66.8	2135
30.	1964	62.0	6.0	68.0	2405
31. Venezuela	1964	62.0	6.5	68.5	555
32. USSR	1928	64.7	5.1	69.8	353

Sources: Rows 1-8, 32, A. Bergson, Real SNIP, pp. 128, 130, 148; A. Becker, "Soviet National Income and Product, 1958-1962," p. 37; Thad Alton, Czechoslovak National Income and Product, 1947-1948 and 1955-1965, p. 87; Alton, Hungarian National Income and Product in 1955, p. 80; Alton, Polish National Income and Product in 1954, and 1956, p. 82; F. Pryor, Public Expenditures in Communist and Capitalist Nations, p. 24. The 1964 Hungarian, Czechoslovak, Polish, and East German consumption figures are extrapolated from the mid-1950's values, using Ernst's Tables 4 and 10. Rows 9-31 from United Nations, Yearbook of National Accounts Statistics (various years).

BIBLIOGRAPHY

Books, Monographs

Alton, Thad. Czechoslovak National Income and Product,
1947-1948 and 1955-1956. New York: Columbia University Press, 1962.
_____. Hungarian National Income and Product in 1955.
New York: Columbia University Press, 1963.
_____. Polish National Income and Product in 1954,
1955, and 1956. New York: Columbia University Press,
1965.

Becker, Abraham, Soviet National Income and Product, 1958,
1962, RM-4881-PR. Santa Monica, California: The Rand
Corporation, May 1966.

Bergson, Abram. The Real National Income and Product of
Soviet Russia Since 1928. Cambridge, Massachusetts:
Harvard University Press, 1961.
_____. The Economics of Soviet Planning. New Haven:
Yale University Press, 1964.

Bornstein, Morris. Soviet National Accounts for 1955. Ann
Arbor: University of Michigan, Center for Russian Studies,
1961.

Chapman, Janet. Real Wages in Soviet Russia Since 1928.
Cambridge, Massachusetts: Harvard University Press
1963.

Czirjak, L. An Index of Hungarian Construction, 1938 and
1946-1965. Alton Project, Occasional Papers. New York:
Columbia University Press, 1967.
_____. Indexes of Hungarian Industrial Production,
1938 and 1946-1965. Alton Project, Occasional Papers,
New York: Columbia University Press, 1968.

Deane, Phyllis, and Cole, W. A. British Economic Growth,
1688-1959. Cambridge: Cambridge University Press, 1962.

Dobb, Maurice. Soviet Economic Development Since 1917.
London: Routledge and Kegan Paul, Ltd. 1960.

Domar, Evsey. Essays in the Theory of Ecomomic Growth.
New York: Oxford University Press, 1957.

Erlich, Alexander. The Soviet Industrialization Debate. Cambridge, Massachusetts: Harvard University Press, 1960.

Fabricant, Solomon. The Output of Manufacturing Industries,
1899-1937. New York: National Bureau of Economic Research, 1940.

Firestone, O J. Canada's Economic Development, 1867 to
1953. Income and Wealth, Series 7. London: Bowes and
Bowes, 1958.

Galbraith, John, K. The Affluent Society. Boston: Houghton Mifflin, 1958.

Gleitze, Bruno. Ostdeutsche Wirtschaft. Berlin: Duncker and Humblot, 1956.

_____. Die Industrie der Sowjetzone. Berlin: Duncker and Humblot, 1964.

Goldberger, Arthur. Econometric Theory. New York: John Wiley and Sons, 1966.

Hansen, Philip. The Consumer in the Soviet Economy. Evanston, Illinois: Northwestern University Press, 1968.

Hoeffding, Oleg. Soviet State Planning and Forced Industrialization as a Model for Asia. Santa Monica, California: The Rand Corporation, August, 1958.

Hoffman, Walter, Das Wachstum der Deutschen Wirtschaft seit der Mitte des nuenzehnten Jahrhunderts. Berlin: Springer Verlag, 1965.

Hoffmann, W. G. The Growth of Industrial Economies. Manchester: University of Manchester Press, 1958.

Holzman, Franklyn, Soviet Taxation. Cambridge, Massachusetts: Harvard University Press, 1955.

Johnston, J. Econometric Methods. New York: McGraw-Hill, 1963.

Kendall, Maurice. A Course in Multivariate Analysis. London: Charles Griffin and Company, 1953.

Köhler, Heinz. Economic Integration in the Soviet Bloc. New York: Praeger, 1965.

Kronrod, Ia. A. Obšestvennyi Produkt i ego Struktura pri Sotcialisme. Moscow: Gosudarstvennoe Izdatel'stvo Poliličeskoi Leteratury 1958.

Kuznets, Simon. Modern Economic Growth. New Haven: Yale University Press, 1966.

Lazarcik, G., and Wynnyczuk, A. Bulgaria: Growth of Industrial Output, 1939 and 1948-1965. Alton Project, Occasional Papers. New York: Columbia University Press, 1968.

Lewis, S. R., and Soligo, R. Growth and Structural Change in Pakistans's Manufacturing Industry, 1954-1964. Research Report No. 29. Karachi: The Pakistan Institute of Development Economics.

Lorimer, Frank. The Population of the Soviet Union. Geneva: The League of Nations, 1946.

Maddison, Angus. Economic Growth in the West. New York: The Twentieth Century Fund, 1964.

Maizels, Alfred. Industrial Growth and World Trade. Cambridge, Massachusetts, Harvard University Press, 1963.

Montias, J. M. Economic Development in Communist Rumania.
    Cambridge, Massachusetts: M.I.T. Press, 1967.
Moorsteen, R., and Powell, R. The Soviet Capital Stock.
    1928-1962. Homewood, Illinois: Irwin, 1966.
Mulholland, D. The Crisis of NEP. Ph.D. Dissertation.
    Harvard University, 1968.
Nutter, G. W. The Growth of Industrial Production in the
    Soviet Union. Princeton: Princeton University Press, 1962.
Okhawa, K. The Growth Rate of the Japanese Economy Since
    1878. Tokyo: Kinokuniya Bookstore Co., 1957.
Politische Ökonomie. Berlin: Dietz Verlag, 1964.
Powell, Raymond. A Material-Input Index of Soviet Construct-
    tion, Revised and Extended. Santa Monica, California:
    The Rand Corporation, September, 1959.
Prokopovic, S. N. Opyt isčislenia narodnogo dokhoda 50
    gubernii evropeiskoi Rossii v 1900-1913 g.g. Moscow,
    1913.
Pryor, Frederic. The Communist Foreign Trade System.
    Cambridge, Massachusetts; M.I.T. Press, 1963.
_____. Public Expenditures in Communist and
    Capitalist Nations. Homewood, Illinois: Irwin, 1968.
Scheffe, Henry. The Analysis of Variance. New York: John
    Wiley and Sons, 1959.
Shimkin, Demitri. The Soviet Mineral-Fuels Industries.
    1928-1958. U.S. Department of Commerce, International
    Population Statistics Reports, Series P-90, No. 19.
    Washington, D.C.:U.S. Government Printing Office, 1962.
Stadnik, Milos. Some Problems Of Economic Growth in
    Czechoslovakia. Prague: Ekonomicky'Ustav Ceskoslo-
    venske Akademie VED, 1968.
Stolper, Wolfgang. The Structure of the East German Economy.
    Cambridge, Massachusetts: Harvard University Press,
    1960.
Williams, E. J. Regression Analysis. New York: John Wiley
    and Sons, 1959.
Die Wirtschaftsstruktur Rumaniens in ihren Wesenmerkmalen
    und Entfaltungsmoglichkeiten. Dresden, 1940.

Public Documents

Budapest Handel- und Gewerbekammer. Ungarns Industrie
    und Handel im Jahre 1935 and 1937. Budapest, 1938 and
    1939.

Canada, Dominion Bureau of Statistics. Census of Manufactures. Toronto, selected years.

Central Administration of Economic and Social Statistics. Socialist Construction in the U.S.S.R. Moscow, 1936.

Central Intelligence Agency. Index of Civilian Industrial Pro-
duction in the U.S.S.R., 1950-1961, CIA/RR Er 63-29.
Washington, D.C.: U.S. Government Printing Office,
September, 1963.

Central Statistical Office, Poland. Concise Statistical Yearbook of Poland, 1966. Warsaw, 1966.

Consiliul Superior Ceonomic. Aspecte Ale Economici Romanesti, 1939. Bucharest, 1939.

Die Deutsche Industrie. Schriftenreihe des Reichsamts für
Wehrwirtschaftliche Planung, Heft 1. Berlin, 1939.

Economic Report of the President, 1968. Washington, D.C.:
U.S. Government Printing Office, 1968.

Glowny Urzad Statystyczny. Rocznik Dochoda Narodowego,
1960-1965. Warsaw, 1966.

_____. Rocznik Statystyczny Przemyslu, 1954-1965.
Warsaw, 1967. Hungarian Central Statistical Office.
Statistical Yearbook, Budapest, selected years.

Jahresbericht des Deutschen Instituts für Konjunkturforschung,
No. 18 (1938).

Joint Economic Committee. Current Economic Indicators for
the USSR. Selected issues.

_____. New Directions in the Soviet Economy. Parts
II-A, III, IV. Washington, D.C.: U.S. Government Printing Office, 1966.

_____. Soviet Economic Performance. Selected
issues. League of Nations. International Trade and Balance of Trade Yearbook. Geneva, various years.

_____. Statistical Yearbook. Geneva, various years.

Ministerstvo Vensnei Torgovli SSSR. Vnešniaia Torgovlia
SSR za 1918-1940 g. g. Moscow, 1960.

_____. Vnešniaia Torgovlia SSSR za 1959-1963 g.g.
Moscow, 1965.

Mitteilungen des Statistischem Amts der Tschecholsovakei,
1933. Prague: Bursik and Kohout, 1933.

Promyslennost' v Khoziastvennom Komplekse Raionov SSSR
Moscow: Izdatel'stvo "Nauka, " 1964.

Staatliche Zentralverwaltung für Statistik, Statistisches Jahrbuch der Deutschen Demokratischen Republik. East
Berlin, various years.

Statističeski Godišnik na Narodna Republika B'lgaria, 1964.
    Sofia.
Statističeski Godišnik na Tsarstvo B'lgaria, 1937. Sofia, 1938.
Svod Statističeskikh Dannykh po Fabрično-Zavodskoi Promyslen-
    nost' s 1887 po 1926 god. Moscow, 1929.
Tsentral'noe Statističesko Upravlenie. Statističeski Spravočnik
    Bulgaria, 1965. Sofia, 1965.
_____. Statističeskii Spravočnik SSSR, 1927 and 1928, M.
    Smith, ed., Moscow: Statističeskoe Izdatel'stvo Ts.
    S. U., 1928 and 1929.
_____. Narodnoe Khoziastvo SSSR. Moscow, selected
    years.
_____. Promyšlennost' SSSR. Moscow, 1964.
United Nations. National Income Statistics, 1938-1948.
    Lake Success, New York, 1950.
_____. Growth of World Industry. New York, 1963.
_____. A Study of Industrial Growth. New York, 1963.
_____. Classification of Industrial Commodities by Industrial
    Origin. Statistical Papers, Series M, No. 43. New
    York, 1966.
_____. The Growth of World Industry, 1953-1965, National
    Tables. New York, 1967.
_____. Demographic Yearbook. Selected years.
_____. Statistical Yearbook. Selected years.
_____. Yearbook of International Trade Statistics. Selected
    years.
_____. Yearbook of National Accounts Statistics. Selected
    years.
United States Bureau of the Census. Census of Manufactures,
    1870.
_____. International Population Statistics Reports, Series
    P-90, Nos. 13 and 14.
Ustredni Urad Statni Kontroly a Statistiky. Statistička Ročenka
    CSSR, 1967. Prague, 1967.

Articles

Bergson, Abram. "Prices of Basic Industrial Products in
    the USSR, 1928-1950," Journal of Political Economy
    (August, 1956).
Chenery, Hollis. "Patterns of Industrial Growth," American
    Economic Review, L, 4 (1960).
Chenery, H.; Shishido, S.; and Watanabe, T. "The Patterns
    of Japanese Growth, 1914-1954," Econometrica, XXX,
    1 (January, 1962).

Chenery, H., and Taylor, L. "Development Patterns: Among Countries and Over Time," Review of Economics and Statistics, L (November, 1968).

Cohn, Stanley, "The Gross National Product in the Soviet Union," in Joint Economic Committee, Dimensionsof Soviet Economic Power. Washington, D.C.: U.S. Government Printing Office, 1962.

Ernst, Maurice. "The Postwar Economic Growth in Eastern Europe," in Joint Economic Committee, New Directions in the Soviet Economy, Part IV. Washington, D.C.: U.S. Government Printing Office, 1966.

Flux, M. A. "Gleanings from the Census of Production Report," Journal of the Royal Statistical Society (May, 1913).

Gershcenkron, Alexander. "The Rate of Industrial Growth in Russia Since 1885," Journal of Economic History, Supp. 7, (1947).

_____. "The Early Phases of Industrialization in Russia: Afterthoughts and Counterthoughts," in W. W. Rostow, ed., The Economics of Takeoff into Sustained Growth. New York: St. Martin's Press, 1963.

Goldsmith, R. W. "The Economic Growth of Tsarist Russia, 1860-1913." Economic Development and Cultural Change, IX, 3 (April, 1961).

Holzman, Franklyn. "Foreign Trade," in Abram Bergson and Simon Kuznets, eds., Economic Trends in the Soviet Union. Cambridge, Massachusetts: Harvard University Press, 1963.

Houthakker, Hendrik. "An International Comparison of Household Expenditure Patterns," Econometrica, XXV (October, 1957).

Kuznets, Simon. "A Comparative Appraisal," in Abram Bergson and Simon Kuznets, eds., Economic Trends in the Soviet Union. Cambridge, Massachusetts: Harvard University Press, 1963.

_____. "Quantitative Aspects of the Economic Growth of Nations: X. Level and Structure of Foreign Trade: Longterm Trends," Economic Development and Cultural Change, XV (January, 1967).

Lee, Pong S. "Structural Change in Rumanian Industry, 1938-1963," Soviet Studies XX (October, 1968).

Melzner, Manfred. "Das Anlagevermögen der mittledeutschen Industrie, 1955 bis 1966," Vierteljahreshefte zur Wirtschaftsforschung, Heft 1 (1968).

Noren, James. "Soviet Trends in Outputs, Inputs, and Pro-
    ductivity," in Joint Economic Committee, New Directions
    in the Soviet Economy, Part II-A. Washington, D. C.:
    U.S. Government Printing Office, 1966.
Nutter, G. W. "The Soviet Economy: Retrospect and Prospect,"
    in Conference on Fifty Years of Communism. Palo Alto,
    California: the Hoover Institution, 1967.
Powell, Raymond. "Industrial Production," in Abram Bergson
    Simon Kuznets, eds., Economic Trends in the Soviet Union.
    Cambridge, Massachusetts: Harvard University Press,
    1963.
Sulmicki, Pawel. "Some Observations on the Rate of Growth
    of National Product," in Alec Nove., ed., Studies on the
    Theory of Reproduction and Prices. Warsaw: PWN, 1964.
Temin, Peter. "A Time-Series Test of Patterns of Industrial
    Growth," Economic Development and Cultural Change,
    XV (January, 1967).
Treml, Vladimir. "New Soviet Inter-Industry Data," in Joint
    Economic Committee, Soviet Economic Performance:
    1966-1967. Washington, D. C.: U.S. Government Printing
    Office, 1969.

ABOUT THE AUTHOR

Paul Gregory is Assistant Professor of Economics at the University of Oklahoma. From 1965 to 1969, he served on the staff of the Russian Research Center at Harvard University. Professor Gregory received his B. A. and M. A. degrees and his PhD from Harvard University. Professor Gregory also has done graduate study at the Free University of Berlin, under a Fulbright Fellowship.